World of Art

...r of Art

...ican

Diaspora, and contemporary visual studies, he has written on topics ranging from primitivism to postmodernism, and has helped organize several exhibitions, including "Rhapsodies in Black: Art of the Harlem Renaissance" for London's Hayward Gallery in 1997; "To Conserve a Legacy: American Art from Historically Black Colleges and Universities" for the Studio Museum in Harlem and the Addison Gallery of American Art in 1999; and "Archibald Motley: Jazz Age Modernist" for the Nasher Museum of Art, Duke University in 2014. His publications include: *The Blues Aesthetic: Black Culture and Modernism*; *Cutting a Figure: Fashioning Black Portraiture*; *Going There: Black Visual Satire*; and *Homecoming: The Art and Life of William H. Johnson*. From 2007 until 2010, Powell was Editor-in-Chief of *The Art Bulletin*.

1 Sylvia Snowden, *Mamie Harrington*, 1985

World of Art

Black Art
A Cultural History
Richard J. Powell

Third edition

For C. T. Woods-Powell

Acknowledgments

In addition to the institutional support and the many people who helped me realize the original 1997 edition of this book, I thank Duke University's John Hope Franklin Humanities Institute. This revised edition has benefited greatly from the intellectual exchange that was generated among my colleagues in the "From Slavery to Freedom" humanities labs, held at Duke's Franklin Humanities Institute, beginning during the academic year of 2018–19. For the time and research assistance to study and revise, I am eternally grateful.

First published in 1997 in the United Kingdom under the title *Black Art and Culture in the 20th Century* by Thames & Hudson Ltd, 181A High Holborn, London WC1V 7QX

www.thamesandhudson.com

First published in 1997 in the United States of America under the title *Black Art and Culture in the 20th Century* by Thames & Hudson Inc., 500 Fifth Avenue, New York, New York 10110

www.thamesandhudsonusa.com

Revised and expanded edition 2002
This edition published in 2021 as *Black Art*

Black Art © 1997, 2002 and 2021
Thames & Hudson Ltd, London
Text by Richard J. Powell

Art direction and series design by Kummer & Herrman
Layout by Adam Hay Studio

British Library Cataloguing-in-Publication Data
A catalogue record for this book is available from the British Library

Library of Congress Control Number 2021935441

ISBN 978-0-500-20466-5

Printed and bound in China through Asia Pacific Offset Ltd

MIX
Paper from
responsible sources
FSC® C136333

Contents

Introduction
The Dark Center

The Alchemy of Black

In 1952, the Martiniquan psychiatrist and cultural theorist Frantz Fanon wrote *Peau noire, masques blancs (Black Skin, White Masks)*: a provocative book that, in its analysis of the damaging psychological effects that racism had on peoples of African descent, shattered the more conciliatory views of race relations that were proffered by social and political apologists during this period. In the section of the book that challenged French philosopher Jean-Paul Sartre's proposal that the black artist's declaration of cultural difference be eventually subsumed by a "future universalism" and "existential attitude," whose dominion meant cultural assimilation, Fanon responded with the following autobiographical disclaimer and "riddle":

The dialectic that brings necessity into the foundation of my freedom drives me out of myself. It shatters my unreflected position. Still in terms of consciousness, black consciousness is immanent in its own eyes. I am not the potentiality of something. I am wholly what I am. I do not have to look for the universal. No probability has any place inside me. My Negro consciousness does not hold itself out as a lack. It is. It is its own follower.

2 Similarly, the late seventeenth-century "slave drum," acquired in colonial Virginia by the physician and naturalist Sir Hans Sloane, raises a racial conundrum for students of black diasporal arts and cultural studies. With its stretched and pegged membrane, indented base, and rotund wooden body covered with decorative blocks and striations, this drum looks very much like percussive instruments found among Akan- and Fon-speaking peoples in West Africa. But even with this resemblance, as well as its African wood (*cordia africana*), and the likelihood that the people who

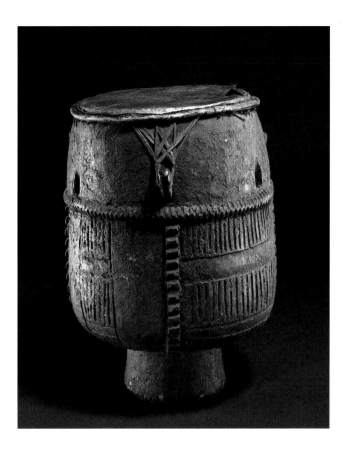

2 Slave drum, late seventeenth century

made it retained Akan or Fon design sensibilities, its new context and possibly new use in colonial Virginia removed it from its Old World frame of reference.

Sloane acquired the drum in the early eighteenth century, at the height of Virginia's involvement in the mass importation of enslaved Africans; his collection ultimately formed the nucleus of the British Museum in London, where the drum is still housed. The drum's specific Akan or Fon ritual identity has therefore been replaced with an identity that is African in kind, American in provenance, interpreted as an artifact through the lens of the Enlightenment, and founded on all the social, political, and cultural austerities of slavery. What students have had to struggle with is the fact that the American-in-origin, African-in-design, and transatlantic-in-praxis lineages of this drum are perhaps more easily understood in the context of an African diasporal experience which, in practical terms, can be summed up by the all-encompassing, historical designation "black."

The intensity, irreducibility, and emphatic nature of the word "black" obviously contradict this drum's complex history and hybrid nature. Yet, following the irreversible impact of the transatlantic slave trade, the English *Black*, the French *Noir*, and the Spanish, Portuguese, and eventually Anglo-American *Negro* became terms that differentiated a largely New World phenomenon of African diasporal cultures and peoples from their ethnic-specific ancestors and relatives. Of course, the Europeans who were engaged in the slave trade had long referred to Africans as "blacks" (in addition to other, frequently disparaging designations), but over time and with a more entrenched colonial foothold in the Americas, ethnic terminologies like "Angolan," "Calabar," "Nago," and "Coromantee" (used for the first and second generations of African-born slaves) were superseded by the short and stinging "black": a term that, in its brusque utterance, contained a white supremacist sense of racial difference, personal contempt, and, oddly enough, complexity that came to define these new African peoples.

Conventional wisdom during and after slavery would have separated the perceived singularity of being black from the inherent multiplicity of being racially mixed, yet these polarities collapsed under their own short-sighted logic and inflexible nomenclature. Given the range of complexions and body types among African peoples, "black" (in spite of its stark, verbal fixity) has always signified more—visually and conceptually—than it has been allowed to represent officially. Sloane and other thinkers of the Enlightenment were often surprised by the variety of physical characteristics that they observed among New World "Negroes." They were certainly aware that this variation from partially African in appearance to almost entirely Caucasian-looking was due to the rape and concubinage of female slaves by white masters and male overseers, but they deluded themselves in classifying these mixed and enslaved entities as "black."

During the colonial period there were other more specific terms for perceived racial and/or cultural mixtures. Apart from the commonly and often loosely used *Creole*, *Mulatto*, *Quadroon*, and *Octoroon*, the Spanish-speaking élite of colonial Mexico invented at least fifty-three different names for various racial intermixtures. In an anonymous Mexican painting of "the castes" from the last quarter of the eighteenth century, sixteen of these race/class categories are illustrated with, surprisingly, those of a perceived African ancestry not always confined to the lowest social rungs. What this caste fluidity suggested was that, rather than one's pigmentation or phenotype, proximity to the

3

3 Anonymous, *Las Castas*, late eighteenth century

4 Arthur Drummond, *The Empress*, 1901

ruling majority's cultural norms in dress, occupation, and wealth was more important in determining status and class. Among the sixteen categories in this painting, an identifiable, New World Africanity—a result of the transatlantic slave trade, colonialism, and miscegenation—vaunted its hybridity and cultural defiance in a litany of imaginative, Spanish-derived labels, such as *Cambujo* (a man with a reddish-black complexion, similar to a horse's coloring), *No te entiendo* (which translated as "I don't get you," meaning someone whose ancestry was indeterminant), and *Salta altras* (which translated as "jump back" or, rather, someone whose African ancestry had unexpectedly reemerged). Although *Negra* in this context meant a female of Sub-Saharan African ancestry with tightly curled hair and a very dark complexion, Mexican social conventions concluded that all of these categories (with the exception of *Español*) were culturally black or, rather, non-white, genealogically heathen and thus subject to the special laws and social boundaries of the Spanish crown and its colonial administration.

The political and economic realities that surrounded the African's encounters with the European (beginning in earnest during the fifteenth century) gave their perceived racial difference a social and cultural dimension: an aspect that, while life-altering for peoples of African descent, was obscured by the fact that blackness was a state of being that was rooted in perception. Notwithstanding the spurious biological basis of the definition of race, "black" has almost always initially meant racial identity, and only thereafter a social and/or political condition: an ingrained way of thinking that has been difficult to overcome. Yet for many people—particularly in England and France, and in response to Europe's colonization of Africa, Asia, and other parts of the non-Caucasian world—blackness is less a color than a metaphor for a political circumstance prescribed by struggles against economic exploitation and cultural domination: a state of consciousness that peoples of various pigmentations have experienced, empathized with, and responded to. Arthur Drummond's *The Empress* (1901), while painted as a tribute to Great Britain's reign over much of the world's population, essentially recognized colonialism's power to render any subject black, as shown in Drummond's dream-like vision of three Africans, two Indians, one Pacific Islander, and three Caucasian females, all kneeling before a heavenly enthroned Queen Victoria. Of course, *The Empress* also communicated the politicizing and genderizing of whiteness, as seen in the painting's focal relationship between Lord Salisbury, King Edward VII, and the seven-year-old future King Edward VIII.

Despite these deep, unstable, and often contradictory meanings for black, one could argue that, by the twentieth

4

century, it had become the most fitting name for a dispersed African peoples, whose common predicament of coming to terms with mass subjugation by Europe (and, later, Euro-America) raised the notion of a Pan-African solidarity that extended from London to Cape Town, as well as across the Atlantic. Even taking into account the more specific and nationalistic vogue—past, present, and, no doubt, future—for hyphenated terminologies such as "Afro-American," "African-American," "Afro-Caribbean," "Afro-Brazilian," etc., "black" embraces a range of African diasporal experiences across national and linguistic borders. All the same—with its past, pejorative connotation, fluctuation between conciseness and ambiguity, and overtures to visual perception—"black" has not been fully appreciated as a way of describing cultural distinctions and peculiarities within the microcosms of African diasporal communities. However, it is with this understanding and acceptance of the problematic nature of blackness—both as a protean identity and as a proactive social presence—that one acknowledges Fanon and others' uses of it in defining, anchoring, and assessing cultural production in a similarly problematic modern and postmodern world.

From Creation to "Making Do"

Sociologist Stuart Hall, in his essay "What is this 'Black' in Black Popular Culture?" (1992), proffered a series of answers and additional questions to his rhetorical query on the occasion of the Black Popular Culture Conference, held at New York's Dia Center for the Arts and the Studio Museum in Harlem in 1991. Although wary of the often insular black nationalist positions espoused by activists and intellectuals, Hall offered the following definition of black popular culture that, while conscious of the ideological pitfalls of categorical absolutes and generalizations, acknowledged the reality, veracity, and even the strategic necessity of such a concept:

It is this mark of difference inside forms of popular culture—which are by definition contradictory and which therefore appear as impure, threatened by incorporation or exclusion—that is carried by the signifier "black" in the term "black popular culture." It has come to signify the black community, where these traditions were kept, and whose struggles survive the persistence of the black experience (the historical experience of black people in the diaspora), of the black aesthetic (the distinctive cultural repertoires out of which popular representations were made), and of the black counternarratives we have struggled to voice.

Filtered throughout Hall's brief definition of "black popular culture" are at least five components that not only define the parameters of the 1991 Black Popular Culture Conference, but demarcate and explain the core factors in this present investigation into visual representations of black diasporal cultures in the twentieth and twenty-first centuries. First of all, these cultures constantly struggle against claims, from both within and without, of racial quintessence, as well as against dominant (and often hegemonic) cultural and political forces. As argued earlier, the intrinsically hybrid nature of blackness complicates these arguments. However, black culture has emerged from clusters of West and Central African cultural sensibilities (which are not reducible to a definitive set of characteristics or traits) and has a common wellspring in the transatlantic slave trade and colonialism. The cultural products of the various black diasporal peoples deserve, therefore, a comparative indexing and critical analysis.

Secondly, black diasporal cultures are defined by having the sufficient demographic numbers and critical mass to proclaim common beliefs, value systems, and goals toward building community-based institutions and products. For example, by the 1980s more than thirty million people of African descent in the United States had forged a separate identity that was frequently referred to by its institutional keystones (that is, African American churches, voluntary organizations, service sector businesses, and schools of higher education). Although indistinguishable at times from the cultural forms of other US ethnic groups, African American styles of religious worship, performance, and verbal and literary expression stand out among US cultural products, representing a shared vision that often resonates with black diasporal counterparts in the Caribbean, Central and South America, Europe, and Africa.

Another characteristic of black diasporal cultures is their structural dependence upon an acknowledged collection of life experiences, social encounters, and personal ordeals, the sum of which promotes a solidarity and camaraderie that creates community. This notion of a collective life experience—racial and cultural discrimination, segregation, recognition, and identification—should not be viewed as a litmus test for blackness *per se*, since peoples of African descent have experienced these to varying degrees. Still, the admission that these social assays are fundamental to black culture, if not actually experienced, is important to its conceptualization and realization.

Stuart Hall's reference to a "black aesthetic," despite the concept's oft-disputed existence, is a fourth characteristic of black diasporal cultures. Because of the modern (and postmodern) derivations of a black diaspora—and the hybrid and complex nature of its various human and cultural products—critics have resisted the perceived "lumping together" of assorted art forms, stylistic approaches, and aesthetic sensibilities under one, seemingly intractable banner, and rightly so. Yet, when explored by Hall as "distinctive cultural repertoires," it is clear that, rather than something singular and unrealistically all-inclusive, a "black aesthetic" is the name for a collection of philosophical theories about the arts of the African diaspora: an aesthetic grounded in the idea of a new, that is, a post-Emancipation and post-colonial, black identity which, from Jazz-Age Harlem and Montparnasse, to the "sound system" societies of west Kingston, south London, and south central Los Angeles, thrives in black communities where artistic creativity and performance are the basic cultural currencies.

Finally, black diasporal cultures are characterized by forms that are not only alternative to mainstream counterparts, but proactive and aggressive in their desire to articulate, testify, and bear witness to that cultural difference. Although usually discussed in the context of traditional African art and religion, the well-known wooden sculpture (or royal *Fa-bocio*) of the Dahomean King Glele (who ruled from 1858–89) introduces the possibility of considering an African-derived work of art in this larger, black diasporal context. Born out of a cosmopolitan period in the West African kingdom of Dahomey, this visually hybrid sculpture of the late nineteenth century by the artist Sosa Adede appropriates imagery from selected West African sculptural traditions, Fon divination signs, European heraldry, and the world under observation, in order to invoke King Glele's strength and ferocity in battle. Adede's king-in-the-guise-of-a-lion motif, rich in metaphor and allusion, directs its argument for King Glele's power and potentiality to residents and outsiders alike, creating a kind of visual and verbal counternarrative: it embodies an artistic departure from the West African norm that recalls the creolized artworks of enslaved Dahomeans and their descendants in Haiti, Cuba, Brazil, and other black diasporal sites.

Therefore, with Stuart Hall's description of "black popular culture" as a point of departure, "black diasporal culture" is defined here as the things that significant numbers of black people do. "Things" that black people "do" can be defined as virtually all that is constructive, inventive, crafted, and produced in various black communities, such as making works of art, participating in religious ceremonies, performing on

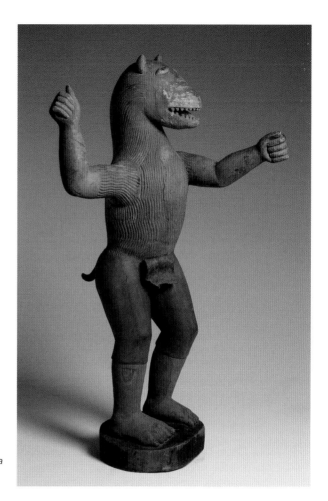

5 Sosa Adede, *King Glele in the Guise of a Lion*, late nineteenth century

the stage, in concert, or on athletic fields, or simply eking out an existence in the most humble of circumstances. And again, what is meant by "black people" are the women, men, and children of African descent who, because of the transatlantic slave trade, European colonialism, western imperialism, and racism, are globally dispersed, culturally hybrid, and narratively engaged in multilingual, Pan-African polemics with each other and with the world-at-large.

Black Cultural Subjectivity

In *Emancipation and the Freed in American Sculpture: A Study in Interpretation* (1916), the pioneering African American art historian and critic Freeman Henry Morris Murray revealed an uncharacteristic and refreshing cynicism in the section of the book that discussed general impressions of enslavement and emancipation. "The fact is," wrote Murray, "the conditions of being exploited, held down, even enslaved in one form or another, are so common and so old, that people, the victims included, come to regard these conditions as natural if not right; at any rate, as necessary and unavoidable." Murray continued his reflections with this observation:

Emancipation—even under the circumstances through which it came about in this country—is conceived and expressed nearly always as a bestowal; seldom or never as a restitution. Hence American art—and foreign art, too, it seems—usually puts it: objectively, "See what's been done for you"; or, subjectively, "Look what's been done for me."

Contained in Murray's comments about slavery and freedom—and in their artistic (and often patronizing) manifestations—was his unabashed concentration on African American concerns, perspectives, and voices in the study and interpretation of art. With the furor over the misrepresentation of black people in D.W. Griffith's 1915 film *The Birth of a Nation* as a likely reminder and concurrent backdrop, Murray believed that the "subject" of art—especially when that subject was "Black Folk"—eclipsed the "art for art's sake" sentiment that members of the European and Euro-American art cognoscenti espoused. For Murray, black subjectivity (as the African American philosopher Alain Locke would affirm in his groundbreaking book, *The Negro in Art*, almost twenty-five years later) presupposed that there was a world in which black peoples and their cultures, rather than always being filtered through white supremacist eyes and mindsets, could be seen and represented differently: either through the non-racist (or at least, multi-dimensional) lens of whites, or through the knowing and racially self-conscious eyes and imaginations of blacks themselves. Unlike other art historians, whose cultural capitals were Florence, Paris, Berlin, or Athens, Murray's mecca of black subjectivity had no single, geographic seat. Given the dispersed, institutionally fragile, and often rootless nature of black lives around 1916, Murray's "dark center" was conceptual: as potentially global and established as it was local and nomadic.

This present investigation continues Murray's "study in interpretation" of black culture by focusing on the exploration of this identity by artists during the twentieth and twenty-first centuries. Cultural historians would probably agree with the assessment that the twentieth century was an unprecedented time for redefining and creating a new image for black culture. In a period rich in historical significance for peoples of African descent, chroniclers of the twentieth century can point to the disenfranchisement (and the eventual reenfranchisement) of blacks; the political and cultural imperialism from outside practiced on various black communities; questions of alliances from both within "the race" and beyond; mass migrations of African peoples to Western metropolises; the flowerings of assorted black cultural "renaissances"; and *ad infinitum* debates over racial discrimination. All of these are proof of that century's importance to the development of black identities, both authentic and collusive. These and other historical developments all contribute to make this era an ideal, chronological period to commence a discussion on black cultural subjectivity in art. A work like Elizabeth Catlett's *Negro es Bello II* (*Black is Beautiful*) of 1969—created in the midst of an ideological and political revolution among African Americans—is emblematic of a black cultural focus in twentieth-century visual arts that not only reflects its particular moment of creation; it also conveys something of a general, modernist-informed African formalism in its idolatry of black physiognomy, as well as a fascination with black culture as a commodity in its Pop Art-like repetition of "Black Panther Party" buttons.

6

Because this book traces through time the changing visual representations of black culture, it could be considered as a survey. But where it departs from the standard surveys of "black art" is in its approach, which is thematic, object-focused, and examines black subjectivity across perceived regional and racial boundaries. In nine mostly chronologically arranged chapters, the theme of visual representations of black culture is developed by looking at specific works of art, and at how those works of art signify: (1) the "souls of black folk" (2) the persona of the "New Negro" (3) a black proletariat (4) race pride and cultural assimilation (5) aesthetic variants on the concept of blackness (6) the artistic commerce in black cultural identities (7) the role of mass media in visualizing blackness (8) the ideological conundrums that arose on the cusp of a new century, and (9) how valuations of black culture have taken different directions in the new millennium.

For the purposes of this particular investigation, the routine regional, ethnic, and racial demarcations of most surveys have been minimized, in order to focus on the thematic implications of black culture in artistic production. Although anyone familiar with a full range of twentieth- and twenty-first century art and artists will see that the majority of examples

6 Elizabeth Catlett, *Negro es Bello II*, 1969

in this study are African American (that is, people of African descent, whose lives and careers are based largely in the United States), this is truly more a consequence of an inordinate African American interest throughout this timeframe in black cultural subjectivity than it is an African American research bias. African artists in the colonial and post-colonial periods have consciously rejected their particular ethnic approaches to art-making (for instance, "Yoruba," "Wolof," "Amhara,") and have replaced these with a Pan-African and/or international art language. African American artists, however, by virtue of a social infrastructure that has included access to training, exhibition opportunities, varying degrees of patronage, and exposure to serious criticism and reviews, still figure significantly among black diasporal artists in their visual self-interrogations and introspective studies of black culture. Beyond any perceived territorialism in this study, the guiding spirit is the claim for black subjectivity, irrespective of, though not totally disregarding, regional, ethnic, and racial categories. In other words, race, nationality, and ethnicity matter (to paraphrase the African American cultural critic Cornel West), but they do not function as omnipotent agents of dismissal, omission, or elucidation. As shown by my selection of works not only by African American artists, but also by European, Asian American, European American, and African artists, and Caribbean, Latin American, and European artists of African descent, black subjectivity is, first and foremost, a choice that, while frequently influenced by the artist's personal identity, is not solely dependent upon it.

Another departure from previous studies is the recognition of artistic media not traditionally discussed in the context of black diasporal arts. Beyond painting and sculpture, a wide range of graphic art techniques, photography, film, video, computer-assisted imagery, and body-centered performance art provides a more complete picture of modern and contemporary black culture. Especially with photography and the advent of film (and, later, television, video, and other electronic forms of visual representation), the twentieth and twenty-first centuries introduced elements of the documentary and the virtual, which (as discussed in Chapters 8 and 9) bring issues of black spectatorship, racial stereotypes, and divergent cultural perspectives to the fore.

Methodologically, this study has been inspired not only by the black subject-based investigations of others (Murray, 1916; Locke, 1940; Parry, 1974; Honour, 1989; Wardlaw, 1989; McElroy, 1990; Pieterse, 1992; Harris, 2003; Farrington, 2005; Mercer, 2005, 2006, 2007, and 2008; Calo, 2007; English, 2007; Cooks, 2011; Fleetwood, 2011; Copeland, 2013; Thompson, 2015; and Murray, 2016), but by notions of an African diasporal culture developed by visual artist Jeff Donaldson (1970 and 1980), cultural theorist Paul Gilroy (1993 and 2000), and art historian Robert Farris Thompson (1969, 1981, 1983, 1993 and 2011). With roots in earlier, Pan-African-informed political and cultural movements, these theorists have revised the image of the African continent, its many peoples, and its dispersed populace as historically grounded yet modern entities, products of socio-political change and cultural self-affirmation in black communities worldwide. Despite the ideological differences between these three theorists, Thompson's exhibitions and publications on a "transatlantic" visual tradition, Donaldson's published writings on "TransAfrican art," and Gilroy's thinking around the highly provocative notion of a "Black Atlantic" all share an understanding that the African diaspora is not so much a monolith as an "infinite process of identity construction" that, in the face of European cultural hegemony and Western technocracy, moves toward an open-ended "black political culture."

In his *Victory in Zimbabwe* (1977–80), Jeff Donaldson committed to relief collage and acrylic paints what he has described in various writings as an "awesome" or "sublime" black diasporal image. With the restored ancient name of the previous British colony of Rhodesia centered and framed by Afrocentric zig-zags, Egyptian-like figures, and contrasting colors, this "Trans African" artist and theorist has put black cultural subjectivity literally at the core of his work. But in addition to the themes of African independence and the linking of black figures across millennia and continental ranges, the subject of *Victory in Zimbabwe* is also black diasporal rhythm: a visual, oral, and performative factor that Paul Gilroy (partially quoting historian Sterling Stuckey) has identified as most expressive and discernible in "the ubiquity of the antiphonal, social forms that underpin and enclose the plurality of black cultures in the western hemisphere." Black cultural subjectivity in art moves beyond a depicted black icon (or illustrative polemic) and, instead, becomes design, word, act, attitude, or what Robert Farris Thompson (in his explanation of Kongo notions of the altar) has characterized as "where the pure power of the dead brings its radiance to the present."

In addition to those texts of art history and cultural studies that focus on issues of identity, culture, and the ever-evolving definitions of an African diaspora, this book has also benefited from feminist writings that, in the aftermath of a period abundant in published works on gender, sought alternative critical strategies related to cultural representations of woman. Examples of these theoretical models are works addressing female subjectivity (de Lauretis, 1984, Trinh, 1989, Broude and Garrard, 1992), the theory of "cultural positionality" (Alcoff, 1988), modern and postmodern engagements with gender (Nochlin, 2001), the meshing of different female experiences (King, 1988, Crenshaw, 1989), and alternatives to representational formulas (Spillers, 1987, hooks, 1992, Gumbs, 2016). Conventional art histories have often separated the critical practices of feminists from those of black cultural advocates, yet it is in a provocative, multidimensional, and circumstantial re-examination of identity in art where more possibilities for understanding and seeing things differently reside.

7

7 Jeff Donaldson, *Victory in Zimbabwe*, 1977–80

Envisaging Blackness for A New Century

Since the 2002 publication of the second edition of *Black Art: A Cultural History*, the status of the visual arts within the African diaspora has undergone considerable change, most notably a greater acceptance in the art world for work by artists of African descent. Increasingly, black artists and their creations were represented in exhibitions at commercial galleries, art institutions, international fairs, trade expositions, and public art sites, often leading to acquisitions by collectors and museums and, eventually, competitive interest in auctions and record prices. The personnel in these cultural venues has also transformed, including black gallerists, museum directors, and curators knowledgeable about the works of black artists, past and present. This enthusiasm surrounding modern and contemporary art from Africa, the Caribbean, and the African diaspora was one of the primary features of a manifestly different art scene beginning in the 1990s, an artistic environment no longer contained within narrow geographical borders or bartered in single currencies but, rather, global and transnational in its purview and influence.

The number of monographs, exhibition publications, and in-depth studies on black artists and their work since 2000 has not been inconsequential. As of 2020, over 150 journal articles, at least 100 exhibition catalogues, and more than 75 scholarly books on individual artists and related topics have expanded the black art bibliography. Some of the writings that reflect the international dimensions of this new scholarly direction are: *The Short Century: Independence and Liberation Movements in Africa, 1945–1994* (Munich, 2001), *Afro-Modern: Journeys through the Black Atlantic* (Liverpool, 2010), *The Image of the Black in Western Art, V, Part 2, The Twentieth Century: The Rise of Black Artists* (Cambridge, MA, 2014), *The Color Line: Les Artistes africains-américans et la ségrégation, 1865–2016* (Paris, 2016), and *Histórias Afro-Atlânticas* (São Paulo, 2018). Each of these weighty and profusely illustrated international imprints editorially acknowledged their art historical antecedents (mainly authored by Anglophone art specialists) while filling large information gaps in the books-in-print category on modern and contemporary art.

Since 2000, five themes or conceptual directions have produced an abundance of new knowledge. First of all, in studies that have concentrated on philosophically cohesive historical periods, many focused on (1) the early twentieth century project known as the Harlem Renaissance, and (2) the circa 1960s and 1970s cultural insurgency known as the Black Arts Movement. Both historical moments, approximately forty years apart from one another, have inspired scholarship that has reshaped earlier interpretations of these artistic uprisings, especially through new foci on each movement's gender and sexual politics, their respective occasions for global outreach, and their shared artistic reimagining via the media arts.

The Harlem Renaissance, or as it was known in the 1920s and 1930s, the New Negro Arts Movement, was an interlude in the larger span of modern history—legendary for a major artistic flowering among African Americans, and celebrated by advocates on multiple fronts. The Black Arts Movement, with its comparable examples of an insubordinate black creativity, has only recently become recognized as another important juncture in African American arts and letters. In tandem with this new appreciation for the Black Arts Movement, cultural historians over the past decade have used the concept of a black artistic "renaissance" to revisit both of these periods, seeing them as anecdotal episodes for a radical rethinking of race and the role of the black artist within societies in flux.

Parallel to the amplified presence of African American women writers in late-twentieth-century literature, artists and historians throughout the African diaspora increasingly explored the lingering questions of sexuality, race, culture, and their often uneasy alliances. These concerns, along with a new disciplinary commitment to highlighting the contributions of gays and lesbians in art history and visual culture, have reshaped black art research. Queer perspectives within visual art practices have unsettled standard gender studies and the attendant critiques of male-dominated, heteronormative institutions and social practices. Instead, black artistic production and academic cognition have been informed by cultural theorists and social scientists who foreground gender, race, sexuality, and class, and the need to address questions of fundamental rights, individual agency, engendering practices, and the full arc of recognition/misrecognition. A number of these investigations have bridged this work with feminist theories and retooled definitions of identity, sexuality, and social difference.

A popular topic in African American art erudition of the twenty-first century was the concept of a "post-black" sensibility in art. The 2001 coining of the term by museum director Thelma Golden and visual artist Glenn Ligon was not only conscious of a shift in the cultural mindsets of the latest generation of African American artists, but was prescient for what was on the horizon: an attitude among artists that embraced the contradictions of making racially informed art without deferring to a platitudinous, archetypal blackness.

Even when the term "post-black" was not cited, its presence hovered over many scholarly undertakings, whether the focus was conceptualism, history and memory, aesthetics, politics, or technology's imprimatur on racial identities. Although most critics who have chronicled this phenomenon examined it from a dispassionate point of view, some scholars questioned the broader implications of taking a cavalier attitude toward history and conclusive truths. It could also be argued that a post-black stance was considered the only way to contend with the psychological damage that racism has inflicted upon subsequent generations, as well as other unspeakable traumas, past and present. The escalation of life-threatening situations and social insecurities for black people also prompted ironic and frequently sarcastic, post-black perspectives: a spectral blackness on which current scholarship endlessly debates and deliberates.

Coinciding with the contemporary art scene's appreciation for works by non-academically trained artists, some historians and theoreticians have begun looking closely at this phenomenon. African and African American artists figured prominently in this socially marginalized group, as did artists located in the global South, therefore much research was indebted to critical race theory and hypotheses that addressed geopolitical center/periphery dynamics. Emphases on the social and economic forces that created this artistic cohort shifted the discussion away from stylistic vagaries and pictorial rawness, or individual eccentricities and, instead, have prompted scrutiny of the market forces and mythologizing around these "gatecrashers." Variously described as "folk," "self-taught," or "outsider," these artists and their champions troubled an already fractious art world that, because of their separate yet vaunted status, provided fodder for viewing the art scene as exploitative, especially in light of more established, professional, yet overlooked black artists and their documented struggles for greater recognition.

Finally, one of the singular characteristics of twenty-first century research on black art has been a fundamental revising of the black art canon, as well as offering correctives to modern art history. This theoretical turn—conterminous with many humanities subfields and their shift toward more exegetic and ideational approaches to history—manifested itself in multiple ways over the past several decades. For example, the often pedantic and moralistic lens through which the history of slavery has been viewed was deconstructed through a part thematic, part theoretical perspective (e.g., in studies of the iconic, late-eighteenth-century, schematic engraving of a slave ship), and a similar multi-pronged tack was undertaken on the subject of black portraiture. Likewise, core themes in African American art such as the African diaspora and the idea of a distinctive black aesthetic have been significantly reconceived, both through the conceptual mechanisms of a discursive approach and synesthetic interpretations, and by traditional processes of historiography and critical analysis.

Scholars working in the early twenty-first century have witnessed a period of creative exchange and intellectual re-engagement with the discipline, in which not only longtime scholars of African American art and culture have participated, but also art historians and theorists from across the geographical, ideological, and racial/cultural spectrum. An intellectual project such as the study of African American art is, both by design and necessity, one that privileges an African diasporal or black perspective. However, the scholarship has argued that the centrality of a black perspective does not as a matter of course mean that blackness can be reduced to an inviolable racial category. In spite of an assumed singularity, blackness and the African diaspora are, as Stuart Hall wrote in 1991, hybrid entities, multilayered in their discursive acts, historically cross-border in scope, and constitutively variable and transitory. It remains to be seen in the advent of the worldwide pandemic and mass protests against anti-black racism if this black artistic efflorescence and its scholarly counterparts will persevere or, in light of constrained social orbits and prescribed artistic circuits, recede into cultural indistinctness or obscurity.

Although this study opens up art history to heretofore overlooked works, different names, and unanticipated concepts and methodologies, this current enlightenment would not exist were it not for the art-historical labors and visual musings that preceded it. Contemporary art historians and cultural critics could not have imagined pursuing the study and analysis of something called "black" or African American art without the field's intellectual substratum, realized by twentieth century scholars such as Freeman Henry Morris Murray, Benjamin Brawley, Alain Locke, Zora Neale Hurston, Melville Herskovits, James V. Herring, James A. Porter, Dorothy Porter Wesley, Cedric Dover, Sidney Kaplan, David C. Driskell, Robert Farris Thompson, Regenia Perry, Elsa Honig Fine, Harry Henderson, Samella Lewis, Jeff Donaldson, Floyd Coleman, Lynn Igoe, Albert Boime, David Boxer, and Okwui Enwezor, among countless others. These forerunners in black art scholarship engaged in intellectual pursuits that, through decades of archival research, bibliographic groundwork, key interviews, and thoughtful, desk-bound authoring, culminated in what theoretician Kobena Mercer has described as a "multi-vocal dialogue on matters of cultural difference, in which the identities of all participants were open to new possibilities." If, in 1916, Freeman Henry Morris Murray had had a crystal ball, magically enabling him to observe how the study of art by and about peoples of African descent would evolve from his insular vantage point to, say, one hundred years into the future, not only would he have marveled at the social and cultural changes that had transpired, but he would have been amazed by a discipline and subfield that, unlike in his more apathetic time, acknowledged the historical importance of black artists, as well as the intrinsic value of studying works that placed questions of race and culture at their very core.

Chapter 1
Art, Culture, and "the Souls of Black Folk"

Turn-of-the-Century Representations

At the end of the nineteenth century a proposal for a gathering of men and women in London to discuss the status of peoples of African ancestry living in Europe, North and South America, the Caribbean, and on the continent of Africa captured the imaginations of black intellectuals and activists the world over. In France the Haitian diplomat Benito Sylvain had initially hoped that the assembly would denounce the scientific community and its allegations of "Negro inferiority": an issue that was being hotly debated among many white ethnologists during this period. In the United States the famous African American educator and spokesperson Booker T. Washington, although generally unsympathetic to political agitation and assertiveness by blacks, gave his tacit approval for such a conference and urged those "colored Americans" who were able to attend to do so. And, in England, the Sierra Leonean Anglican cleric, Bishop James Johnson, leaving to take up his appointment as the church's spiritual leader in the Lower Niger Delta area of West Africa, proclaimed that the "Pan-African Association" and its congress of black people from all over the world was "the beginning of a union I had long hoped for, and would to God it could be universal!"

This call for black people throughout the world to meet and discuss their collective condition at the dawn of the twentieth century was an extraordinary event. The 1900 Pan-African Conference and the context that produced it—the cultural and psychological colonization of African peoples worldwide, their economic exploitation, and rampant racism and genocide from the Belgian Congo to the southern United States—all suggested that, at this early stage in the formation of a post-Emancipation black identity, there was the sense among many peoples of African ancestry that they had certain concerns, fears, aspirations, and even cultural values in common.

Indeed, in the months just prior to London's Pan-African Conference the Exposition Universelle in Paris had rallied scores of black visitors to see and take pride in the "American Negro Exhibit" on the Rue des Nations. Comprising photographs, books, industrial and fine arts products, handmade objects, miniature architectural models, machine patents, and other materials made by independent black artisans and students from historically black US schools, this display served as a shining example of what was possible for any oppressed people, whether in Africa, Europe, or the Americas, once the veil of slavery had been lifted, and they had a chance to do something for themselves.

The belief that black people, apart from physiognomic and genealogical ties with the inhabitants of Africa, had comparable experiences, identical struggles for full acceptance in society, and shared destinies, was widely held by social commentators and thinkers in the second half of the nineteenth century. For ethnographers, the lowly status of black peoples in the United States, the Caribbean, and Latin America, and what was considered the "primitive" culture of their African forebears, were "evidence" that all blacks were cut from the same coarse "biologically-determined" cloth, and that the policies of white paternalism and social control were necessary for world order and Western progress.

In contrast, there were a few nineteenth-century thinkers who took a position that might be described as "Pan-Africanist" or "black nationalist." For them, the same historical "facts"— the shared African origin, the social dissolution that afflicted African peoples through the transatlantic slave trade, the hope (and, in many instances, the futility) of universal emancipation, and the social/economic vacuum, which resulted from Western imperialism and white racism—all suggested that the world's African peoples, in spite of having experienced different forms of slavery, dispersal, and economic exploitation by the West, had more in common with one another than with their white brethren. These various interpretations of an African-derived presence in the world created particular stereotypes and perceptions of black people and their cultures, which differed dramatically from either earlier pre-Emancipation representations of blacks or images of indigenous African peoples.

Several approaches in representing this African-derived, but new and distinct "black culture" reveal both the possibilities

8 Cover of sheet music for "All Coons Look Alike to Me" by Ernest Hogan, 1896

and the limitations of black life as perceived during this period. One tendency developed around a burgeoning African American performance tradition. Its roots in slave plantations, and in parodies of this culture by white blackface minstrels, and also in post-Civil War politics and social customs, spawned a whole commerce in comic, music-and-dance-oriented, and racist representations of black people.

Like many literary and visual portrayals, whose principal incentive is a satirical or "humorous" view of "the other," these images took the form of outrageous characterizations of blacks, their communities, and their alleged cultural practices. These grotesque, garishly dressed beings, with black skins, protruding red lips and bulging eyeballs, were usually shown in impoverished settings with yard fowl, watermelons, and so on. Alternately backward, shiftless, ridiculous, childish, criminal, these characterizations faithfully appeared in turn-of-the-century European and American theatrical productions, popular literature, advertisements, children's toys, and other cultural documenta. Countless graphic artists and illustrators established themselves in this field of commercial art. Edward W. Kemble, literally created his own one-man Negro-stereotype industry, with dozens of racist illustrations for books and journals, including his 1896 "classic," *Kemble's Coons.*

Ironically, among those most responsible for putting the pejorative word "coon" into common usage was the black American vaudeville performer and composer Ernest Hogan. His celebrated (and notorious) 1896 song, "All Coons Look Alike to Me," catapulted the "coon" craze and racist representations of blacks into worldwide popularity.

An entirely different approach invested black people with a more truthful humanity, as in the novels of French and American writers, such as Emile Zola, Guy de Maupassant, Henry James, Stephen Crane, and Theodore Dreiser. American visual artists such as Thomas Hovenden, Thomas Eakins, Winslow Homer, and Henry Ossawa Tanner, developed a similar realism, which also challenged the prevailing assumptions of black inferiority, shallowness, and bestiality.

Tanner, who based himself in Paris, was one of a small number of African American artists, including sculptor May Howard Jackson, painter Alfred Stidum, and photographer C.M. Battey, who were producing new images of black life at the turn of the century. Tanner's early training at the Pennsylvania Academy of the Fine Arts (under Thomas Eakins) and in Paris at the Académie Julian (with John-Joseph Benjamin-Constant and Jean-Paul Laurens) gave him the painting skills and realist credentials which, with his innate talent, imagination, and interest in morally charged subject matter, led to the creation of such early masterpieces as *The Banjo Lesson* (1893). In Tanner's hands this familiar scene of an old man teaching a young boy how to play the banjo, set in the domestic warmth and genteel poverty of a hearth-lit cabin, was transformed into a painted Negro spiritual: a luminous, pictorial narrative about learning, cultural nourishment, and cross-generational affection. Tanner was principally a painter of Biblical allegories, and during the fifty-odd years of his career only intermittently explored these sympathetic themes featuring black subjects. Yet these loving and remarkably sober images of blacks have long been paragons of positivism for the African American popular imagination in the welter of cultural stereotyping and ridicule.

A third source of representations of black culture at this time was what Richard A. Long has described as the "folk-rural" tradition. Both the racist and realist/idealist strains of black imagery emerged from artists and perceptions outside typical black communities; in contrast, the folk-rural orientation developed from within them. The memory of an African legacy, the institution of slavery, confinement within a socially instituted caste system, and a position on the margins of the economy—all these influenced the self-taught and vernacular style, like many of the crafts that were on display in the "American Negro Exhibit" for the 1900 Exposition Universelle in Paris.

The *Bible Quilt* (c. 1895–98) by the Georgia seamstress Harriet Powers had its genesis in this culturally insular, folk-rural world, conditioned by Bible stories, subconscious affinities for West African design sensibilities, and the politics of race, gender, and class. Powers did not explicitly portray black culture or black people, but expanded the representational discourse through sign-like, heraldic emblems and her own description (written at her dictation) of each appliquéd panel of the quilt. Although masked by standard Biblical narratives, Powers's *Bible Quilt* and her earlier version of 1886, covertly interrogated the worldly affairs of women and men who, like those in Powers's tiny community outside Athens, Georgia, had their own share of Old and New Testament-like temptations, trials, betrayals, and sacrifices.

The clashing and colliding sentiments in Hogan's "coon" imagery, Tanner's impressionistic scenes of black life, and Powers's rural folk artistry showed what was being flaunted by 1900 in the popular imagination as "Negro." What was harder to discern were the underlying significations of black culture, both in its actual forms and in its representational constructs.

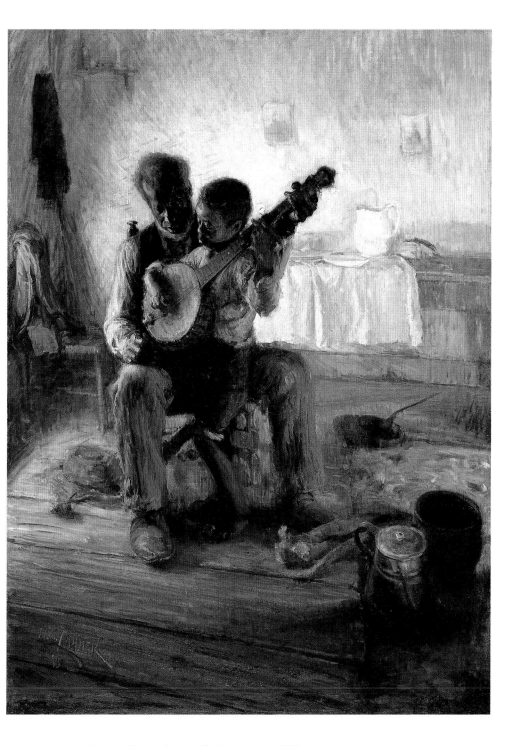

9 Henry Ossawa Tanner, *The Banjo Lesson*, 1893

10 Harriet Powers, *Bible Quilt*, c. 1895–98

Lifting Every Voice

Part of the answer surfaced at this time in the writings of the African American educator, attorney, diplomat, and author James Weldon Johnson, who is best known for his 1900 song "Lift Ev'ry Voice and Sing" (commonly referred to as the "Negro National Anthem"). His 1912 novel, *The Autobiography of an Ex-Colored Man*, published anonymously and remaining so until 1927, traced the racial and cultural evolution of the protagonist, from his "illegitimate" and mixed racial beginnings in the segregated South, to his equally "illegitimate" end as an African American who tragically "passes" for white at the novel's conclusion. The ex-colored man's anxieties about having sold his birthright "for a mess of pottage" are framed by his admiration for the various African American cultural idioms of the day—ragtime music, Negro spirituals, African American religious oratory, and the popular black dance known as "the cakewalk." He saw them as ultimately on a par with the very best of European art, and felt that their originality, evocative nature, and universal appeal (as indicated in the revealing caption of H. M. Pettit's 1899 photomontage of cakewalkers for *Leslie's Weekly*) gave "evidence of a power that will someday be applied to the higher forms."

But how does one reconcile Johnson's eloquently articulated celebration of black popular culture with the legion of racist "coon" images that usually accompanied the era's ragtime music and cakewalking black dancers? Can the black theater scene of this time, with its roots in black-face minstrelsy and background of post-Civil War disenfranchisement and white-on-black violence, be redeemed with the universalizing and humanizing language of art and cultural relativism?

The black cultural demi-monde with its stereotypes, portrayed in *The Autobiography of an Ex-Colored Man*, was well known to Johnson. As the lyricist for such ragtime hits as "Under the Bamboo Tree" and "Congo Love Song," Johnson used many of the standard black clichés of the day, seeing great mastery in the cakewalk and ragtime music, and praising a range of cultural expressions from the "racist" to the "authentic."

Of course, Johnson did not view his theatrical activities and those of his fellow black vaudevillians as "racist" or necessarily disparaging to black people. Rather, he recognized the importance of the African American musical and performance tradition, and understood its major contribution to the transformation of American art from a mere imitation of older European models to a significant, world-class statement of artistic modernism in its own right. In spite of the broad dramatizations, crude jokes, and outrageous portrayals in black

11

11 H. M. Pettit, *Close Competition at the Cake Walk*, 1899

popular music, theater, and dance of this period, the musical richness, rhythmic complexity, highly stylized treatments, and multi-layered messages were evidence of an artistry and creative genius whose source was a black vernacular.

Several visual artists joined James Weldon Johnson in his curious fusion of seemingly stereotypical imagery from the black theatrical scene with profound, telling representations of black popular culture. Stuart Davis, a future proponent of a school of indigenous, American abstraction in painting, began his career as a newspaper illustrator, drawing various aspects of urban life in the northeastern United States. One of those early drawings, *Negro Dance Hall* (1913), depicted the unrefined black folk who frequented disreputable barrelhouses and nightclubs to gamble, dance, fraternize, and listen to the latest piano rags. In this quickly sketched, gestural drawing, his black subjects are invested with a contradictory yet provocative range of characteristics, from the dreamy, contemplative woman in the picture's foreground, to the lasciviously squatting wisp of a woman in the picture's central middleground.

A year later and across the Atlantic, in the garish stage lights and outrageous milieu of Berlin's lively cabaret scene, the German Expressionist artist Ernst Ludwig Kirchner too turned to African American performers as part of his wider quest to visualize the primitive energy of modern life. In one of Kirchner's lithographs, *Tapdancing Negro* (1914), the gestural drawing techniques, which appeared in Davis's *Negro Dance Hall*, have been taken to extremes with jagged scrawls and heavy, built-up markings echoing the rapid-fire movements

12

13

12 Stuart Davis, *Negro Dance Hall*, 1913

and staccato dance steps of the black performer. Kirchner's subject, while on the surface nothing more than a "tapdancing Negro," embodied an artistic spontaneity and "Nietzschean vitalism" which many European artists thought would further propel their work into a modernist trajectory.

While these artistic overtures to black popular culture can be viewed as part of a bigger, international movement in modern art away from bourgeois, academic conceits and toward expressive, emotionally liberating sources of artistic inspiration, many African American artists opposed this view. In sharp contrast to James Weldon Johnson, most educated blacks of this period rejected those aspects of black culture that perpetuated certain notions of black servility, racial jokes, derogatory pictures, and other disparaging displays. Black vaudeville, representations of the black working class, and their shared nineteenth-century slave lineage were considered throwbacks to an inglorious past, vulgar, and embarrassing to "the race." Literary critic Henry Louis Gates Jr. has argued convincingly on the subject of this rejection of the so-called "old Negro" and a fixation on the so-called "new Negro" by members of the black élite of the time, and how these choices, despite the progressive nomenclature, often prevented them from confidently articulating a broad and nuanced African American self.

One exception among the conservative black élite in this rejection of the past can be found in the writings of the sociologist, historian, and black activist William Edward Burghardt Du Bois. At the beginning of Du Bois's 1903 classic, *The Souls of Black Folk*, he described his intended literary goal as a delineation "in vague, uncertain outline" of "the spiritual world in which ten thousand Americans live and strive." In the fourteen chapters that follow, Du Bois's objective is fully realized through a poetic, historically rooted, and highly literate voice of reason, authority, and appeal. He introduced cultural metaphors, such as a "double-consciousness" and living one's life within "the Veil" of racial segregation, and he directed one of the most persuasive and fearless arguments against the then powerful Booker T. Washington and his racially submissive "Atlanta Compromise" speech of 1895. *The Souls of Black Folk* branched out into previously uncharted territories for black scholarship, fusing psychology, philosophy, ethics, and old-fashioned political debate.

13 Ernst Ludwig Kirchner, *Tapdancing Negro*, 1914

Du Bois embraced the historical past, while renouncing contemporary black popular culture; this is evident in his poignant treatise on African American spirituals, or what he termed "the sorrow songs." "The Music of Negro religion," he wrote in *The Souls of Black Folk*, "is that...which, despite caricature and defilement, still remains the most original and beautiful expression of human life and longing yet born on American soil." For Du Bois, the spiritual life and cultural expressions of black people—inherently fundamentalist, ethical, and born of a great, social injustice—are the guiding lights in the vast gloom and darkness of the years after the American Civil War. Like the similarly idealized representations of black life found in Tanner's *The Banjo Lesson*, or in the photographic frontispiece for Paul Laurence Dunbar's 1901 book of verse, *Candle-Lightin' Time*, Du Bois allowed African Americans a metaphysical reality and an inner being, which refuted the absurdities of everything that was then commonly touted as "Negro," from popular culture's "coon" imagery to Booker T. Washington's widely sanctioned message of black acquiescence.

14 Leigh Richmond Miner, frontispiece for Paul Laurence Dunbar's *Candle-Lightin' Time*, 1901

15 John Henry Adams Jr.,
The Modern Cyrenian's Cross,
or *The Black Man's Burden*, 1907

The Modern Cyrenian's Cross, or the Black Man's Burden

    The sophisticated frontispiece for *Candle-Lightin' Time*
was taken by a member of Hampton Institute's Camera Club.
The Institute had been founded in 1868 in Hampton, Virginia,
for the children of ex-slaves and reservation-bound Native
Americans, and by the year 1900 it had almost one thousand
students enrolled; photography was only one among the many
trades and industrial art forms taught there. This frontispiece
was photographed in dramatic chiaroscuro by Institute faculty
member Leigh Richmond Miner following the pictorialist
tradition of Clarence H. White. It implicitly communicated
an image of African Americans that stressed both their slave
heritage and what Du Bois described in the African American
psyche as "that transfigured spark of divinity."
    Like Du Bois, many other black artists were harsh critics
of a white and largely racist status quo in the United States.
John Henry Adams Jr., a Professor of Art and Drawing at Morris
Brown College in Atlanta, Georgia, and a contributor to the
Atlanta-based monthly *Voice of the Negro*, frequently lent his
talents to a biting, visual analysis of Du Bois's notion of life
"within the Veil." Adams's *The Modern Cyrenian's Cross,* or
The Black Man's Burden (1907) presented to *Voice of the Negro*
subscribers a rogues' gallery of political and literary "deities"

15

Art, Culture, and "the Souls of Black Folk"

16 D. W. Griffith, *The Birth of a Nation*, 1915

whose anti-black rhetoric or neglect of African American social
and political concerns qualified them for this ignoble status.

Adams's perception that many influential white Americans—
from Thomas Dixon, the author of the notorious bestsellers
The Leopard's Spots (1902) and *The Clansman* (1905), to Theodore
Roosevelt, the twenty-sixth president of the United States—
were the main barriers to black advancement was shared
by other radical black thinkers of the day. In response to
President Roosevelt's decision to discharge with dishonour,
and without legal recourse, an entire battalion of black soldiers
in Brownsville, Texas, Du Bois boldly wrote in the African
American monthly *The Horizon: A Journal of the Colored Line*,
"...Mr. Roosevelt by his word and deed...has slammed [the door
of opportunity] most emphatically in the black man's face."

Roosevelt's successors in the White House, William Howard
Taft and Woodrow Wilson, proved equally unsympathetic
to African American concerns. Taft's call in 1912 for African
Americans to accept their fate "under the guardianship of

the South," and Wilson's abject silence in the face of a rash of racially motivated lynchings throughout the United States caused many African Americans in the years just before World War I to doubt that there was any hope of justice from the federal government.

In these years, the social policy of segregation and the rise in white-on-black violence precipitated images of blacks in the visual arts that conformed to the worst stereotypes imaginable. Interestingly it was the literary racism of novelist Thomas Dixon that inspired the pioneer movie maker D. W. Griffith to create the period's most scathing depictions of blacks. *The Birth of a Nation* (1915)—Griffith's cinematic adaptation of Dixon's two novels about the Civil War, the Reconstruction period, and the rise of the Ku Klux Klan—transformed racist pronouncements and injurious words into larger-than-life, moving truisms for predisposed audiences. President Wilson's widely reported endorsement of *The Birth of a Nation*, saying that it was "like writing history with lightning," prompted Du Bois to organize a nationwide protest against the film, but it was not successful.

Almost simultaneously with this culture of ridicule and slander, an African American élite (especially in New York, Philadelphia, and Washington, DC) began to defend itself with its own ammunition—"colored" literary societies, industrial fairs, and art exhibitions featuring the creative talents of its best and brightest. Even on the racial killing fields of the segregated south, the Arkansas-based African American sculptor Isaac Scott Hathaway waged his own campaign. He created larger-than-lifesize commemorative plaster busts of educator Booker T. Washington; the nineteenth-century antislavery activist Frederick Douglass; poet Paul Laurence Dunbar; and the founder of the African Methodist Episcopalian Church, Bishop Richard Allen. He sold casts of his four heroic heads ("$1.50 each/4 busts for $5.00") by mail order and through local agents. He combined the need for more uplifting, positive black images with a quintessentially American, entrepreneurial approach, advertising "The Isaac Hathaway Art Company" in *The Crisis*, the monthly journal published by the National Association for the Advancement of Colored People (NAACP).

In contrast to Hathaway's homage to four historic black achievers, Meta Vaux Warrick Fuller developed a more allegorical approach to black culture. Following studies in her native Philadelphia and in Paris at L'Ecole des Beaux-Arts, Académie Colarossi, and privately with Auguste Rodin, Fuller embarked on a series of sculpture projects, which documented her evolving racial consciousness, as well as her expanding artistic talent. Her experimental, fourteen-part *tableau* for the

Jamestown Tercentennial Exposition, illustrating the "Negro's progress" from Africa to Afro-America (1907), was followed some years later by a more accomplished group of figures entitled *Emancipation* (1913), created for a New York City exposition on the same theme, and echoing the style of Augustus Saint-Gaudens, the Irish-born American sculptor.

Fuller's most important sculpture, *The Awakening of Ethiopia* (*c.* 1920), depicts a woman of African ancestry dressed in the classical headgear and apparel of an ancient Egyptian pharaoh, turning, gesturing, and extracting herself from the mummy-like bandages that wrap the lower half of her body. There are obvious allusions to similar subjects in mid-nineteenth-century neoclassical statuary, and to Rodin's legendary *Balzac* portrait of 1893–94, but, according to art historian Judith Wilson, an important source of inspiration for *The Awakening of Ethiopia* may also have been the utopian, Pan-Africanist novel *Ethiopia Unbound* (1911) by the Gold Coast activist and newspaper

17 Isaac Scott
Hathaway, *Frederick
Douglass*, 1919

18 Meta Warrick Fuller, *The Awakening of Ethiopia*, c. 1920

publisher J.E. Casely Hayford. Both Casely Hayford and Fuller (who had ties to the Pan-Africanist movement) employed the metaphor of an enshrouded and awakening "Ethiopia" (synonymous with Africa and also with the greater black diaspora). Physically restrained yet emotional and visually rich, *The Awakening of Ethiopia* served the representational needs not only of a disillusioned but hopeful black élite, but also of successive generations of "race" men and women.

Souls at War

On the global front, the years between the outbreak of war (1914) and Germany's ultimate defeat (1918) was a period of consternation for peoples of African ancestry. The African continent was further partitioned by France and Great Britain, and the island republic of Haiti, the first black independent nation in the Americas, fell under the humiliating occupation of the US Marines in 1915. That same year saw the death of Booker T. Washington, arguably the most influential black man in the world, leaving a major void in black leadership. Thousands of black soldiers—largely from the United States and the continent of Africa—joined forces on European battlefields to fight, risk injury, and die for the democratic ideals and liberties of others that were unavailable to them.

Representations of black soldiers revealed the ambiguities and conflicts of their position. The image of a smiling Senegalese artilleryman, or *tirailleur*, in the advertisements for

19

Banania (1917), a popular French breakfast cereal, conveyed, in equal proportions, a sense of good humor, comfort, the exotic, and the savory (as voiced in the picturesque Afro-French caption, "Y'a bon"). To the French, these subliminal messages were further colored by (1) the positive propaganda surrounding the contributions of the Senegalese *tirailleurs* to the French war effort, and (2) France's colonial relationship to Senegal and its legacy of exploiting West African agricultural products, as in bananas and cocoa, Banania's main ingredients.

20

In sharp contrast, Edwin A. Harleston's *The Soldier* (1919) presented a portrait of the black soldier—proud, undaunted, admirable, and disquieting—that embodied much of what African Americans felt about their wartime service. Like Fuller's *The Awakening of Ethiopia*, Harleston's enlisted man expresses the frustration and simmering anger of knowing that duty to God and country will not be sufficiently acknowledged or rewarded. Harleston, a product of The School of the Museum of Fine Arts in Boston, was certainly familiar with the story of Colonel Charles Young, a West Point graduate and one of the highest ranking black officers in the country who, because of the Army's reluctance to promote black officers into the brigadier general's ranks, was forced to retire in 1917. Harleston's black veteran, wearing medals, insignia, and an expression that tells of campaigns against both the Germans and his fellow white Army officers, epitomized the growing realization among many blacks that World War I was merely a prelude to greater and more overwhelming battles on the home front. For instance, the promise of racial equality, which was symbolized in the triumphant February 1919

19 Advertisement for Banania, 1917

20 Edwin A. Harleston, *The Soldier,* 1919

promenade up New York's Fifth Avenue by the all-black, 369th Regiment, was resoundingly negated (beginning that June) by a wave of lynchings, race riots, and other forms of racial violence across the United States, infamously referred to as the "Red Summer" of 1919.

However, at the beginning of 1919—a moment of optimism for many people in the world—a second international gathering of peoples of African ancestry took place, this time in Paris, and concurrent with the Versailles Peace Conference. Unlike the 1900 Conference, this "Pan African Congress" was organized through the efforts of Du Bois, who was in Paris as part of the Peace Conference press corps, and Blaise Diagne, a Senegalese member of France's Chamber of Deputies. While the primary topics of discussion revolved around the current conditions and future of the "Mandated Colonial Territories" in Africa, there was the belief among the participants that these African concerns, in spite of their distance from Europe and the Americas, had serious ramifications for blacks everywhere. Du Bois boldly articulated this position in the pages of *The Crisis* that same year: "The African movement means to us what the Zionist movement means to the Jews...the centralization of the race effort and the recognition of a racial fount."

Du Bois's notion of a common, Africa-centered "racial fount," though dangerously moving toward a kind of essentialism through identity politics, acknowledged (through his example of Zionism) the importance of the shared experiences of oppression, economic exploitation, and discrimination in the construction of such an ideological wellspring. By the end of 1919, with colonialism fully installed and racism endemic to much of the world, the quest for this "racial fount," or, to use another Du Bois metaphor, "the souls of black folk," drifted between romantic platitudes and "Red Summer" realities. In the world of art, Romanticism and Social Realism were the hallmarks of largely European, mid-to-late nineteenth-century aesthetics and, consequently, only capable of representing black "souls" within those cultural and theoretical strictures. It would not be until the early 1920s—with the rediscovery of what James Weldon Johnson described as the folk-inspired "creative genius of the Negro"—that Du Bois's racial fount would be located to a manifest "Ethiopia," (that is, Chicago's South Side, New York City's Harlem, and Paris's Montparnasse) and then, like an oasis to the parched in spirit, wholly absorbed.

Chapter 2
Enter and Exit the "New Negro"

Ethiopia: Reborn and Re-Presented

In *Making the Modern: Industry, Art, and Design in America* (1993), art historian Terry Smith traced the American obsession in the 1920s and 1930s with the creation of a contemporary aesthetic: a sensibility that he described as polished, efficient, progressive, democratic, and pure, as well as one that functioned with "only the newest structures" in mind. What Smith's investigation of modernism revealed was the deliberate construction of modernity out of an American marketplace of ideas, dreams and, in many instances, distinct winners and losers.

With this American compulsion as a backdrop, one can look at Henry Louis Gates Jr.'s "trope of a New Negro" and compare the applications of the twin concepts of the New and the Modern to the larger black cultural endeavor of this period. This phenomenon, variously called the "New Negro Arts Movement," a "Negro Renaissance" or the "Harlem Renaissance," was a myriad of different things to different people. For Alain Locke, Howard University professor of philosophy, and Charles S. Johnson, sociologist and director of research and publicity for the National Urban League, the "New Negro Arts Movement" was their carefully orchestrated effort to place African American social issues at the forefront of the national agenda. They used African American arts and culture as the vehicles for promoting "the race," and directed their publicity toward various philanthropic organizations and social agencies.

For composer George Gershwin, publisher Frank Crowninshield, theatrical agent and music publisher Irving Mills, and mobster and nightclub owner Owney Madden, the Harlem Renaissance was, to use American slang, "the hook": a marketing strategy for New York's publishers, theater producers, nightclub and cabaret owners, and other business people in the 1920s and 1930s.

For black artists like Paul Robeson, Langston Hughes, Duke Ellington, and Ethel Waters, as well as black intellectuals like Locke, Du Bois, James Weldon Johnson, and others, this "Negro Renaissance" was an auspicious moment in American cultural life: African Americans had unprecedented access to, and an active role in, the organizations of the mass media, the venues of mainstream entertainment, and cultural institutions.

Finally, for many people this "New Negro" entity was not so much a movement, a moment, or even an actual person, as a mood, or a sentiment in which black culture and its practitioners were seen as a valuable part of the larger cultural scene. In a society that had recently suffered a war of tremendous proportions, and was increasingly changing into an urban, impersonal, and industry-driven machine, black culture was viewed, interchangeably, as life-affirming, a libidinal fix, an antidote for ennui, a sanctuary for the spiritually bereft, a call back to nature, and a subway ticket to modernity. The "New Negro" was the perfect metaphor for this moment of great social rupture because, like a medicine-show elixir, it was perceived as the cure for everything.

The term "New Negro," meaning an enlightened, politically astute African American, sprang from the turn-of-the-century, progressive race rhetoric of Booker T. Washington, of Fannie Barrier Williams, advocate of black women's rights, and from the illustrations for *The Crisis* and *Voice of the Negro* of artist John Henry Adams Jr. As a cultural movement, the term "New Negro" entered into popular usage with two, influential publications in 1925: a special edition of the magazine *Survey Graphic*, entitled *Harlem: Mecca of the New Negro*; and an anthology of essays, short fiction, photographs, drawings, and a short play, entitled *The New Negro: An Interpretation*. Alain Locke, the driving force behind these two publications, dislocated the "New Negro" concept from its original socio-political connotations to an aesthetic of progress and race redefinitions.

Of course, comparing Smith's modernist iconology of the newest structures (that is, skyscrapers, department store displays, and Cadillacs) to the large cast of characters who comprised the "New Negro" arts movement might at first seem incongruous. Yet the classic images of this period—for instance, Winold Reiss's portrait of the twenty-three-year-old poet Langston Hughes (*c.* 1925)—perfectly captured the common ground from which these newest structures and racial pre-occupations sprang.

Winold Reiss, a product of Munich's Academy of Fine Arts and School of Applied Arts, came to the United States in 1913 and very soon opened his own Art School and Design Studio in New York City. Reiss divided his talents between commercial graphic and

21 LEFT Winold Reiss,
Langston Hughes,
c. 1925
22 OPPOSITE Aaron
Douglas, *Dance*
Magic, 1929–30. Mural
in the College Room
Inn, Sherman Hotel,
Chicago (destroyed)

interior design projects, and his renowned pastel renderings of "representative" world racial types. The creation of a modern design look and the study of the world's races through their exterior cultural expressivity were clearly evident in the Hughes portrait. From the painstaking delineation of Hughes's face, to the cubistic background of Art Deco marginalia, musical notes, and whimsical "Negro" decorations, Reiss situated the "New Negro" in the world of product and display, where the commodity (Hughes) was clearly placed between modernity and a persistent, pliable folk temperament.

Was it ironic that Alain Locke and the other promoters of the "New Negro" chose Winold Reiss—a Caucasian artist of German nationality—to portray this modern, black persona? Perhaps, but, on another level, the choice made sense given Reiss's cultural distance from the assorted forms of American racism. He had artistic affinities with both pictorial realism and modern industrial design, qualities that Locke and the other creators of the "New Negro" considered essential for constructing an African American identity in art. This no doubt inspired them to arrange for Aaron Douglas, a twenty-six-year-old African American artist who had recently arrived from Kansas City, to receive art instruction from Reiss.

Reminiscing about his apprenticeship, Douglas recalled that Reiss constantly urged him to explore "that inner thing of blackness." That Reiss, a European, encouraged Douglas, an African American, to explore a black identity was, again, not surprising given Reiss's earlier explorations (in the US, Germany, Sweden, and Mexico) into the visible manifestations of racial identity. Douglas's investigations took him into Harlem's cabarets and soirées where the proponents of the "New Negro" displayed their talents, into the Brooklyn Museum's gallery of African art where he could study black classical forms, and into the cogwheels of his own mind where he attempted "to objectify with paint and brush what [he] thought [were] the visual emanations...that came into view with the sounds produced by the old black songmakers...." Judging from a photograph of a Douglas mural, *Dance Magic* (1929–30), created for the Sherman Hotel's College Inn in Chicago, Illinois, Douglas's investigations transformed him from skeptical art student to nationally recognized black Modernist.

22

While indebted to Winold Reiss and his experiments with a kind of "Afro-Deco" art vocabulary (chevrons, mask-like designs, and bold color juxtapositions), Douglas eventually evolved his own style. For example, Douglas's mural *Harriet Tubman* (1931), celebrating the nineteenth-century antislavery activist, showed his signature use of silhouetted figures, overlaid and gradated chromatically with diagonal and concentric bands of color. His paintings were color abstractions, punctuated by environmental forms and action figures, portrayed like figures from ancient Egyptian wall paintings and reliefs; they conveyed inspirational messages which, in the spirit of the "New Negro," fused modernism with historical and vernacular themes. In 1925 Douglas said that he wanted to create an art that was, "Transcendentally material, mystically objective. Earthy. Spiritually earthy. Dynamic." This desire provided his *Harriet Tubman* mural, and his other works in this distinctive style, with a fluid, metaphysical framework.

A photograph of Aaron Douglas (1933) taken by New York theater critic, social gadfly, and "New Negro" patron Carl Van Vechten showed the artist standing in front of one of his hard-edge, Modernist murals (painted in Van Vechten's bathroom). As with Reiss's portrait of Hughes, Van Vechten's portrait of Douglas captured the impetuous, brazen spirit of

23

24

23 BELOW Aaron Douglas, *Harriet Tubman*, 1931. Mural at Bennett College, Greensboro, North Carolina
24 OPPOSITE Carl Van Vechten, *Aaron Douglas*, 1933

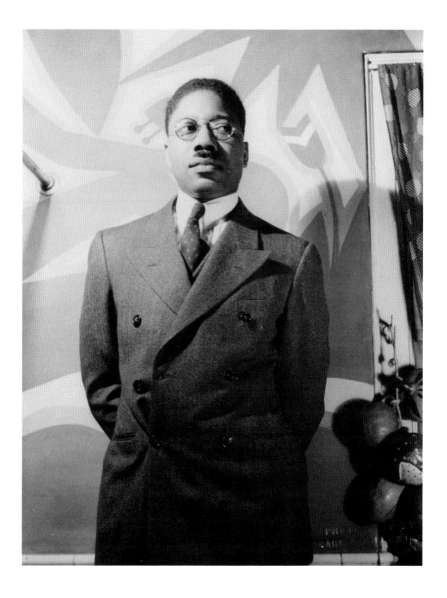

this black cultural moment, when younger African American
artists, without excuses or apologies, presented their work to
the wider public with the declaration that, "If white people
are pleased we are glad. If they are not, it doesn't matter.... If
colored people are pleased we are glad. If they are not, their
displeasure doesn't matter either. We build our temples for
tomorrow, strong as we know how, and we stand on top of the
mountain, free within ourselves."

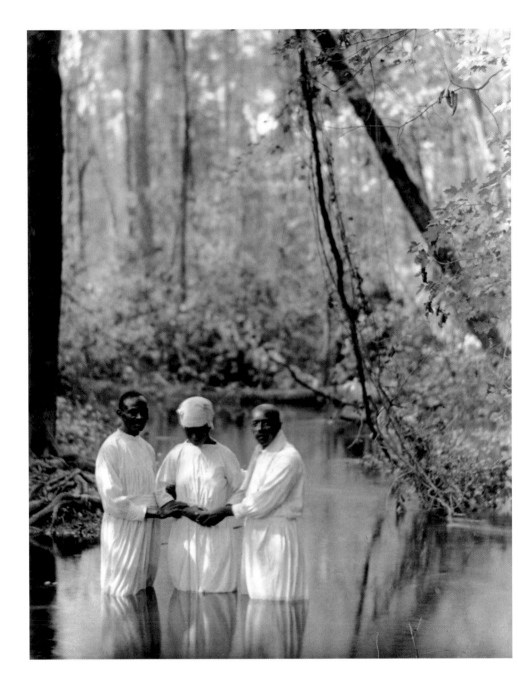

25 Doris Ulmann, *Baptism*, 1929–30

This exultation, penned by poet Langston Hughes as part of his essay "The Negro Artist and the Racial Mountain" (1926), ventured far beyond the theoretical musings presented in Locke's 1925 anthology *The New Negro*. Hughes confronted those critics who would limit the artistic expressions of African Americans to narrowly defined, skewed notions of what was beautiful, appropriate, uplifting, or "authentically Negro." Although the visual arts occasionally provided these debaters with examples of what they liked or disliked, the literary arts were more frequently interrogated in regard to "representative racial types." For example, Langston Hughes often came under attack for his literary portrayals of working-class black subjects. In many poems, such as "The Weary Blues," "Jazzonia," "Elevator Boy," and "Red Silk Stockings," Hughes painted with words his vivid, moving portraits of blues singers, jazz musicians, common laborers, and street hustlers: hardly the types of black people conservative African Americans wanted as cultural representatives for the race.

With the multitude of artistic products by and about African Americans that were available to consumers of culture, it was natural that critics like Locke and more established commentators like Du Bois and James Weldon Johnson would address the merits of certain works of art in regard to race relations and the more thorny question of racial representations. The breadth of what constituted the "New Negro" was staggering, with everything from depictions of the urbane and affluent, of the black poor and working class, of those in the high-profile world of entertainment, to visions of a kind of idyllic, black Arcadia. Although that part of the "New Negro" concept that emphasized urbanity, progress, and youth dictated the form and content of much of the art and rhetoric of the period, the "New Negro's" associated, often glossed-over message of rediscovery, growth, and rebirth also informed much of the movement's subject matter, as seen in works as varied as Oscar Micheaux's motion picture *The Homesteader* (1919), Jean Toomer's book *Cane* (1923), DuBose Heyward's hit play *Porgy* (1927) and, of course, Doris Ulmann's dreamlike, otherworldly photographs of blacks, such as *Baptism* (1929–30).

One could argue that the concept of the "New Negro" was meaningful only in relationship to the "Old Negro" or to an eternal, primordial "blackness." The "New Negro" was a metaphor of self-discovery for blacks (as well as for whites) in that the black vernacular was viewed as the panacea for centuries of stagnant, European cultural hegemony and the "zoo restrictions" (to quote from Jean Toomer's *Cane*) of a rigid, Victorian code of morality. By the mid 1930s, with the

25

26 LEFT William H. Johnson, *Self-Portrait*, 1929
27 OPPOSITE Laura Wheeler Waring, *Anna Washington Derry*, c. 1927

social demands of a worldwide economic Depression, this emphasis on the black vernacular eclipsed the fixation on the "progressive" and the "uplifting," ushering in an altogether different ideological movement among artists.

The representational extremes of the "New Negro" were present in two of the period's better-known African American portraits. The Philadelphia-based artist Laura Wheeler Waring incorporated impressionistic brushwork and an illusionistic background into her award-winning portrait of 27 *Anna Washington Derry* (c. 1927), the elderly mother of one of her friends. Waring's painting style—the conservative product of her years of academic training—resulted in the creation of this sentimental tribute to a proud black matriarch. An obvious 26 departure from Waring's nostalgia was William H. Johnson's much reproduced *Self-Portrait* (1929): an image of the artist in the guise of a "New Negro" bohemian. Johnson's formative years at the National Academy of Design in New York, and three years in France (between 1926 and 1929) gave his art a more expressionistic style.

In spite of their very different approaches to painting, both Waring and Johnson received gold medals and monetary awards from the William E. Harmon Foundation, a New York-based philanthropic organization that served as the principal patron for many African American visual artists between 1926 and 1933. Although the Harmon Foundation continued to provide limited support for many black artists after this period, the 1933 termination of their juried exhibitions and awards (coinciding with the shift in US art patronage to the government's Public Works projects) essentially ended the "New Negro" arts movement as it was known in America.

Harlem: Mecca and Metaphor

This historic moment—when black culture flourished and received wide, interracial and intercultural recognition—had several descriptive names beyond the more germane "New Negro Arts Movement." In a 1927 essay, literary scholar and cultural historian Benjamin G. Brawley referred to the proliferation of important creative writing in this period as a "Negro Literary Renaissance." In his autobiography *The Big Sea* (1940), Langston Hughes used the phrase "Manhattan's black Renaissance," to describe the black literary talent that was centered in and around the predominantly African American, New York City neighborhood of Harlem. Historian John Hope Franklin, in the first of several editions of his classic history, *From Slavery to Freedom* (1947), called his chapter on New York's burgeoning black arts scene—largely literary, but also theatrical and visual—"Harlem Renaissance." Almost twenty-five years later, historian Nathan Huggins entitled his ground-breaking book on this important moment and place in American cultural history *Harlem Renaissance* (1971). And sixteen years later, with the art exhibition "Harlem Renaissance: Art of Black America," and its accompanying publication of the same name (1987), the concept of the "New Negro" was further rooted in the idea of a Harlem-based racial fount of artistic accomplishment.

This brief account of the term "Negro Renaissance"—and the more frequently employed "Harlem Renaissance"—is useful if only as a demonstration of how, over time and depending upon the operative disciplines and methodologies employed, the significance of the concept has subtly shifted. In these several transformations from a literary term to a generic designation, from a generic designation to a visual arts phenomenon, and from a cultural motif to one defined by race, culture, and, most significantly, location, "Harlem Renaissance" has come to define the "New Negro" movement as a broad-based, multidisciplinary program, concentrated in New York's black community. The problem is that the term "Harlem Renaissance" is wanting as an accurate yet elastic description of the levels and range of black creativity in the 1920s and early 1930s.

Before entering further into a critique of the term, it is worthwhile to look at the historical and cultural factors that have led some scholars to locate this regenerative impulse in Harlem. Of primary importance was Harlem's large and growing black population. In 1925, it numbered about 175,000; by 1930, with steady migration from the southern States and immigration from the Caribbean and other parts of the black diaspora, it had expanded to over 200,000, making it the largest African American urban community of its kind. The new arrivals found advocates for their collective interests among several major black organizations with headquarters there. The NAACP, the National Urban League, the Universal Negro Improvement Association, and literally dozens of churches, fraternal organizations, sororities, social clubs, weekly newspapers, and businesses helped define and shape this Harlem-based "Renaissance."

Harlem was, of course, a racially and culturally distinctive community within New York City, yet one should resist the temptation to isolate Harlem's fame and fortunes in the 1920s and early 1930s from those of greater Manhattan. New York City's flamboyant Mayor in the second half of the 1920s, Jimmy "Beau James" Walker, encouraged the economic development of cultural forces in the city—radio broadcasters; book, magazine, and newspaper publishers; concert promoters; Broadway producers; song writers; cabaret owners; and various other entrepreneurs, legitimate and underworld—who, in their own way, helped to stimulate the vogue for Harlem. The roster of Harlem-based writers, actors, and musicians whose talents were advanced by these assorted cultural forces in New York City was a *Who's Who* of African American arts and letters around 1925. Similarly, the mystique and symbolic status that New York enjoyed from the late nineteenth century—as a destination full of opportunity for immigrants, as an escalating architectural wonder, and as a city that thrived on the extraordinary and "the New"—was increasingly shared with Harlem as its own reputation grew.

In contrast to the factors that enhanced Harlem's undeniable status as a cultural capital, its importance as the site of a renaissance in the visual arts in the 1920s and early 1930s is questionable. The "renascence in Negro art" that was promised by a small, Harlem-based exhibition (held in 1921 at the 135th Street branch of the New York Public Library) was, revealingly, not realized until 1927 when the important exhibition "The Negro in Art," opened, but this was in Chicago rather than in New York.

Apart from the artistic presence in Harlem of Aaron Douglas, James VanDerZee, and painter Malvin Gray Johnson, its place in African American art history during the 1920s is incompatible with the notion of a major artistic groundswell. James Weldon Johnson argued in his book *Black Manhattan* (1930) that Harlem had not yet produced a Negro painter of the stature of a Henry Ossawa Tanner. Similarly, art historian James A. Porter noted that, despite the local acclaim of Harlem sculptor Augusta Savage, her commitments to teaching and her own artistic training significantly compromised her work during the "renaissance."

28 James VanDerZee, *Untitled (West 127th Street, Harlem)*, 1932

Although Harlem's artists and patrons benefited from their
proximity to the annual Harmon Foundation art exhibitions,
these traveling shows (as well as the Foundation's overall
support for the visual arts) affected black communities
and artists not just in Harlem but across the nation. Of the
top award winners in the Harmon Foundation's annual art
competitions between 1926 and 1933, only Malvin Gray Johnson
could be considered a true Harlem-based artist. The rest
represented black artists across the US, such as Hale Woodruff
in Indianapolis, Laura Wheeler Waring in Philadelphia, Sargent
Johnson in San Francisco, Archibald J. Motley Jr. in Chicago,
and James Lesesne Wells in Washington, DC. The two other
Harmon Foundation award winners who have often been
linked with Harlem—artists Palmer C. Hayden and William
H. Johnson—spent the most important parts of their careers
during this period in Europe, and were not substantially
involved with Harlem's arts scene until the second half of the
1930s, just after the so-called Harlem Renaissance period.

Besides the Harmon Foundation exhibitions, the other
major "New Negro" art shows in Manhattan during this period
were the two critically acclaimed 1928 solo exhibitions by the

Mexican caricaturist Miguel Covarrubias and Chicago painter Archibald J. Motley Jr. Like their literary counterparts, Sterling Brown and Zora Neale Hurston, Covarrubias and Motley related to Harlem not in a documentary way but in more subliminal ways, with an emphasis in their work on African American folklife rather than on a distinct Harlem topology. Although sculptor Richmond Barthé (who moved from Chicago to New York in 1929) had two solo ventures in the early 1930s, these shows were largely harbingers of greater things to come during Barthé's more accomplished post-"Renaissance" phase.

While Harlem was extremely important as a cultural center for many people—and especially writers—during the period of the "New Negro," to imply that it was also the cradle of that period's visual arts scene—as the designation "Harlem Renaissance" is often taken to mean—is an exaggeration. While several visual artists certainly emerged with artistic authority from that community during this period, they had equally accomplished counterparts in other metropolitan cities. The most notable of the Harlem artists, painter Aaron Douglas and photographer James VanDerZee, used Harlem in their respective works not merely to map it out or to illustrate it for the thrill-seeking tourist but, rather, to make Harlem a modern, racial motif that transcended a specific black place or black people. The degree to which they succeeded in making Harlem what literary critic James de Jongh called "an ethos of race renewal" was demonstrated in the breadth of the community's patronage: the Harlem institutions that sponsored Douglas's earliest murals; the countless literary figures—Locke, Johnson, Van Vechten, and Hughes, among others—who commissioned Douglas to illustrate their Harlem-centered texts; and the ordinary people of Harlem who dressed up, posed for and bought VanDerZee's photographs. As can be seen from VanDerZee's well-known *Untitled (West 127th Street, Harlem* (1932), it was important even in the depths of the Depression for "commoners" and "high society" alike to maintain Harlem's image as a "black mecca" and symbol of material wealth and glamour in order to advance community, culture and "the race" in general. Still, these artists, their works and patronage, as important as they were, did not alone constitute a "renaissance." As an art-historical term, "Harlem Renaissance" works best when removed from its regional connotations and is placed within the more inclusive concept of a metaphoric racial landscape, where this born-again black culture is realized in a range of artworks, visual artists, and artistic meccas.

28

Revue Negre

The almost hallucinatory energy that the anonymous illustrator for Paramount Records poured into an advertisement for Memphis Julia Davis's blues recording, "Black Hand Blues" (1925), evoked the "black magic" that consumers of black popular culture felt in the "New Negro" arts movement. Here, the artist used Davis's blues narrative about a female philanderer receiving her just deserts, in the form of anonymous, threatening "black hand" letters, as a discursive overture on African American superstition and on the omen-like potency of "blackness." Carl Van Vechten, in a memoir of another performer from Memphis, the blues diva Bessie Smith, used imagery that was similarly supernatural in tone:

Her face was beautiful with the rich ripe beauty of southern darkness, a deep bronze, matching the bronze of her bare arms. Walking slowly to the footlights, to the accompaniment of the wailing, muted brasses, the monotonous African pounding of the drums, the dromedary glide of the pianist's fingers over the responsive keys, she began her strange, rhythmic rites in a voice full of shouting and moaning and praying and suffering, a wild, rough Ethiopian voice, harsh and volcanic, but seductive and sensuous too, released between rouged lips and the whitest of teeth....

For Carl Van Vechten, Bessie Smith's physical presence as well as her artistic talents invited this atavistic interpretation of her 1925 performance at the Orpheum Theater in Newark, New Jersey. The expressive power of black performance—whether incorporated into an advertisement for a blues recording, or reported by someone as *au courant* as Carl Van Vechten—was an important theme in the culture of the "New Negro," and an aesthetic issue that has yet to receive its deserved analysis in art-historical research.

Although in 1912 James Weldon Johnson had already drawn attention to the importance of black dancers, singers and musicians in the construction of a modern American cultural identity, it was the writers and visual artists of the "New Negro" arts movement who placed these black performers at the theoretical center of the culture. In a profusion of art forms, they cast the entertainers as cultural intermediaries who articulated in their acts the problems, hopes, desires, and aspirations of the "New Negro."

This sense of the oracular powers and "race" advocacy of the black entertainer figured strongly in many of the paintings and prints by the Paris-based, African American artist and jazz musician Albert Alexander Smith. His *A Tap Dancer* (c. 1928),

29 LEFT Albert Alexander Smith, *A Tap Dancer*, c. 1928
30 BELOW Advertisement for Memphis Julia Davis's "Black Hand Blues", 1925

featuring a young black vaudevillian, wearing a top hat and oversized tuxedo, on stage and under the intense glare of a spotlight, could be interpreted as simply a homage to a fellow black trouper. But the nature of Smith's parallel work—as an illustrator for *The Crisis*, *Opportunity*, and the Harlem-based, Puerto Rican bibliophile Arthur Schomburg—could also lead one to see *A Tap Dancer* as an allegorical statement about the preparedness and "performance" capabilities of "the race."

Smith was just one of many black artists who lived and worked in Paris in the 1920s and 1930s. Like Smith, many African Americans had their first encounter with French culture during World War I when black soldiers quickly realized that there was a personal freedom in France that was inconceivable back home. Following World War I and spurred on by economic prosperity and a spirit of optimism, Paris began to attract people from all parts of the globe, including significant numbers from the United States. Many of the African American newcomers were stage and nightclub performers, eager to take advantage of Paris's international reputation as Europe's entertainment capital.

The French novelist Paul Morand, reflecting on Paris as an ideal site for a critique of black performance as art, wrote in 1928:

31 BELOW Archibald J. Motley Jr., *Jockey Club*, 1929
32 OPPOSITE Jean Renoir, *Sur un air de Charleston*, 1926

*So sublime, so heartrending, are the accents of jazz, that we all
realize that a new form is needed for our mode of feeling.... Sooner or
later...we shall have to respond to this summons from the darkness,
and go out to see what lies behind this overwhelming melancholy that
calls from the saxophones. How can we stand still while the ice of
time is melting between our warm hands?*

About a year after Morand's plaintive, surrealistic call for
an acknowledgment of the power and presence of jazz, the
Chicagoan Archibald J. Motley Jr.—no stranger to the calls from
the saxophone himself—painted several canvases on the subject
of Paris's lively black music scene. *Jockey Club* (1929), Motley's
painting of the famous, American-owned nightclub where the
international art crowd gathered, responded to Morand's challenge
in its shadowy, unsettling portrayal of the club. Clearly, Motley had
decided in *Jockey Club* to turn the discriminating spotlight away
from the black performers (the subject of *Blues*, his other, well-
known painting of that same year) and toward the club's clientele,
with their affectations, trysts, and voyeuristic tendencies.

    French filmmaker Jean Renoir (son of the famous
Impressionist painter, Auguste Renoir) also turned to the period's
black performance tradition in his short film, *Sur un air de
Charleston* (1926). But, like Motley's painting, Renoir's film fantasy
about the mesmerizing, redemptive power of the popular black
dance step, the Charleston, shifted the focus; it is a white dancer
(played by Renoir's wife, actress Catherine Hessling) who, in a

31

32

post-Armageddon Europe, teaches the moves to a visiting African astronaut (played by the African American mime and blackface minstrel, Johnny Hudgins).

Renoir's implicit message in *Sur un air de Charleston*—that black creativity was modern society's only salvation and hope for human perpetuity—was influenced by the looming presence in Paris of the African American dancer Josephine Baker. When this nineteen-year-old dancer from St. Louis appeared on the stage of the Champs-Elysées's Music Hall in the 1925 stage show, *La Revue Nègre*, virtually nude and carried upside down, like a wounded gazelle, on the back of the robust, Martiniquan dancer Joe Alex, even the most cosmopolitan Parisians were stunned. When, in the following year, she appeared on the stage of the world-famous Folies Bergère, wearing nothing but a *cache-sexe* made of rubber bananas, and dancing a frenetic Charleston, she single-handedly defined the "New Negro" in Paris.

Theatre critic André Levinson's exclamation that Josephine Baker and Joe Alex's "*pas de deux sauvage* reaches the heights with wild and superb bestiality" epitomized the primitivist response to black culture exploited by both black and white, not only in France, but in much of the Western world. Despite the racism and sexism of images like Paul Colin's lithograph of a caged and simian-like Josephine Baker (from the *c.* 1927 portfolio *Le Tumulte Noir*), one should not forget that, for all the aspirational elements of the "New Negro" arts movement, there was another side of the "race renewal" agenda: one that probed uninhibitedly the more sordid and often stereotypical terrains of a black identity. Josephine Baker, as a willing subject and participant in this forbidden exploration, was joined by a long list of cultural primitivists, including Hughes, Covarrubias, the Jamaican writer Claude McKay, and (as seen in the previous literary examples) Carl Van Vechten, and Paul Morand.

Unfortunately, the peoples and cultures of Africa were the principal objects of this primitivist mindset. An almost universal ignorance of Africa, coupled with a legacy of exploitation of African peoples, created an atmosphere in which Westerners—usually taking their cues from Edgar Rice Burroughs novels and Hollywood jungle movies—saw "Africa" as either exotic and passionate, or dangerous and fearsome. Both attributes—the sensual and the sinister—were frequently combined, as in Alfred Janniot's sculptural reliefs covering the entire facade of Paris's Palais de la Porte Dorée (1931) and in Richmond Barthé's *African Dancer* (1933). Both works relied on stylized and animated renderings of nature to convey impressions of African peoples that, apart from an undeniable beauty, stressed savagery and carnality.

33 Paul Colin, from *Le Tumulte noir*, c. 1927

34 LEFT Richmond Barthé,
African Dancer, 1933
35 OPPOSITE Alfred Janniot,
sculptural relief, 1931, for
the facade of the Palais de
la Porte Dorée, Paris.

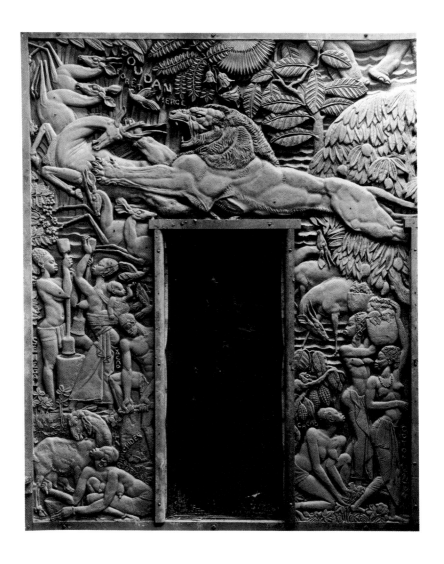

Enter and Exit the"New Negro"   69

Of course, there was also a movement during the period of the "New Negro" to redefine Africa and to make it a symbol of pride and accomplishment for the world's darker peoples. In the forefront was the Universal Negro Improvement Association (UNIA), founded by the Jamaican activist and visionary Marcus Garvey. Although the rhetoric of the Garveyites often yielded to images of a despotic black world, their message of black pride and economic self-sufficiency was followed in black communities throughout the northeastern United States and the English-speaking Caribbean.

Beyond Garvey's domain, what philosopher V. Y. Mudimbe described as "the invention of Africa" took place in another "New Negro" laboratory of cultural and economic revitalization: namely, Chicago. There, artist Charles C. Dawson created several African-inspired emblems for products targeted at African Americans. For his 1925 advertising campaign for Madagasco, a hair straightener of "no regrets" that softened the "naturally" kinky hair of blacks, he chose a blend of Ancient Egyptian motifs, East and West African references, and industrial-era "product efficiency" allusions, which urbanized and deprimitivized "Africa" for the "progressive" black consumers.

Despite Alain Locke and Marcus Garvey's celebration of Africa as an important source of inspiration for African Americans, many members of the "New Negro" rank and file were still challenged by the very notion that Africa could mean

36 Charles C. Dawson, advertisement for Madagasco Hair Straightener, 1925

GENTLEMAN, for the first time viewing a work of African sculpture: "What sort of a woman is that?"

37 Miguel Covarrubias, "To Hold as t'Were the Mirror Up to Nature", 1929

"To Hold, as t'Were the Mirror Up to Nature"

37

something significant to them. Like the anxieties about an African past posed in Countee Cullen's 1925 poem "Heritage" ("...Africa? A book one thumbs, Listlessly, till slumber comes..."), most African Americans could not (or perhaps refused) to acknowledge their racial and cultural ties with Africa. Artist Miguel Covarrubias, in a 1929 cartoon for *Vanity Fair*, expressed the inability of the typical African American to see him or herself in Africa's sculptural arts (or, in Covarrubias's primitivist thinking, "the Mirror"). But what Covarrubias had lost sight of was that, while some people were content to continue looking for the most racially representative image of the "New Negro" (the "primitive," the urban sophisticate, and so on), for many more the search had long been abandoned, and replaced by explorations of a more political, class-based nature. Even Locke came to believe that the so-called "Renaissance" was succeeded by a "Reformation" of sorts, characterized by "more penetrating," "even handed," and "less illusioned" portrayals of black life.

Claude McKay, creator of a range of "New Negro" types in his poetry and fiction, eventually felt that the necessity for African Americans, especially in the midst of the Great Depression, was the acquisition of "a group-soul." But unlike Du Bois's rarefied, romantic notion of "the souls of black folk," McKay's group-soul was structured around the day-to-day issues of race solidarity and labor: themes that took on a life of their own as the "New Negro" gave way to the plight of the world's black masses. What art audiences increasingly encountered was not so much a denunciation of modernity, primitivism, and the explorations of the urban versus rural paradigm, as an attempt to place these "New Negro" themes in a broader social context. Sensing that the Depression and its aura of dispossession and a renewed social activism would usher in yet another aspect of the "New Negro," the movement's advocates increasingly abandoned its sensational and more commercial trappings and, in their place, adopted other, more altruistic icons: specifically those of the "people," the "worker," and the ever-ambiguous "folk."

Chapter 3
The Cult of the People

From "New Negro" to "New Deal"
A few years after Richmond Barthé created *African Dancer*, the San Francisco Bay Area sculptor Sargent Johnson created
38 *Negro Woman*. Although both artists were products of the "New Negro" arts movement, in this particular instance their respective sculptures—both representing women of African ancestry—could not have been more dissimilar, stylistically as well as in emotional content. As discussed in the previous chapter, Barthé's *African Dancer* grew out of a European and American fascination with "the dark Continent," a Western conceit that frequently employed exotic, sexually charged representations of Africans and their cultures. By contrast, Johnson's *Negro Woman* portrayed the black female subject as modern, unpretentious, and devout: a stereotype of another kind, but free of the more degenerate connotations.

Of course, in any historical period, one is bound to find artists simultaneously pursuing different artistic directions. But by 1933, the primitivist attitudes of much of the art produced under the auspices of the "New Negro" arts movement were gradually being supplanted by more sober and prosaic perspectives on black representation. While Barthé's *African Dancer* certainly had its champions—it was acquired in 1933 by the Whitney Museum—Johnson's *Negro Woman* showed a heightened emphasis on the black vernacular in the arts; during the Depression, people found this not only relevant to their social situation, but also marketable in a culture of idealized working-class images.

The reasons for this ideological shift were varied. In Europe and the United States, the stock market crash of 1929 and the ensuing world economic Depression created an atmosphere in which the concerns of working-class people

38 Sargent Johnson, *Negro Woman*, c. 1935

dominated the international agenda. The rise of several Fascist governments during this period (in Germany, Italy, and Spain) also sparked populist political movements in Europe and America. For some, the political and economic programs of Socialism and Communism seemed to be the way to resolve the plight of the proletariat. Many others, especially in the US, questioned the effectiveness of Socialism and Communism in providing meaningful employment for the masses and in saving a collapsed, free market economy. After Franklin Delano Roosevelt's election as US president in 1932, his administration's "New Deal" (massive welfare and work-relief programs) made the United States one of the world's major laboratories for social and economic planning and a hub of social consciousness.

Among Roosevelt's various job creation measures was the establishment of the Federal Art Project (1935–43) which employed artists to create easel paintings, sculptures, photographs, motion pictures, posters, graphics, and murals, as well as to provide arts-related services to the federal, state, and municipal branches of the US government. Most government art patronage was humanitarian, didactic, and propagandist in purpose, and so, despite the array of American artists from different cultural, social, and ethnic backgrounds employed by the WPA/FAP (Works Progress Administration's Federal Arts Project), the predominant artistic style was figurative, naturalistic, and narrative-driven. While neither *African Dancer* nor *Negro Woman* was made under the auspices of the WPA/FAP, both, but especially *Negro Woman*, reflected the government's implicit "style" prototype: the human figure conceptually placed within a "social" narrative.

What were the narratives that visual artists most often utilized in creating an art of "social consciousness"? Scenes of both rural and urban communities at work or at leisure, family groupings, and historical themes were the most frequent, both under the auspices of the WPA/FAP and in independent projects.

Contrary to the conventional wisdom that would have predicted a pessimistic world view during the Depression, painters Archibald J. Motley Jr., and Palmer C. Hayden saw the world as teeming with life, leisure, and a touch of the lowbrow. *The Picnic* (1936), which Motley painted while employed by the WPA/FAP in Chicago, mixed the period's interest in common folk with his modernistic uses of color and compositional density. *The Picnic* certainly recalls the chromatic warmth and easy intelligibility of content found in works by contemporaries such as Thomas Hart Benton, but Motley's forms—colorful,

39

39 ABOVE Archibald J. Motley Jr., *The Picnic*, 1936
40 OPPOSITE Palmer C. Hayden, *Midsummer Night in Harlem*, 1936

organic, and provocatively situated to fit the artist's own
logic and sense of rhythm—subverted the standard label of
"American scene" often attached to his work, and replaced it
with something far more metaphysical.

Motley's fanciful, densely packed composition had
40   similarities with Palmer C. Hayden's *Midsummer Night in
Harlem* (1936): another brash, expressionistic scene of blacks
relaxing in an outdoor, urban setting. Numerous other
works of the Depression era took as their subject people at
leisure, such as Philip Evergood's *Dance Marathon* (1934) and
Reginald Marsh's *Twenty Cent Movie* (1936), but Hayden's use
in *Midsummer Night in Harlem* of the stereotypes of wide-eyed
and grinning blacks gave his work a troubling air, especially
in its visual corroboration of common racist sentiments. Yet
Hayden was not alone during this period in representing blacks
irreverently; we see the same treatment in the bawdy, culturally
contentious works of such "progressive" artists as novelist
Richard Wright in the manuscript of *Lawd Today*, written
around 1936, and actor Paul Robeson in his 1937 film *Big Fella*.

In his book *Blues and Evil* (1993), African American cultural
critic Jon Michael Spencer described the Dante-like journey

of Depression artists into the deep recesses of a mentality inveterately demarcated by race and class: a realm, like Hayden's outrageous black world in *Midsummer Night in Harlem*, fraught with real-life absurdities, insults, horrors, and hyperboles. The cultural spokespersons for the black masses in the 1930s—blues musicians, gospel singers, number runners, exhorting preachers, and "soap-box" radicals—painted their own pictures of black life that were just as absurd as Hayden's midsummer scene under the full moon.

Because economic issues were of central importance during the Great Depression, these pictures of communities and leisurely activities were overshadowed by other more serious images that explored the world of work. Even Hayden's *Midsummer Night in Harlem*, appearing just one year after Harlem experienced its first major riot, could also be interpreted as a satirical response to that community's real anxieties in the face of high unemployment and economic hardship. Consequently, representations of industry, agriculture, employment, and the associated problems that these issues brought were of particular interest to socially committed artists and audiences alike.

Even during the more optimistic years of the "New Negro," labor issues and their impact on black communities captured the imaginations of several writers and visual artists. Publications like *The Crisis*, *Opportunity* and the leftist monthlies *The Messenger* and *New Masses* featured articles and art editorials on the subject of black labor by such "New Negro" figures as W.E.B. Du Bois, Charles S. Johnson, Aaron Douglas, and James Lesesne Wells. Wells's book jacket for Lorenzo J. Greene and Carter G. Woodson's *The Negro Wage Earner* (1930) anticipated the appeal of the black worker theme that preoccupied artists and intellectuals throughout the 1930s. In the details of Wells's stark black-and-white design, the black worker was, at once, agriculturist and industrialist, a professional as well as a blue collar worker and, at his most metaphorical level, a waiter, balancing (or serving) the city, while bestraddling "progress" from ancient pyramids to modern skyscrapers. By 1930 Wells had clearly taken the "New Negro" movement's quest for racial progress to a higher plane: one that rejected superficial barometers of success and class-based privileges for black economic development across class lines.

Agitation on the economic front was often combined with political activism. The battles fought in the US over such issues as full employment, optimum on-the-job environmental conditions, and union representation were frequently associated with political efforts to combat racism and job discrimination. The John Reed Clubs, the Artists' Union, and the American Artists' Congress were the principal organizations through which American artists participated in political activities—protesting against American racism and

41 James Lesesne Wells, book jacket for *The Negro Wage Earner*, 1930

42 Ernest
Crichlow, *Lovers*,
1938

world Fascism, picketing employers who engaged in unethical
hiring and firing practices, conducting voter registration drives,
and persuading workers to join trade unions.

As subjects for visual artists, labor struggles and racial
inequity surfaced in a variety of art forms, from Diego Rivera's
widely seen mural cycle, *Portrait of America* (1933), created for
New York City's New Workers School, to Margaret Bourke-White's
Life magazine photograph of unemployed blacks lined up for
food supplies in front of a billboard which ironically proclaims,
"There's no way like the American Way" (1937). In African
American artists' circles, the most celebrated example of a work
of art created with a critique of US economic and racial realities
in mind was Aaron Douglas's *Song of the Towers* (1934), one of
four panels from his *Aspects of Negro Life* mural (commissioned
by the 135th Street branch of the New York Public Library). Ernest
Crichlow, while working alongside Douglas on the New York City
WPA/FAP, contributed to this growing body of protest imagery
42   with *Lovers* (1938): a politically charged yet voyeuristic depiction
of a hooded Klansman sexually assaulting a black woman.

The Cult of the People   **79**

While images like Crichlow's *Lovers* were dismissed as hopelessly "ideological" and "propagandist" by succeeding generations of art critics, the art reviewers of the 1930s could neither deny nor escape the expressive power and validity of such works. For example, the 1935 NAACP-sponsored exhibition, "Art Commentary on Lynching" (exhibited at the Arthur U. Newton Galleries in New York City), received a review in *Parnassus* magazine concluding that the works (by artists like Benton, Marsh, Paul Cadmus, and Isamu Noguchi, among others) were "chosen not merely for the clarity and intensity with which they state their case or plead their cause but with an eye definitely set for their artistic value." The socially explosive realities of US race relations in the 1930s—exemplified in the decade-long, international cause célèbre surrounding the trumped-up rape charges against nine young black men in Scottsboro, Alabama—created a whole new school of artists informed by African American culture who, even under the sponsorship of the WPA/FAP, found their own, independent voices.

One such artist was Augusta Savage. In 1932, after several years of studying, exhibiting, and traveling throughout Europe, Savage returned to Harlem where she opened the first of several of her community art schools. Savage, taking on the colossal role of art educator and community activist in Depression-era Harlem, renounced the elitist advantages of an artist's life in favor of its more altruistic aspects. Although this meant channeling her creative energies away from her own work and toward teaching, the achievements of many of those whom she taught and advised (Crichlow, William Artis, Gwendolyn Knight, Jacob Lawrence, and Norman Lewis, among others) demonstrated her tremendous, long-term impact on Harlem's visual arts scene.

That Savage's commitment to Harlem's artistic future was not a complete obstacle to her own art was confirmed by her last major commission: the sixteen-foot (five-meter) tall plaster sculpture *Lift Every Voice and Sing* (also known as *The Harp*), created for the 1939 New York World's Fair. Savage's sculptural homage to the illustrious author, composer, and fellow Floridian James Weldon Johnson (who had died the previous year) was a radical departure for her, with its figural distortions and part anthropomorphic, part architectonic symbolism. The community spirit in this piece—a by-product of Savage's years as a Harlem art teacher and workshop director—clearly resonated with Claude McKay's expressed notion of an African American "group-soul" and prophetically looked ahead to the flowering of black culture in the early 1940s.

43

43 Augusta Savage, *Lift Every Voice and Sing* (*The Harp*), World's Fair, New York, 1939 (destroyed)

In Search of the Black Proletariat

A preoccupation with representations of the black working class during the 1930s was not only confined to artists of African American or European American backgrounds. In the early 1930s, British painter Edward Burra spent almost a year in New York City, feverishly jotting down (in a style similar to that of Miguel Covarrubias and George Grosz) quick impressions of everyday African American life, which he later developed into larger, finished watercolors. Burra's *Harlem* (1934), with its perspectival view of brownskinned pedestrians and brownstone buildings, represented the community and its inhabitants as a study in urban harmony. Indeed, in a letter of 1934 to a friend in England, Burra described Harlem as "lovely, rather like Walham Green gone crazy."

Burra's *Harlem* was also like a mosaic of several street scenes including blacks by the US photographer Walker Evans, most notably Evans's *42nd Street* (1929) and *Citizen in Downtown Havana* (1933). The black man dressed in a brown suit and green hat in *Harlem* recalled the pose and demeanor of the black man in a white suit and straw hat in *Citizen in Downtown Havana*. In both works, these urban sentries pictorially anchored the compositions, exalting a kind of working-class archetype which, from Harlem to Havana, was the object of much concern from both the left and right of the political spectrum.

Cuba, where *Citizen in Downtown Havana* was photographed, was in the throes of a social and cultural uprising by the time Walker Evans arrived there in 1933. The dictatorship of Cuban President Gerardo Machado, largely supported by US business interests, prompted great political unrest, from massive student demonstrations to police attacks against academics, journalists, and union organizers. On the cultural front, Cuban artists had begun to embrace their African and, by extension, vernacular roots, resulting in a kind of renaissance in Cuban literature, visual arts, and performing arts not thematically different from the recent "Negro Renaissance" in the US. Although Evans's documentary manner in *Citizen in Downtown Havana* initially orients the viewer away from a consideration of these social and cultural upheavals, a closer look at this photograph—and especially Evans's use of media and popular culture imagery—presents the possibility here of a covert, socio-cultural critique: one that places Cuba's non-white masses in conflict with imperialism and cultural dominance from abroad.

The theme of a social and cultural uprising inspired by the black working class also shaped much of the art of black artists and intellectuals in France and the French-influenced Caribbean. One strain of this distinctly francophone artistic

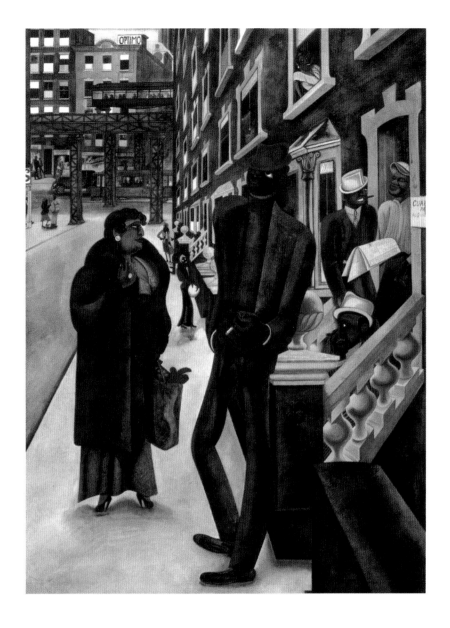

44 Edward Burra, *Harlem*, 1934

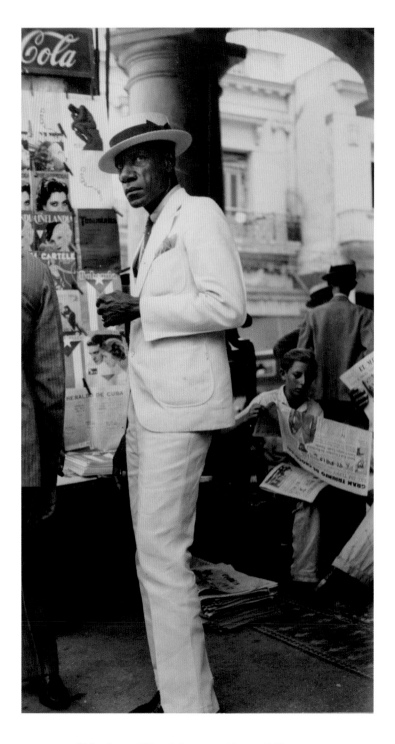

45 Walker Evans, *Citizen in Downtown Havana*, 1933

phenomenon—known as *Negritude*—inadvertently grew out of Paris's 1931 International Colonial Exhibition, which brought public attention to the affairs of France's African, Asian, and Caribbean colonies. Although in many instances this exhibition perpetuated exotic and primitivist representations of black cultures (for instance, Alfred Janniot's cast reliefs for the exhibition's newly constructed Palace of the Colonies), the event also encouraged black intellectuals from Africa, the Caribbean, and the US to come together, discuss the exhibitions and related programs, and, most importantly, to mobilize their various talents toward reporting their own firsthand accounts of "the black world."

With the exception of an Aaron Douglas illustration, which appeared in the first issue of the *Negritude* journal *La Revue du Monde Noir*, the artists of African ancestry who figured most prominently in the *Negritude* movement were literary. It would not be until 1937, when the African American painter Lois Mailou Jones arrived in Paris, that painting would provide an important visual link to the writings of such *Negritude* authors as Aimé Césaire, Léon Damas, and Léopold Sédar Senghor. Jones was an accomplished academician, trained at the School of the Museum of Fine Arts in Boston, but during her year's stay in Paris she broke free from this training with her painting *Les Fétiches* (1938): a post-Cubist and post-primitivist study of African masks. In her pictorial gathering of assorted African personae—ethnographic and imaginary—Jones prefigured the declamatory yet surrealistic visions of the Martiniquan poet Aimé Césaire who wrote that his *Negritude* "plunges into the red flesh of the soil,...into the blazing flesh of the sky,...[and] riddles with holes the dense affliction of its worthy patience." In spite of the fact that Jones, like Césaire, relied on an illusory rather than documentary passage into African culture, *Les Fétiches* displayed its *Negritude* with an urgency and definitiveness that was unprecedented among the artists of the Depression.

Haiti, the world's first independent black republic and occupied by the US Marines between 1915 and 1934, was the site of the other francophone, proletariat-inspired cultural phenomenon, known as the *Indigenist* movement. With a history of achievements in the literary and visual arts dating back to the late eighteenth century, Haiti reemerged in the late 1920s with a spirited, folk-inspired arts scene that was largely instigated by the ethnographic writings of Jean Price-Mars and the literary efforts of a group of younger Haitian writers. A black American academic painter, William Edouard Scott, visited Haiti in 1931 and lived there for a year, teaching the fundamentals of painting to a whole generation of aspiring artists.

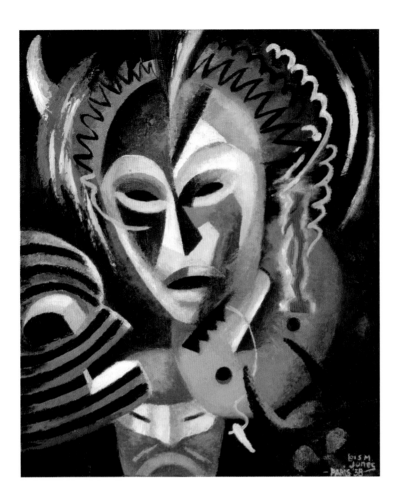

Like the contemporary black cultural activities in the United States, France, and Cuba, Haiti's *Indigenist* movement had political implications. In the novel *La Case de Damballah* (*Damballah's Hut*) of 1939, Haitian author and visual artist Petion Savain voiced subtle criticisms of the Haitian élite and governmental authorities, while endowing Haiti's large peasant class with creole-inflected spiritual entitlements. Savain's accompanying illustrations, although shaped by his 1931 apprenticeship with Scott, adopted a straightforward, slightly untutored look that responded to his fellow *Indigenist* artists and to the overwhelmingly illiterate Haitian masses.

The main protagonist of Petion Savain's novel—the West African-derived serpent deity Damballah—is a key component of the popular Haitian religion known as *Vodun*. During the 1930s

47

numerous writers and scholars looked closely at heterodox black religions like *Vodun* in their attempt to understand the spiritual and ethical dimensions of the black peoples of the whole African diaspora. Studies conducted by Charles S. Johnson, Zora Neale Hurston, and Melville Herskovits, among others, explored topics such as the emergence of African-based religions in the New World, the sundry characteristics of black religious expression, and the high frequency within many black religions of "spirit possession." These sociologists, anthropologists, and artists found that black religions had a powerful, all-encompassing authority over their followers: an authority that even the political panaceas of Communism and Socialism could not override.

48   *Pocomania* (1936), a work of sculpture created by the Jamaican artist Edna Manley, took its name from the revivalist Jamaican religion, partly African and partly Christian, that by the early 1930s had come to symbolize that Caribbean island's fundamental, non-European cultural identity. Although the dynamic figure in *Pocomania* certainly echoed the actual "jumpin' and trompin' " of its ecstatic, religious devotees, the figure's bowed head, raised arm, and hand-on-chest gesture were allusions to the making of oaths and the pledging of allegiances: nationalist displays that Manley knew as the wife and political partner of N. W. Manley, one of Jamaica's leading advocates of abolishing British colonial rule. In contrast to the viewpoint that religion thwarted the revolutionary aspirations of its followers, Manley's *Pocomania* suggested that black religion was capable of invigorating the black masses and inspiring them toward real political change.

46 OPPOSITE Lois Mailou Jones, *Les Fétiches*, 1938
47 BELOW Petion Savain, untitled block print from *La Case de Damballah*, 1939

That the enthusiastic dance—or battle—against evil forces in Manley's *Pocomania* had both spiritual and political implications could be argued from the perspective of another black proletarian image from the 1930s. Robert Riggs's 1939 painting of the Joe Louis and Max Schmeling fight of 1938 was also dependent upon cultural symbolism for its multiple connotations. Louis, the best heavyweight boxer since Jack Johnson, was an American hero during the Depression era, with a string of boxing victories and a stoic, humble demeanor that endeared him to blacks and whites alike. Louis's larger-than-life stature in the American imagination made his defeat in 1936 by the German heavyweight Max Schmeling more than a disappointment: it was an American tragedy for the already demoralized, economically beleaguered nation. In addition, the US government's apprehensions concerning Adolf Hitler's Germany added a socio-political dimension to the 1936 Louis/Schmeling fight, and (as seen in the Robert Riggs painting) to their much anticipated 1938 rematch.

49   The title of Riggs's painting—*The Brown Bomber*—makes clear the degree to which Americans used the African American boxer Joe Louis as a metaphor for their own fantasies on the economic, political, and racial fronts. For some, Louis was the ultimate working-class hero: of common origins but equipped with a grace and physical prowess that made him exceptional. For others, Louis was Nazi Germany's worse nightmare: a Negro weapon, ready to prove to the world that democracy, in spite of inconsistencies, would prevail. For many blacks, Louis embodied racial and cultural vindication after centuries of abuse, discrimination, and ridicule on their native soil. Riggs's photographically inspired work, depicting those initial minutes following Louis's famous one-round knock-out punch, presented the boxer as an avenging angel, body arched and tightly drawn, and miraculously suspended in space over his fallen opponent. In Riggs's dark arena, the photographers, reporters, and other spectators—visible in the foreground and along the boxing ring's distant, artificial horizon—played awe-struck eyewitnesses as Louis became the symbol of the apotheosis of the black proletariat. President Roosevelt's modest, pre-fight admonition to Louis that the people "were depending on those muscles for America" underscored just how pervasive was the tendency to objectify black people in this populist, morale-boosting era.

          Yet the spiritual core of the black masses—as articulated in works as diverse as Manley's *Pocomania* and Hurston's black vernacular novel *Their Eyes Were Watching God* (1937)—separated them from the rest of the proletariat of the period,

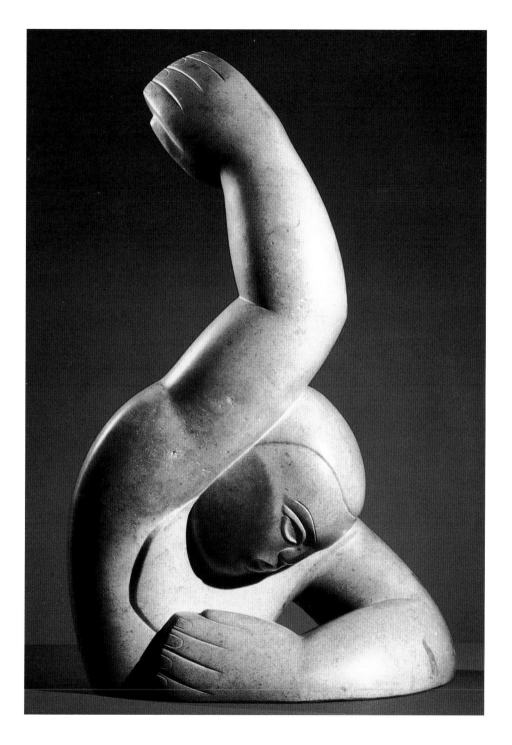

48 Edna Manley, *Pocomania*, 1936

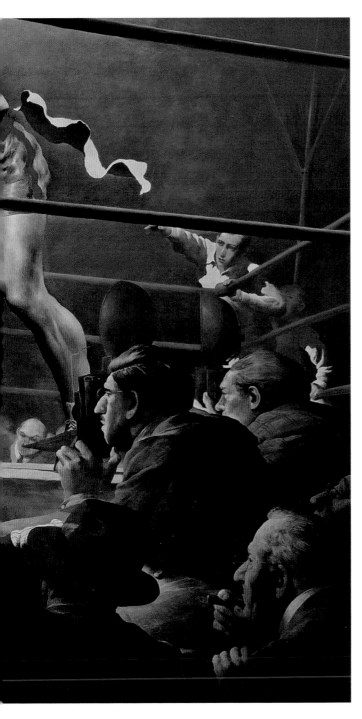

and sustained them through these difficult years. It would not be very long before this interest in a spiritually endowed black proletariat led many American artists and intellectuals to musical, oral, and visual arts that (in their estimation) were the "authentic" creative expressions of "the folk." In addition to satisfying the societal desire to understand more fully the mind and imagination of the "pre-industrial" segments of the population, the documentation, assembly, and study of a range of American "folk" arts fueled an often nationalistic sentiment concerning America's cultural roots.

This celebration of "the folk," however, did not come without its critics. Harold Preece, in his 1936 essay "The Negro Folk Cult," questioned the value of celebrating the black vernacular without an associated examination of the political, economic, and social issues that affected black practitioners and audiences of this culture. Preece specifically objected to Zora Neale Hurston's excavations of the colorful lore and language of poor, working-class blacks, seeing her largely uncritical efforts as those of a naive, black sycophant or, worse, of a duplicitous, "literary climber." To Hurston's credit, her motives for exploring black folklore did have a political agenda, and that agenda was to remove the pathological stigma (as promulgated by social scientists like E. Franklin Frazier and others), and to invest black folk culture with an artistic worth and universal importance which it had been long denied. "Hurston rejected the pathological stereotype," wrote her biographer Robert E. Hemenway in 1977, "because she knew that material poverty and ideological poverty were distinct entities...." Hurston tried to show in her writings and research that "normality is a function of culture, that an Afro-American culture exists, and that its creators lead lives rich with ideological and esthetic significance, a fact demonstrated by their folklore."

Harper's Bazaar photographer Louise Dahl-Wolfe's "discovery" of the African American, Tennessean "folk" sculptor William Edmondson, and her successful lobbying to have his work exhibited in 1937 at New York's Museum of Modern Art, attested to the aesthetic appeal of this art from the racial and cultural margins. Works like Edmondson's *Angel* (*c*. 1932–37)— originally created as grave markers and garden ornaments for the impoverished yet art-loving members of Nashville's black community—became coveted "folk art" collectibles once Edmondson was given the imprimatur of a solo exhibition at MoMA. *Angel* and other sculptural products of Edmondson's "God-given" vision fueled the modernist nostalgia for an existence that was simpler and morally uncomplicated, and the modernist fantasy about the "primitives" among them.

50

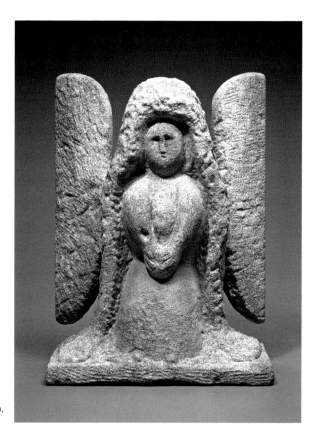

50 William Edmondson,
Angel, date unknown

Scholarly studies on the spiritual lives of the black masses showed that their relationship to God was anything but simple and uncomplicated. In the mid-1930s, a sociological study examining the religious conversion experiences of ex-slaves concluded that one of their striking characteristics was the process of discerning the presence of the holy spirit and, then, coming to terms with the "reborn" self. For Edmondson, the answer was to let his art become God's vehicle for spiritual renewal. For Elijah Pierce, artist, barber, and itinerant preacher based in Columbus, Ohio, it was to dedicate his carved and painted wooden panels to the literal teaching of God's word. These two examples of a folk aesthetic springing out of black communities extended the image of an art "of, by, and for the people" beyond governmental and other proletariat-inspired artistic orientations and into a broad-based representational enterprise that was unimaginable for the proponents of the "New Negro."

51

51 Anonymous, *Elijah and Cornelia Pierce*, c. 1935

Many of these works of the Depression era were included
in the debates in the art world on nationalistic tendencies
in modern art and the threats of politically imposed artistic
boundaries. Ranging from Social Realism to Regionalism,
these boundaries were described by New York painter Romare
Bearden as "profoundly social," or, rather, indicative of African
American artists succumbing to the aesthetic tyranny of an art
based solely on lived "experience." What none of these artists or
theorists anticipated was that this humanistic impulse would
carry them and their art toward mid-century and a shifting
fascination in the art world between racial distinctiveness and
the total disappearance of race, cultural markers, and figural
representations.

Chapter 4
Pride, Assimilation, and Dreams

An Overview

Between 1940 and 1963, the image of black culture underwent several major transformations. The year 1940 was the seventy-fifth anniversary of the ratification of the Thirteenth Amendment, which abolished slavery; in 1963 over 200,000 people converged on Washington, DC, to protest against restricted job opportunities for African Americans and de facto segregation in housing and education. Throughout this period, which was also a time of war and major political change, black culture alternately shifted from the spotlight to the periphery and, ultimately, to the center of the world's stage: shifts that were analogous to black people's changing social status.

In one sense, World War II fueled an international desire for political freedom and individual self-determination that many of the world's peoples took to heart during the 1940s. For some there was the belief that with an Allied victory African Americans would attain full citizenship and finally reap the benefits of living and working in a model democracy. For blacks in Africa and the Caribbean, the liberation of Europe also kindled hopes for the collapse of colonialism and a chance at self-rule. Many saw Fascism as a not-so-distant relative of racism and colonialism and, consequently, also something that blacks needed to fight against. This view was underscored by the fact that black soldiers, particularly from the US, Africa, and the Caribbean, were fighting in the war against Germany, Italy, and Japan.

In England the numbers of black residents from the Caribbean and Africa grew during and after World War II. At least 7,000 men from the Caribbean served in the Royal Air Force alone. After the war, many of these veterans and their families (both "nuclear" and "extended") made their

52 John
Robinson,
Self-Portrait,
c. 1945

way to England in the hope of finding jobs, decent housing,
educational opportunities, and a future for their children.
Instead what they frequently encountered were unemployment,
overcrowding, discrimination, and physical attacks (as
experienced during the infamous riots in London's Notting
Hill in 1958). The thousands of North African and Southeast
Asian immigrants in post-war France hardly fared better, with
the escalating tensions between the French government and its
overseas territories making life in Paris and other French cities
especially intolerable for Algerians, Tunisians, Vietnamese,
and other colonial subjects.

However, as journalist Roi Ottley suggested in *New World
A-Coming* (1943), his book on contemporary black life, African
American expectations for a promising future were, at least
initially, high during this period. In Washington, DC, John
Robinson conveyed this decidedly optimistic racial mood in
his *Self-Portrait* (*c.* 1945), where painter, artworks, environs,
and reflections in glass formed a picture in which creativity

52

53 Karl Broodhagen, *The Poet*
(George Lamming), c. 1945

and introspection are paramount. Thousands of miles away, in
Barbados, sculptor Karl Broodhagen, ventured into his own brave
new world with his portrait bust of the local budding poet (and
future novelist) George Lamming. Broodhagen's *The Poet* (*c.* 1945)
shared with Robinson's *Self-Portrait* an introspective quality
of young manhood, as well as an exploration of the African
facial characteristics of his subject that, in both works, made
"blackness" an irrefutable, fixed reality and badge of honor.

By the end of the 1940s, however, Robinson and Broodhagen's
images of progressive, idealized black youth were superseded
by more pessimistic or ambivalent racial themes. In literature,
blackness as an insignia of social estrangement first emerged
in the writings of novelist Richard Wright but, increasingly,
Wright's voice of protest was joined by the more troubled
writings of novelists Chester Himes, Ralph Ellison, James
Baldwin, and even Broodhagen's George Lamming, author of
In the Castle of My Skin (1953). In 1949, the artist Harlan Jackson—
born in Texas, based in New York City—applied this notion of

53

54 Harlan Jackson,
Mask No. II, 1949

54 a problematic black identity to his painting *Mask No. II*. Split
between a racial pride that was embodied in a "tribal" mask
and a desire to assimilate that black identity within the "white"
cultural practice of abstract painting, *Mask No. II* illustrated
the contradictions that were increasingly felt by proponents
of black culture. Toward the end of this period the options
for black cultural expression and its reception went beyond a
simple dialectic of "pride" versus "assimilation" and, instead,
embraced models that were either inclusive of both, or were
derived from an entirely different set of social and aesthetic
values. These new options emerged just at the moment when
black cultural groups became conspicuous, cosmopolitan,
and candid about their universality and growing political
importance in world affairs.

"Flying Home"

Precursors of a vibrant, black cultural scene were already evident during the final years of the Great Depression. African American artists and their creations were key elements in America's cultural fare around World War II, from the literary works of Richard Wright to the theatrical performances of Paul Robeson. Well into the 1940s, these artists and others in literature, theater, music, dance, and motion pictures, helped shape perceptions of a black identity that were especially diverse. Lionel Hampton's swinging persona in his jazz recording "Flying Home," Marian Anderson's dignified presence in her classical interpretations of Negro spirituals and German *lieder*, Eddie "Rochester" Anderson's light-hearted, gravel-voiced, radio respondent to Jack Benny, choreographer Katherine Dunham's ballets influenced by Afro-Caribbean dance and jazz, and novelist Richard Wright's brooding, angry characterizations of black men all figured prominently in the American popular imagination.

In the late 1930s and early 1940s the visual arts experienced an explosion comparable to the "Negro Renaissance." Beginning with the show that was organized for the Texas Centennial Exposition's "Negro Building" in 1936, there were at least ten other major "all Negro" art exhibitions in the following decade, ranging from the widely discussed "Contemporary Negro Art" at the Baltimore Museum of Art (1939), to the much heralded "The Negro Artist Comes of Age" at the Albany Institute of History and Art (1945). In contrast to the earlier, "all Negro" art shows sponsored by the Harmon Foundation, these exhibitions received endorsement and critical analysis from two of the period's leading art critics: Alain Locke, the author of *The New Negro* and that movement's elder statesman, and James A. Porter, Master of Arts from New York University's prestigious Fine Arts Graduate Center and a professor of studio arts and art history at Howard University. Both Locke and Porter published important books on the subject in the early 1940s, thus contributing to this period's growing enthusiasm for African American themes and subjects in art.

Locke's theoretical premise in *The Negro in Art* (1940) was that work by black diasporal artists, as well as work by white artists who explored black subject matter, formed a body of cultural evidence worthy of close study. In addition to tracing just how ubiquitous black subjects had been throughout Western art history, Locke's *The Negro in Art* was ahead of its time in that it addressed the issue of race and its catalytic role in cultural representations.

Porter's *Modern Negro Art* (1943), although less prophetic than Locke's book, was perhaps the more historically important work, both in its own day and later. Solidly researched and painstakingly documented, this pioneering study traced the art-historical record of African Americans from their colonial beginnings to the "Negro art" boom of the early 1940s. What pushed Porter's study beyond the boundaries of a standard text was his willingness to criticize, question, and evaluate the works of African American artists without succumbing to racial favoritism. As a traditionalist and aesthetic conservative, Porter made harsh but informative criticisms of artists Aaron Douglas, Archibald J. Motley Jr., Palmer Hayden, and William H. Johnson. However, Porter also exhibited a remarkable tolerance in his favorable critiques of the works of such "naive" artists as William Edmondson, Horace Pippin, and the twenty-six-year-old "popular" artist and "virtuoso" Jacob Lawrence.

Lawrence, a product of New York's American Artists School and Harlem's community art centers of the Depression era, painted local, contemporary scenes as well as historical subjects with an unusual eye for overall design, small details, and thematic essences. These attributes—along with his ambitious undertaking of several multi-paneled, gouache and tempera works on black history—singled him out among his peers as early as 1938, and championed a radical way of visualizing black culture. Lawrence's strategy of imposing high-key color contrasts and spare, planar treatments on his pictorial vignettes of African American life (as seen in his 1946 painting *Going Home*) elicited enthusiastic responses from a broad spectrum of viewers during the 1940s which, in turn, helped to facilitate an interest in visual representations of a black culture that was both modernist and folkloric.

William H. Johnson, after his auspicious New York debut in 1929, abruptly departed for a long stay in Europe. On his return to New York in 1938, he soon encountered Lawrence's expressive work. This visual meeting, combined with Johnson's own distillation of European Post-Impressionism and African American folk culture, resulted in works like *Jitterbugs (V)* of *c.* 1941–42: a faux-naïve yet modernistic interpretation of a Harlem couple performing the fast urban dance known as the Jitterbug.

Johnson's folk/modern art fusion—couched within the over-arching presence of Jacob Lawrence, as well as Johnson's attempt to articulate something special about contemporary African American life—was clearly in the air, as seen in the popular "all Negro" movie musical *Cabin in the Sky* (1943). Film director Vincente Minnelli, who had previously forged close working

55 OPPOSITE Jacob
Lawrence, *Going
Home*, 1946
56 RIGHT William
H. Johnson,
Jitterbugs (V),
c. 1941–42

57 Vincente Minnelli, *Cabin in the Sky*, 1943

relationships on Broadway with some of the leading black
entertainers of the day, brought those experiences to this film
fantasy. Ostensibly about a humble, black couple (played by
Ethel Waters and Eddie Anderson) struggling between the forces
of good and evil, *Cabin in the Sky* was, in truth, a Hollywood
discourse on the reconciliation (rather than the struggle)
between spirituality—folk culture and traditional black values—
and materialism—the trappings of modern society and black
urban lifestyles. The extraordinary cast of black performers
(with Waters and Anderson joined by Lena Horne, Kenneth
Spencer, Rex Ingram, and Louis Armstrong, among others) did
not so much play on standard stereotypes as operate in their
own, customarily sophisticated and theatrical manner. The
end results, in keeping with Minnelli's cinematic interest in
show business splendor and illusionism, depicted black culture
as eternally bound to an invented folk past, even under the
dazzling lights of the city (and of the MGM studios).

The construction of this pictorialized folk past—whether
codified in the expressionist shacks, hair braids, and gnarled
58   human features in a work like John Biggers's *Manda* (*c.* 1945), or
built into the folkloric mien and stylized gestures in a painting
59   such as Robert Gwathmey's *Work Song* (1946)—proclaimed an

58 RIGHT John Biggers,
Manda, c. 1945
59 BELOW Robert Gwathmey,
Work Song, 1946

60 LEFT Eldzier
Cortor, *Room No. V*,
1948
61 OPPOSITE John
Dunkley, *Back to
Nature*, 1939

aspect of US culture that, though light years from the aesthetic
rumblings of Abstract Expressionism, fulfilled the desire
among members of a polarized arts scene to seek identification
with America's roots. African Americans, in spite of their
slave legacy and in spite of being the epitome of everything
undesirable in white America, embodied at the end of World
War II the social conscience of the United States and the
country's test case for true democracy.

 Artist Eldzier Cortor understood black America's role as a
social catalyst and a reminder of promised freedoms, as seen
in *Room No. V* (1948), his painting of a nude reflected in the
mirror of a wooden dresser, in an interior with newsprint-

covered walls and a chipped linoleum floor. With its jarring
mix of sensuousness, hardcore poverty and, most notably,
a folk-derived collage whose sarcastic commentaries on
the American dream literally shouted from the walls,
Room No. V confronted post-World War II complacency
with a humble habitat, a ruminating black woman, and a
catnapping feline.

Cortor's travels in 1944 and 1945 (sponsored by the Julius
Rosenwald Fund) among blacks who lived on the largely
isolated Sea Islands off the coast of South Carolina and Georgia
strongly influenced his vision, which was partly folkloric and
partly surrealistic. In this respect, Cortor joined scores of other
Americans and Europeans in their emulation of artists who
worked beyond the art scene's borders. As with the latter-day
reverberations of the "New Negro" arts movement, the vogue
around 1940 for "Negro folk art" had its beginnings a decade
earlier, in the "discovery" of artists like William Edmondson
and Horace Pippin, and in the WPA/FAP's efforts to research,
document, and promote America's homespun arts and
"folkways." By the 1940s, this passion for "the folk" intensified,
with "folk art" receiving accolades from the American and
European avant-garde.

In 1949, Cortor received a Guggenheim Fellowship to
conduct research in Jamaica, Cuba, and Haiti: three sites in
the Caribbean where, as in his Sea Islands sojourn of several
years earlier, he hoped to encounter black people "whose
cultural tradition had been only slightly influenced by whites."
Interestingly, artworks by John Dunkley, Jamaica's foremost

Hector Hyppolite, *Pan de Fleur (Basket of Flowers—Voodoo)*, 1947

intuitive painter during this period, challenged the common misconceptions that artists like Cortor and other "folk art" enthusiasts took from this kind of work. Dunkley's *Back to Nature* (1939), which transformed the Jamaican landscape into a dark, organic, and symmetrical valentine, had a lot in common with Cortor's *Room No. V* and other Modernist art in spite of Dunkley's cultural distance and social isolation from the contemporary arts scene. Yet one could also argue that it was precisely this enigmatic quality in "folk art" that made it both perplexing as well as fascinating to viewers in the 1940s.

During Cortor's stay in Haiti (where, coincidentally, he was accompanied by abstract painter Harlan Jackson), he became aware of this sympathy between the "moderns" and the "primitives." This artistic bond, appearing first in the 1930s with the Haitian *Indigenist* movement, was later strengthened by the American art teacher, DeWitt Peters, and his founding of the Centre d'Art in Haiti in 1944. It was perhaps best characterized in the visit of the Surrealists André Breton and Wifredo Lam in 1945. Breton, the Surrealist movement's leading theorist, and Lam, a Surrealist painter of Chinese and African Cuban ancestry, became enamored with the paintings of Hector Hyppolite: a self-taught artist, ex-merchant marine, and *Vodun* priest. Hyppolite painted wondrous, symbolic compositions, like *Pan de Fleur (Basket of Flowers—Voodoo)* of 1947, which employed dramatic juxtapositions and thematic leaps in a manner similar to the Surrealists. In an essay of 1947, published in a later edition of his 1928 book *Surrealism and Painting*, Breton described Hyppolite's artistic integrity as "entirely unalloyed, ringing as clearly as virgin metal," and Hyppolite as the guardian of a universal, all-important secret.

What Breton did not understand was that Hyppolite—through the discursive strategies of art and religion—created an alternative universe for himself and his people that seemed to be surreal and secret but was, in fact, (to paraphrase the Martiniquan critic Edouard Glissant) a picture of "a seldom-seen side of reality." For Hyppolite and the other artists who were neither academy-trained nor a part of the art scene proper, these representations of a fantastic world and their innermost visions were more intellectually tangible and functional than Breton and the Surrealists could have ever imagined.

For example, James Hampton's glittering, monumental assemblage, *The Throne of the Third Heaven of the Nations Millennium General Assembly* (c. 1950–64), was meant to be a liturgical display within his "all black" church in Washington, DC. But its public unveiling after this reclusive artist's death in 1964—and its artistic premiere a few years later in the

63 James Hampton, *The Throne of the Third Heaven of the Nations Millennium General Assembly*, c. 1950–64

Pride, Assimilation, and Dreams

64　Minnie Evans, *A Dream*, 1959

Smithsonian Institution—cloaked its devotional and culture-specific purpose. Paintings by the self-taught black artist Minnie Evans, apparently spiritual and cathartic works of the subconscious, actually spoke volumes about the effects of racism and segregation on black aspirations and dreams in Jim-Crow-era North Carolina. The white angelic choir in Minnie Evans's *A Dream* (1959) was entirely conceivable in a society where, for blacks as well as whites, a spiritual and divine realm—and all that was considered "good" and "beautiful" in the culture—had to be white. The creations by these artistic "outsiders," while highly praised in this period, were routinely misunderstood, removed from their aesthetic and social contexts, and inserted into a catch-all "folk art" category that accommodated the mainstream art world's unwritten policy based on exclusion by race and class. It would not be until the late 1970s, with a diversified, highly profitable US art market, that these popular works and their artists would stand as equals beside the works and practitioners of the so-called professional art world.

Freedom Through Abstraction

Like Eldzier Cortor a few years earlier, Rose Piper, a New York City artist, received Rosenwald Fellowship funds (in 1946 and 1947) to travel throughout the southern United States and conduct research on African Americans, in order to create a series of paintings on "the folk Negro." One of Piper's works from this series was *Slow Down Freight Train* (1946): a semi-abstract, colorful figure study executed in a style similar to that of the American precisionist painter Ralston Crawford. The catalyst for Piper, however, was the African American musical form, the blues; her paintings therefore presented a rebel strain of abstract art in the late 1940s.

Through the sometimes fracturing, blurring, subtracting or interactive practices of painterly abstraction, Piper created impressions rather than illustrations of what she described as "the imaginative experiences evoked by the world of Negro folk song." In *Slow Down Freight Train*, bands, arcs, and fields of color, punctuated by thin, black outlines, made oblique yet germane references to the images, sounds, and sensations that

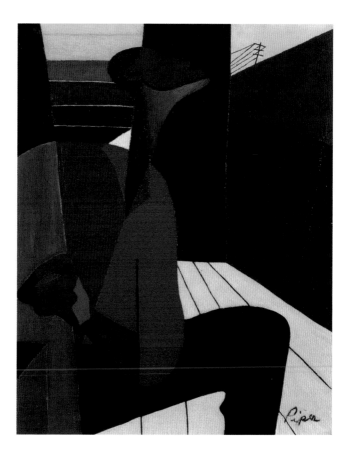

65 Rose Piper,
*Slow Down
Freight Train,*
1946

the blues conjured. Piper's technique and impetus, similar to those of painters William H. Johnson and Robert Gwathmey, reconstituted the black folk experience, making it discernible and evocative, yet also condensed and abstract.

By the mid-1940s, many US artists were abandoning figurative and narrative subjects and shifting to abstraction. Apart from those who simply saw abstraction as the latest trend, many artists genuinely believed it was the only viable route away from the formal and ideological limitations of Social Realism: a tradition that, since the American Artists' Union and Popular Front days of the 1930s, was increasingly viewed as constrained by politics, various schools of cultural nationalism, and an overwhelming social agenda. With significant numbers of European Surrealists and abstract artists settling in the US before and during the war years, American artists also felt this current from abroad, especially with regard to non-figurative art and Surrealism's fondness for irrational, accidental, and subconscious impulses in art. In summary, abstraction offered American artists a sense of personal freedom and creative license that was virtually alien in US visual culture.

While many African American artists gravitated to abstraction for these reasons, for others abstraction took on a larger and more complex meaning. Historically confined to exhibiting their works in "all Negro" art exhibitions and left out of the national forums on American art, several African American artists extended abstraction's call for individual and artistic freedom to the art world's racial front. Beyond an aesthetic affinity for abstraction, some African American artists also saw their move to abstraction as a personal and professional step toward artistic integration: a step that symbolized their willingness to subordinate blackness—and all that was associated with it—and to place themselves and their work in a larger, wider and, ultimately, whiter art world that provided more opportunities to exhibit, sell, and enter into artistic dialogue with others. In 1958, *Ebony* (a monthly magazine founded in 1945 by publisher John H. Johnson and directed toward an expanding African American readership), carried an article remarking on this shift to abstraction among younger black artists, speculating (based more on wishful forecasts than actual demographics) that the turn from "Negro subject matter" was "a natural consequence of living in a more integrated world."

Abstraction was only a partial stylistic presence in the work of Piper and Jackson, but for Norman Lewis and Hale Woodruff, both African Americans, abstraction was an important pathway to artistic freedom and individual self-discovery. As early as

66 Norman Lewis, *Every Atom Glows: Electrons in Luminous Vibration*, 1951

1945, Norman Lewis painted colorful, linear compositions that alluded to the riotous sounds of bebop, or the throngs of pedestrians, rushing aimlessly down crowded New York City streets. However, other paintings like *Every Atom Glows: Electrons in Luminous Vibration* (1951) revealed Lewis's more iconoclastic side, moving beyond the typical issues centered in black culture, and instead tackling such "universal" themes as atomic energy and nuclear fallout. Indeed, Lewis was a product of a divided, contradictory world view: painting abstractly and participating in the mainstream art scene of the 1950s, yet also maintaining close ties with the Harlem scene and its mid-century mood of social separateness and cultural bravado (best exemplified in Ollie Harrington's cartoons and Langston Hughes's short stories that appeared in the black press during this period). Because Lewis based his paintings on more social and, by extension, culturally informed themes, his works were frequently in conflict with the more enigmatic, private mythologies of much American abstract art. Consequently, Lewis's abstractions reveled in an aesthetic predicated on painted gestures that, while camouflaged by artistic overtures to Abstract Expressionism, made analogous overtures toward a Harlem-inspired art of visual and verbal "signifying."

Hale Woodruff—who had made forays into a School of Paris modernism, a Mexican-influenced historicism, and an African American brand of southern US Regionalism—also embraced painterly abstraction in the late 1940s, seeing in it not only another kind of visual authenticity, but an occasion for "extending [one's] vision" beyond the ordinary scope of comprehension. *Art of the Negro* (1950–51), Woodruff's six-paneled mural in the Art Museum at Clark Atlanta University (formerly Atlanta University), conceptualized the history of the visual arts within the black diaspora in terms of six thematic groupings, each occurring at selected historical junctures over several millennia. Panel 5, subtitled *Influences*, examined the enduring, potent nature of African art and design in imagery as diverse as the paintings of Amedeo Modigliani and the sculptures of Henry Moore, the ground drawings (or *vèvè*) of Haiti, and other abstract and semi-abstract forms. Woodruff had been interested in African art throughout his career; in *Influences* he recorded abstract art's debt to Africa, and abstraction's fundamental position in world visual culture.

In 1947, Woodruff—with sculptor Richmond Barthé, Howard University art professor James V. Herring, and abstract artist Romare Bearden—convinced the International Business Machine (IBM) Corporation to remove all racial references in the catalogue of their art collection, and to abolish all racial

67 Hale Woodruff, *Art of the Negro* murals, Panel 5: *Influences*, 1950–51

preferences in their art acquisition policies. "In light of the
Negro artist's present achievements in the general framework
of American art today," wrote Woodruff to another artist
involved in the 1947 IBM venture, "there does not exist the
necessity to continue all Negro exhibitions which tend to
isolate him and segregate him from other American artists."
Behind the righteous tone of this group's call for integration
was the faint hope that black artists would be brought into the
larger fold of the American art scene. These were optimistic
years after World War II, when President Truman established
his Committee on Civil Rights in 1946, and Jackie Robinson
made the giant, symbolic step in 1947 of becoming the first

African American to play major league baseball. Yet, as art historian Ann Gibson suggested in her study of African American abstract painters, this proclamation of "belonging" by Woodruff and the others was essentially ignored with a continuing, if not escalating, neglect. When Harold Rosenberg, one of Abstract Expressionism's most articulate spokespersons, was asked in the early 1960s to name a few of the leading African American artists, he allegedly brushed off the request, saying that he did not know of any.

By the mid-1950s—and continuing well into the early 1960s—abstract art functioned for several black (as well as white) artists as a passport into mainstream acceptance and—for a very select few—artistic renown. Chicago sculptor Richard Hunt was one of the period's more successful abstract artists, with improvised,

68 LEFT Richard Hunt, *Arachne*, 1956
69 OPPOSITE Aubrey Williams, *Guyana*, 1965

68 open-form works like *Arachne* (1956) revisiting and updating the experiments in iron-welding and metal assemblage by the early twentieth-century Spanish artist Julio González. Around the same time that Hunt was becoming better known, abstract painter Aubrey Williams was exhibiting his dense, chromatic canvases in various galleries and exhibition spaces in London. However, unlike Hunt in the 1950s, Williams did not get recognition until 1965, almost a decade later, when he was awarded the prestigious Commonwealth Prize for Painting, 69 and exhibited his latest, abstract composition, *Guyana* (1965), in London's Royal Academy of Arts.

In 1959 in an article about Williams's paintings, Jan Carew, a London-based journalist and writer (like Williams, from Guyana) wrote that "superimposed" on Williams's nature-inspired art were "the new images of science, shapes under a microscope, pictures of nebulae in popular magazines, the bright blurs of trick photography, and *the torment of a uprooted man searching for an image of himself and his people*" (author's emphasis). In this description, Carew's juxtaposition of scientific and technological analogies with an allusion to Williams's personal ordeal as a social and political being illustrated just how malleable abstract art could be, especially

70 Ollie Harrington, "No, it don't make sense to me neither Bootsie. But white folks jus' won't buy nothin' if it makes sense!," 1959

when the artist was black or the context of the work evoked blackness and, thus, fit into an observer's pre-existing, social interpretation.

Still, abstract art had its black opponents as well as its black advocates, as demonstrated in Ollie Harrington's cartoon on the subject from the *Pittsburgh Courier*, "No, it don't make sense to me neither Bootsie..." (1959). In framing abstract art as nothing more than "The Emperor's New Clothes," Harrington—along with the cartoon's largely sympathetic black audience—saw his black artist as an ignoble "con artist," yet with plenty of common sense, putting "a big one" over on a mercurial and gullible white clientele. As reactionary as Harrington's cartoon was, it raised the critical issue of accountability and communication in cultural production: a problem that all black artists, abstract as well as representational, would continue to ponder and debate in the future.

Black Orpheus
Since 1951, Ollie Harrington had lived and worked in Paris, France. There, he joined a group of African American artists

who, having been stung once too often by American racism, chose to live in the racially tolerant and intellectually stimulating community in and around Saint-Germain-des-Prés. These artists, in addition to the many African and Caribbean artists who already lived in Paris, and the many African American artists who passed through the city during these years (including Romare Bearden, Edward Clark, Bill Rivers, and others), established their own, black expatriate community, which forged important alliances with Paris's influential intellectuals and philosophers.

The philosophy of Existentialism—with its emphasis on the predicament of being, and the crises of social action and personal responsibility—resonated strongly with black artists during these post-war years. For African American artists, Existentialism articulated their feelings of isolation in a society that was largely deprecating of or blind to black humanity. For African and Caribbean artists, Existentialism addressed these same emotions, in addition to voicing strong arguments against colonialism. But what Existentialism and its French advocates especially communicated to black artists was black culture's affinities with other creative forces in the world. For example, in 1947 three prominent French writers—André Gide, Albert Camus, and Jean-Paul Sartre—served on the advisory board of *Présence Africaine*, a publishing house and literary journal devoted to the writings of black intellectuals working in Africa, Europe, and the Americas. The stated mission of *Présence Africaine*—"to define African originality and hasten its entrance into the modern world"—reverberated with Sartre's theory that the black man "wants to be both a beacon and a mirror; the first revolutionary...who will tear Blackness out of himself in order to offer it to the world...."

Sartre's thoughts on black culture, first published in his widely discussed essay "Orphée Noir" ("Black Orpheus," 1948), fused the creative genius of such black writers as the Martiniquan Surrealist Aimé Césaire and the Senegalese literary critic Léopold Sédar Senghor with: (1) the revolutionary aspirations of Marxist ideology; and (2) the all-embracing, universal impulses of Western civilization. In his analysis of Césaire's poem "Return to My Native Land" (1939), Sartre observed that "negritude..., inserted into Universal History,... is no longer a *state*, nor even an existential attitude" but, rather, "a *Becoming*," or a kind of inprocess experience which leads black intellectuals to form alliances with other oppressed peoples throughout the world. "Like the Dionysian poet," remarked Sartre, "the Negro attempts to penetrate the brilliant phantasm of the day, and encounters, a thousand feet under

71 Wifredo Lam,
*The Eternal
Presence*, 1944

the Apollonian surface, the inexpiable suffering which is the
universal essence of man." Although Sartre's universalizing
objective for *Negritude* signaled its eventual death and (as
argued in 1952 by the Martiniquan psychiatrist Frantz Fanon)
the destruction of "black zeal," Sartre also seemed to believe
that the only viable place for this blackness to exist and live out
its purpose in the interim was in poetry and the arts in general.

This notion of a volatile, dynamic, black presence in the
world (with revolutionary and redemptive implications),
although directed toward Césaire's writings, could equally
have been a caption for Wifredo Lam's painting *The Eternal
Presence* (1944). Lam, an associate of Césaire, shared his
colleague's fascination with the "black epic," as revealed by the
carnival of African Cuban deities, Caribbean flora, and other
life and death forces on display in this painting. Transcending
his youthful infatuations with Pablo Picasso and a second-
hand appropriation of African art, Lam demonstrated in
The Eternal Presence and other works from his post-1941 period
(during which he lived and worked mostly in his native Cuba)

71

his acknowledgment of a black diasporal "self," via Sartre's
duly termed "Orphic" descent into a "black substratum" of
religion, music, and poetry.

Sartre's betrothal of *Negritude* with the universalizing
philosophies and symbols of the ancients—especially those
associated with the musician and poet Orpheus—was a thesis
that a number of artists explored during the post World
War II period. Richard Hunt's *Arachne*, James Wells's and
Romare Bearden's various classical subjects of the 1940s, and
Ralph Ellison's sweeping, Homeric novel *Invisible Man* (1952)
all contributed to this cross-over impulse in black diasporal
arts. But the work of art from this period that established the
penultimate accord between blackness and the universality of
the Western world's classical heritage was the 1959 film *Orfeu
Negro* (*Black Orpheus*).

Adapted for the screen from the stage play *Orfeu da Conceiçào*
(by the Brazilian poet Vinicius de Moraes), *Black Orpheus*
transplanted the ancient Greek legend of the ill-fated lovers
Orpheus and Eurydice to modern-day Brazil and its mostly
poor and illiterate descendants of African slaves. Director
Marcel Camus placed this archetypal story about love, death,
fate, and perpetuity in Rio de Janeiro during Carnival week.
With the added attractions of an irresistible Afro-Brazilian
music sound-track, a talented and handsome cast of black
actors, and a part documentary/part theatrical format filmed

72

72 Marcel Camus, *Orfeu Negro* (*Black Orpheus*), 1959

in dazzling Eastmancolor, Camus turned *Black Orpheus* into an instant film classic and a huge commercial and critical success with international audiences. Camus's borrowing of the title and tenor of Sartre's 1948 essay, along with his unprecedented celebration of both racial and cultural blackness (culminating in his remarkable documentary film footage in *Black Orpheus* of an Afro-Brazilian *Macumba* ceremony), transformed black culture into an entity with worldwide appeal and an aesthetic integrity of its own.

Camus's realization of Sartre's Afro-Orphic excavation of the black soul—largely accomplished through his innovative mix of sound, movement, and color—had its counterpart during

73 Bob Thompson,
Garden of Music, 1960

this period in the figurative expressionist paintings of the
African American artist Bob Thompson. Although Thompson
did not directly encounter this Sartrean rationale until he
traveled to Paris in 1961, by 1959 (the year of his move from
Kentucky to New York City) he was already incorporating into
his large color canvases an Orpheus-like sense of fatality,
mystery, and spirituality. Thompson's *Garden of Music* (1960),
his homage to New York's avant-garde jazz scene, accentuated
the hallucinatory, transfigurative states that jazz musicians like
Ornette Coleman, John Coltrane, and others invoked in their
audiences. Like a mid-twentieth-century, black Hieronymus
Bosch, Thompson introduced chromatic brilliance and

73

moral enigma into American figurative painting and, like his intellectual comrades Lam and Camus, created an artistic bridge between black cultural expression and the elusive notion of universality.

Among the Paris-based black artists whose paths may have crossed Thompson's in the early 1960s were the African American painter Beauford Delaney and the Ethiopian painter Alexander "Skunder" Boghossian. Delaney, the eldest of the three and a resident of France since 1953, arrived at a similarly colorful, mysterious, and universal place in his work as Thompson, but by an entirely independent route. Around 1944, after many years of fairly traditional portrait painting in New York's Greenwich Village, Delaney, like so many American painters, began to imbue his compositions with more paint and less realistic form, so that, by the time he left for Paris in 1953, his work had taken on the appearance of textured, swirling topologies. Ironically, Delaney's approach, rather than taking him further away from the humanistic concerns of his earlier work, actually brought him closer to a heartfelt, universal statement and (when applied to black subjects like his 1962 *Self-Portrait*) an all-encompassing declaration of what the American writer Henry Miller in a broadside of 1945 described in Delaney's work as displacing metaphoric "blackness" with divine "solar radiance."

Skunder lived and worked in Paris from 1957 until 1966, where he found himself, like Thompson and Delaney, in the midst of a lively international arts scene. He had access to a whole range of black expressive culture: *Présence Africaine*; Camus's *Black Orpheus*; the music of Paris-based African American jazz musicians such as Kenny Clarke; Jean Genet's influential, absurdist play *The Blacks*; and the city's major collections and archives of African art. All this significantly altered his work, curiously making it both "Pan-African" and "universal." Skunder reworked a calligraphic approach reminiscent of Paul Klee, of the European proponents of action painting, and of the illuminated scrolls and manuscripts of the artist's native Ethiopia. This reworking functioned in paintings like

75 *Ju-Ju's Wedding* (1964) as cross-cultural markers: characters and figures whose symbolism leapt over conventional boundaries and became a kind of multi-signifying lingua franca.exhibitions on three continents during this period, as well as acquisitions by art institutions as divergent as New York's MoMA and Virginia's Hampton University Art Museum illustrated Skunder's successful—and largely indiscernible— merging of cultural specifics with philosophical abstractions: an artistic balancing act that he, along with his fellow universalists, had perfected, and one that Sartre believed would push them out of "past particularisms" and into "future universalisms" which, in turn, would ultimately enact "the twilight of [their] negritude."

The Other Movement
For artist Gerard Sekoto, Sartre's philosophical platitudes about black culture and universalisms could not have been more foreign or more fanciful. Although Sekoto was a contributor to *Présence Africaine* and a participant (as was Skunder) in the Second Congress of Negro Writers and Artists in Rome in 1958, his firsthand experience of racial oppression in South Africa— initially in his native, rural Transvaal and later in Johannesburg and Cape Town—limited his appreciation of Sartre's idea of a white recognition of black humanity. Sekoto had arrived in Paris in 1947, just after South Africa's white minority government first formulated the concept of apartheid, and had been painting under the exigencies of racial discrimination
76 for a number of years. *Woman Ironing* (c. 1940–41), one of several paintings inspired by Sekoto's stay in Sophiatown (a poverty-stricken black township in Johannesburg), revealed his understanding of black life under white racism, as seen in his evocation of that township's murky, claustrophobic atmosphere, with a torch-like candle providing the scene's only source of light and, by poetic association, its only rays of hope.

Yet many artists and intellectuals, sensing that racism and oppression were not disappearing but, rather, becoming more entrenched, responded in fiercer ways than shown in Sekoto's *Woman Ironing*. Unlike the expressions of universal goodwill or the circumventions of politics and race in much of the work from the post World War II period, several US artists adopted a humanitarian stance in their work and, reminiscent of the activist politics of artists in the 1930s, directed their efforts toward an art of social engagement and protest. These artists, frustrated rather than heartened by race relations in the post-war years, joined organizations like the NAACP and the National Negro and Civil Rights Congresses; they exhibited in

76 Gerard Sekoto,
Woman Ironing,
c. 1940–41

galleries and art venues that—in this period of abstraction and thematic disengagement in the arts—promoted figurative or Social Realist work; and they aligned themselves with like-minded, civil rights activists both in the US and abroad, risking from right-wing factions the dreaded "Communist" label.

In spite of legitimate concerns about being "blacklisted" for one's political beliefs, or anxieties about one's work being considered irrelevant by an increasingly abstract art-oriented scene, several socially engaged African American artists persevered in the late 1940s and throughout the 1950s, producing work that not only challenged a racially biased, white status quo, but reinvigorated the black subject in American art. In her *Negro Woman Series* (1946–47), Elizabeth Catlett extended the historical dimensions of her pictorial study of black women's experiences into an impassioned yet lucid, first-person affidavit against racism. One of the most riveting images from the series was *...and a special fear for my loved ones* (1947). This linocut print revisited a grisly theme that so many American

77

artists had explored a decade earlier, and took on a new urgency from Catlett's inclusion of three, cropped-off pairs of feet, so placed as to suggest either spectators, standing in perspective, or more lynch mob victims, hanging above the body that had already been cut down.

Like Elizabeth Catlett's work, the drawings of Charles White (her former husband) emerged during this period of the artistic "triumph" of Abstract Expressionism. But unlike Catlett (who found an ideological refuge and a more fulfilling, personal existence for herself in Mexico), White not only survived in the US in this 1950s atmosphere of action-painting and "red-baiting," but blossomed into a major figure of the New York art world. White's drawings of black people were large-scale, moderately expressionistic, and meticulously rendered. Much of their success hinged on their being seen within the larger cultural context of black life in the 1950s. Lorraine Hansberry, author of the Broadway play *A Raisin in the Sun* (1959), the catalogue essayist for White's 1961 exhibition at New York's ACA Gallery and, like White, from Chicago, recognized this requirement, observing that she and White were "of the same sidewalks and acres of 'rocking storefront churches'" and that they both "drew breath hearing certain music, watched by certain eyes, chastised and comforted again by certain voices." In White's *Oh, Mary, Don't You Weep* (1956), Hansberry's allusions to stalwart, church-going black mothers became concrete, resonating with real images of black women, and extending those images into a sympathetic display of human emotion, frailty, and strength.

These dramatic images by Catlett and White—of black men dying and black women comforting one another in dignified anguish—became all too common as American race relations began to receive greater media attention and public scrutiny.

78

77 OPPOSITE Elizabeth Catlett, *...and a special fear for my loved ones*, 1947
78 BELOW Charles White, *Oh, Mary, Don't You Weep*, 1956

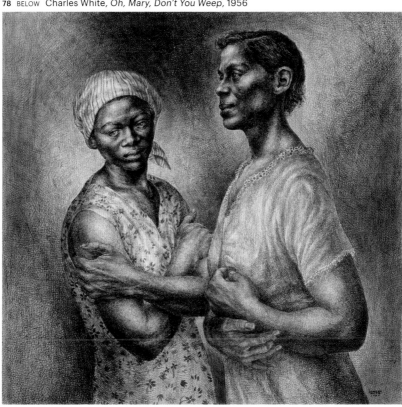

Beginning in 1955 with the bus boycott in Montgomery, Alabama, after Rosa Parks, an African American woman, was arrested for refusing to give her bus seat to a white male passenger, the African American struggle for full citizenship increasingly took center stage in the cultural consciousness of the United States. Catlett and White's works, along with those by artists Philip Evergood, Robert Gwathmey, Jacob Lawrence, and others, raised the specter of inequality in a so-called American democracy, drew attention to the frightening truths about white-on-black violence, and focused on examples of endurance and moral tenacity in the face of these obstacles.

In spite of the contributions that Catlett, a printmaker and sculptor, and White, a draughtsman, made on behalf of an art of social consciousness, the medium of photography seemed to be the ideal and most frequently used art form for addressing these social issues. Perhaps it was the misconception that photography was primarily a journalistic endeavor rather than an art form that made these photographic images of the American racial landscape more acceptable, or at least allowed them within the margins of the art world. Gordon Parks's *Life* magazine photo-essays on racial issues, Roy DeCarava's collaborative portrait (with author Langston Hughes) of the "Negro experience" in *The Sweet Flypaper of Life* (1955), and Robert Frank's penetrating look at an often myopic, racially polarized society in his book *The Americans* (1958) were a few of the more noteworthy, social documentary photographic projects during this period.

79 BELOW Ernest C. Withers, cover of *Complete Photo Story of Till Murder Case*, 1955
80 OPPOSITE Norman Rockwell, *The Problem We All Live With*, 1964

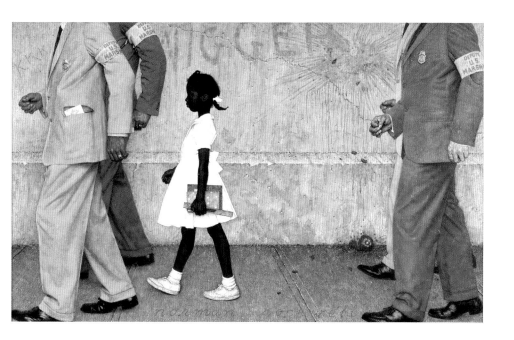

Ernest C. Withers, although not as well known as Parks, DeCarava, and Frank, worked as a freelance photographer in Memphis, Tennessee. His twenty-page, self-published *Complete Photo Story of Till Murder Case* (1955) was created in response to the notorious incident involving Emmett Till, a black teenager who, having casually spoken to a white woman in Mississippi, was abducted from his house by two white men and brutally murdered. Sold in African American communities for a dollar and prominently featured in *Jet* magazine (Johnson Publishing Company's small format, news and photo weekly), Withers's *Complete Photo Story of Till Murder Case* was a powerful, graphic example of photojournalism, and helped to galvanize the burgeoning civil rights movement throughout the country. Even a conservative artist like Norman Rockwell—after a decade of boycotts, sit-ins, marches, efforts to desegregate schools, and often ugly, violent retaliations against these actions—eventually had to bring the race issue to the attention of his audiences, as seen in his 1964 *Look* magazine cover, *The Problem We All Live With*, a painting of US marshals assisting an act of school desegregation.

More revealing than Rockwell's photographic-like scene was the painting's title which, with perhaps intended ambiguity, did not make clear exactly where "the problem" resided. Was the problem simply the evils of racism and bigotry, or

79

80

was it (from the vantage point of the white, homogeneous, self-righteous "We" of the title) an African American population, no longer invisible and demanding civil rights? Even if one conceded that his sympathies rested with this brave little girl, there is no denying that, in the larger scope of things, Rockwell regretted the entry into his escapist, "problem" free, *Saturday Evening Post* world of an indelible presence, whose very being was defined in stark "black and white" terms. By the mid-1960s, this presence would do more than merely provide "local color": it would transform the Reverend Martin Luther King's dream of racial integration into a reality, insist upon a permanent place within the cultural landscape and, eschewing the racial and cultural ambivalences of the past, declare itself "Black."

Chapter 5
"Black is a Color"

The Name Game

Around 1965, African Americans began to find the racial and cultural designation "Negro" not only antiquated, but suggestive of a less transcendent and revelatory time than the one in which they were currently living. In those first few years of the 1960s, African Americans had already experienced a significant number of political and cultural firsts, as well as moral encouragement from the society-at-large. Still, there were times when race relations seemed far from hopeful, as in 1964, when the slain bodies of three civil rights workers were discovered in a shallow grave outside Philadelphia, Mississippi, or in 1965, when the Los Angeles community of Watts erupted into a major civil unrest following clashes between its African American residents and a mostly white police force. But even at such times, many African Americans were in accord with the opinion of the poet and playwright LeRoi Jones (soon to be renamed Amiri Baraka) that "there are some of us who will not be Negroes, who know that indeed we are something else, something stronger...." Although this shift from the purportedly acquiescent "Negro" to the seemingly assertive "Black" was viewed by many older, more conservative African Americans with confusion, suspicion, and amusement, the younger and more outspoken members of the race saw the change as not only symbolic, but an emphatic proclamation of an oppressed people's psychological reorientation.

In the art world, this rejection of being "Negro" and the embracing of "Blackness" was embodied in the professional and aesthetic transitions of New York artist Romare Bearden. In 1963, after almost two decades of painting abstractions, Bearden joined forces with a group of other New York-based African American artists (who adopted the name "Spiral") to explore

81 Romare Bearden,
Summertime, 1967

ways in which they could respond to the issues and needs
of African Americans. In spite of the group's indifference to
Bearden's proposal to collectively create a collage of cut and torn
magazine images, Bearden took on the project himself and—in
a stark departure from his totally abstract, stained and dripped
paintings of the 1950s and early 1960s—began assembling
disparate bits from *Look*, *Life*, *Ebony*, and other photo-magazines
into loosely structured compositions on various "Negro"
themes (the urban experience, the rural south, black music and
musicians, African American spirituality, and so on).

When photographed and blown-up versions of these collages
were first exhibited in 1964 (under the title "Projections"), critics
responded enthusiastically, prompting Bearden to all but forget
his previous life as an abstract painter and to embark upon
a new career as a collagist, inspired by "the innerness of the
Negro experience." In interviews Bearden resisted the critical
tendency to align his collages with what Americans were
seeing on television and reading in books and newspapers
about "the Negro's struggle for civil rights," but the analogy took

shape anyway and often to Bearden's advantage. By the time many African Americans had espoused the tenets and rhetoric of "Black Power," works like Bearden's *Summertime* (1967) perfectly articulated the period's racial moods, swinging between a sentimental, four-part harmony about brownstone stoops and syrup-laden ice cones, and a tabloid-style exposé of an impoverished and potentially explosive black inner city.

81

In Paris, amid the political and intellectual furor triggered by the war in Vietnam, the anticolonial rumblings in Algeria, and the student revolts at the Sorbonne, African American sculptor Barbara Chase-Riboud also encountered an emerging black consciousness. Born in Philadelphia, trained at the Yale School of Art, widely traveled and a resident of Paris since the early 1960s, Chase-Riboud was perhaps the quintessential Sartrean "universalist." Yet her work of the early 1970s—bronze and aluminum castings of layered, semi-geometric forms, in combination with cascades of wool and silken cords, braids, and knotted ropes—subverted the art world's emphasis on a detached minimalism, and also undercut Sartre's theory of an in-process, but doomed, *Negritude.*

82

In sculptures like *Confessions for Myself* (1972), Chase-Riboud's black bronze and mane-like extensions of black wool appropriated the process-oriented "anti-form" strategies of artists like Eva Hesse and Robert Morris, but in a completely self-referential, introspective manner. Chase-Riboud's interjection of the autobiographical into this usually soulless mode of object-making, and her subtle yet unmistakable allusions to gender and race, strongly resonated with the then popular writings of Frantz Fanon. In Fanon's *Black Skin, White Masks* (1952; English translation, 1967), his declaration that he was "not the potentiality of something," but rather, wholly himself and the product of a universal, self-evident, black consciousness, bore comparison with Chase-Riboud's emphatic, resolutely "black" *Confessions for Myself.*

The San Francisco Bay artist Raymond Saunders, although sympathetic to individual quests for an alliance between the "artistic" and the "personal," had little or no tolerance for the misguided uses of race or ethnicity in the formulation, creation, and interpretation of art. In his self-published pamphlet, *Black is a Color* (*c.* 1968), Saunders lashed out at the "uptown critics" and "politico-sociologists" who, in this era of the heightened black conscience, burdened African American artists with civil rights battles, an eternal pessimism, and narrow inquiries that led nowhere. The pamphlet—with its vibrating, Op Art-like white letters on black pages—chided both the black nationalist and minimalist schools of thought

82 LEFT Barbara Chase-Riboud, *Confessions for Myself*, 1972
83 OPPOSITE Raymond Saunders, *Jack Johnson*, 1972

with its clever word play on the conceptual—and thus, subjective—implications of the term "black."

When Saunders, at the end of his essay, questioned the feasibility of rising above "racial-hang-ups" in order to "recognize the wider reality of art, *where color is the means and not the end*" (author's emphasis), one is still confronted with the question of what was the perceived role of color—specifically blackness—in the production of art? Was it purely political, a cultural presence, a chromatic affair, or (like Bearden's *Summertime*) subject to a multiplicity of meanings?

If one looks at Saunders's art, it was clear, in spite of his disdain for political and racial formulae, that "black," in addition to being a "color," was much more. Saunders's *Jack Johnson* (1972) was a portrait of the boxer who became the first black heavyweight world champion in 1908, and was known for his flashy demeanor and life-long defiance of the white status quo. *Jack Johnson*, transcending conventional portraiture, represented Johnson as a black chimera, placed against a red backdrop and "identified"

83

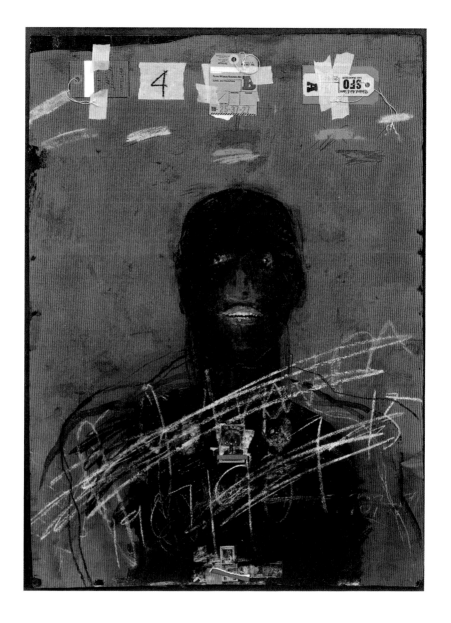

"Black is a Color"

by airline luggage tags, crayon erasures, foreign stamps, and advertising labels. By insisting on the material nature of things and on the malleability of content, in *Jack Johnson* Saunders lifted blackness out of a purely political category, and deposited it within his "wider reality" of visual perception, racial illusion, and an improvisational space that put artistic risk-taking and process in the forefront.

The strategies for visualizing blackness that artists like Bearden, Chase-Riboud, and Saunders developed represented only three of the many approaches available to artists in the 1960s and 1970s. The emphasis within the larger American society on the goals of the civil rights movement, the problems of the mostly black inner cities, and the historically under-valued position of African Americans in mainstream life fueled a dramatic change in contemporary culture that, in conjunction with other societal shifts, made black peoples and their cultures pivotal. The relative affluence of the United States before the oil crisis, the ever-expanding and influential mass media, the burgeoning youth culture, political unrest, and a social atmosphere of moral leniency, formed a backdrop for the emergence and rise to prominence of a partially autonomous black culture. From African American dance crazes to African American inspired acts of political agitation, blackness became a cultural lightning rod that attracted controversy, commentary, and acclaim. Visual corollaries for these representations of black culture during the 1960s and 1970s took the form of abstractions, artistic expressions of social and political realities, and testaments to the metaphysical aspects of blackness, and can also be seen in the documented careers and personal experiences of artists who persevered during these two decades of major social change.

Abstract Truths

In spite of the history surrounding Chase-Riboud's *Confessions for Myself*, the sculpture essentially remained an enigma: a mass of metal and fiber that challenged eye and mind with its mysterious, intractable form. By the mid–1960s, art audiences had resigned themselves to the realization that the main ingredient in abstract art was its obscure and elusive nature. Yet mystery did not denote senselessness. Any work of abstraction is a multileveled store of interpretative possibilities, accessible to anyone with attuned senses and a desire to respond to its labyrinthine character.

Although abstraction was perceived to be in an antithetical relationship to such issues as race and ethnicity, several artists in the 1960s and 1970s experimented with forms of abstraction that, if not explicit in their aesthetic or ideological ties with social themes, were engaged in an implicit discourse about a black consciousness. The crux of this conceptualization was that the identity in question was not the monolithic, political notion of a black consciousness (most often represented through Social Realism and cultural nationalism) but, rather, one that could conceivably embrace a multiplicity of personae or states of blackness.

Alma Thomas and Sam Gilliam, for example, the two African American "members" of the renowned "Color School" of Washington, DC, both painted brilliant, fractured abstractions in the second half of the 1960s. While conversant with the works of fellow Washington Color School artists (Gene Davis, Morris Louis, and Kenneth Noland), they also addressed, through rhythmic and high key color abstract painting techniques, the social aspirations of Washington, DC's African American middle class. Thomas was Howard University's first fine arts graduate in 1924 and, until her retirement in 1960, had been a teacher in DC's public schools. She turned her back on an earlier representational style that, by the late 1960s, would have been seen by DC's art community as ideologically conservative. Instead, with the encouragement of the Washington colorist Jacob Kainen, she embraced an abstract style inspired by horticulture, scientific color theory, and music. Thomas's *Red Azaleas Singing and Dancing Rock and Roll Music* (1976) proffered a literate and moderately expressive mode of abstraction that, while skillfully negotiating the slippery pathways between nature and society, epitomized the integrationist mood of the times.

Sam Gilliam settled in DC in 1962 and, like Alma Thomas, taught in the District's public schools. By 1966 Gilliam had expanded his professional vistas, regularly exhibiting and experimenting with a painting technique involving acrylic stains and drips on folded and draped canvas. Viewing the figurative, explicitly race-conscious works of many African American artists as the products of an "aesthetic conservativism," Gilliam represented a perspective in this era of black consciousness that was rarely acknowledged: dissatisfaction with the reigning figurative or explicitly political black art status quo and the subsequent creation of an alternative. Like the revolt among avant-garde musicians and the proponents of "jazz fusion" during this same period, Gilliam's abstractions articulated the emotional and cerebral musings of an intelligentsia, black and white, as they rebelled against politically prescribed and aesthetically bound art conventions. Even in works as late as the 1981 triptych *Lion's Rock Arc*, Gilliam sought a

84 ABOVE Alma Thomas, *Red Azaleas Singing and Dancing Rock and Roll Music*, 1976
85 RIGHT Sam Gilliam, *Lion's Rock Arc*, 1981

86 Hervé Télémaque, *Othello No. 1*, 1960

redefinition of blackness that (through abrupt breaks in form
and color contrasts visible through scored, impasto surfaces)
was more evocative than a painted black figure or a cultural
slogan.

Beyond experiments with color and pigment, implied
gesture and movement dictated the direction of much abstract
art during the early 1960s. Jagged, twisted forms in sculpture,
or sweeping, flailed brush strokes in painting, reminded
viewers of this work's aesthetic debt to the gestural paintings
of the Abstract Expressionists of the 1950s. Yet, as a black
consciousness grew more popular, two questions arose:
(1) was there such a thing as a black gesture, or forms of
expressive movement that could be classified under what
Bearden had described as the "innerness of the Negro
experience," and (2) if black gestures existed, how could one
reconcile them with abstraction?

Painters Hervé Télémaque and Emilio Cruz supplied answers
86   to both questions. In Hervé Télémaque's *Othello No. 1* (1960),

his brushwork—frenetic, disjointed, and covering the whole surface—camouflaged an underpainting of cartoonish forms that, while not immediately seen as black, used heads, skulls, and the name of William Shakespeare's Moor as the potential components for a cultural meaning. Similarly, New Yorker Emilio Cruz's *The Dance* (1962)—with several loosely painted, racially non-specific figures in poses that evoked crouching, genuflecting, and choreographed movement—had links to an array of performative acts in the early 1960s, from the vogue for experimental theater and modern dance, to the fad for popular black dance steps like the African American "twist" and the Afro-Cuban "mambo." Both Télémaque and Cruz represented examples of gestural artists whose paintings, while profoundly psychological, included within their respective ranges of interpretation cultural aspects that provided oblique yet definite allusions to race. In contrast, the inheritors of this gestural tradition embraced these socially rooted tendencies in non-objective art with far less ambiguity or secrecy about their role in the creation of a race-conscious, rather than a

87

87 Emilio Cruz, *The Dance*, 1962

"Black is a Color"

88 Sylvia Snowden, *Mamie Harrington*, 1985

race-consumed, art. This can be seen in the works of artists like
88 Sylvia Snowden, the Washington figurative expressionist, and
89 John T. Scott, the New Orleans kinetic sculptor.
   In a similar push toward a visual and cultural radicalism in
abstraction beginning in the 1970s, Joe Overstreet combined
painted geometries with stretched and tied expanses of canvas,
while Al Loving assembled small, geometrically shaped pieces
of painted canvas into larger, wall-mounted installations. These
works—building on the experiments with non-rectangular
paintings during the 1960s by Gilliam and Frank Stella—were
a dramatic departure from these earlier reformulations,
and were based on thematic and perceptual echoes of non-
European prototypes, such as Native American tent structures
for Overstreet, and West African masquerades and textile arts
for Loving. Yet, for all their cultural references, works like
90, 91 Overstreet's *Saint Expedite* (1971) and Loving's *Self-Portrait No. 23*
(1973) maintained abstraction's mysterious, anti-illustrative
position, much like the innovative writings during this period
by novelist Ishmael Reed, or the "new black music" by jazz
performers such as the Art Ensemble of Chicago.

89 John T. Scott, View of the Ruggles Street Station Installation, Boston, 1986

90 Joe Overstreet, *Saint Expedite* from the *Flight* series, 1971

What was perhaps most significant about these forays into abstraction by black painters, beginning in the mid-1960s and culminating in the 1970s, was their sense of a shared language, especially in the face of popular, politically explicit art. Al Loving, reminiscing about those years, stated: "When we showed together at the Studio Museum in Harlem in the early 1970s we could see that we all had arrived at a kind of abstraction that emphasized materials.... We didn't talk about it, didn't write it down, but it was a common link and it was there." The "we" that Loving referred to—Gilliam, Overstreet, Frank Bowling, Edward Clark, Bill Hutson, Howardena Pindell, Jack Whitten, William T. Williams, and himself—were all black painters, exhibiting in New York, and (as Loving suggested) engaged in an intra-disciplinary dialogue with one another, whose aesthetic thesis (if not about blackness) was that abstraction had the breadth and ability to convey the

91 Al Loving, *Self-Portrait No. 23*, 1973

moods, ideas, and strategies of all artists, but especially of
black painters.

Edward Clark and Jack Whitten, two of the period's
practitioners of non-figurative painting, employed techniques
and compositional formats that, in addition to re-energizing
an art of geometries and gestures, were influential in their
circle of New York-based abstractionists. In the 1974 painting *Ife
Rose* (named in part after the historic Nigerian city that Clark
visited in 1973), the novel use of a pushbroom over an elliptical,
horizon-like perimeter was a reminder that as early as 1957
Clark had worked with large, sweeping passages over shaped
canvases. In Jack Whitten's *Dead Reckoning I* (1980), the artist
reminded viewers that the theoretical point in the cosmos
where "it [is] no longer viable to turn around and go back," was
present in visual data ranging from technical diagrams, to the
concentric grooves from an "afro-comb."

92

93

When asked about the role of a black consciousness in his work, Whitten replied:

I can't define what is black in my work. I think it's not necessary that I have to define it as much as I should know that it's there.... I'm black, and my sensibility derives from my being black. But I'm also dealing with art...on the highest universal level. And that's what I want to be known for. I want to maintain that search for what it means to be black, whatever it is.... But at the same time, I must deal with this within the issues that have grown out of the history of art....

Whitten's acknowledgment of a black presence in his abstractions was not only corroborated by the products of his fellow black abstractionists in New York, but supported by the paintings of black abstractionists living and working abroad. The Nigerian painter Uzo Egonu (a British resident since 1945) launched an impressive series of colorful, abstract pattern paintings in London in the mid-1960s. Works like Egonu's *Deserted Asylum* (1964)—curiously conversant with as well as alien to London's contemporary arts scene— emphasized the conscious and often effective insertion of a black cultural sensibility into such Western art protocols as painterly abstraction.

92 BELOW Edward Clark, *Ife Rose*, 1974
93 OPPOSITE Jack Whitten, *Dead Reckoning I*, 1980

Besides Egonu and Aubrey Williams, the other leading proponent in England of this ideological merger was artist and critic Frank Bowling. Bowling, who was active during this period in both London and New York, stood in the forefront of painters working with a type of chromatic, cultural abstraction, as seen in the impressionistic *Night Journey* (1968–69). This and other paintings by Bowling dealing with geography, belonging, and the fluid, often transitory notions of pigmentation, catapulted this Guyanese-born, British-trained artist into wide recognition, but it was his critical essays that earned him special notice and, in many instances, discredit him among advocates of an explicit black consciousness in art. In his Saunders-inspired essay, "Is Black Art About Color?" (1971), Bowling was perhaps at his bluntest, saying that "Were we not afraid...of being considered white, we would be truly black. We would be wholly black (this new entity) and tackle our 'instruments' and language the way the leading jazz musicians and writers do...." Apart from his analogy here between abstraction, free jazz, and experimental writing, Bowling

95

94 ABOVE Frank Bowling, *Night Journey*, 1968–69
95 OPPOSITE Uzo Egonu, *Deserted Asylum*, 1964

claimed that a new form of racial and cultural authenticity could result from excavations of materials, methods, and the self. This assertion carried deep, though problematic implications, since identical claims were also made by the period's black cultural nationalists.

"Correction: The Revolution *Will* Be Televised"

H. Marshall McLuhan's mid-century prediction of an increasingly influential and often intrusive mass media was proved right, and this influence on people's lives in fact extended far beyond expectations. For the first time, wars, disasters, political campaigns, major cultural figures, and social trends were surveyed by the Cyclopean eye of the press, and either affirmed or negated by radio, television, and the media's newest abitrator: the public opinion pollster.

Never before had activists in the civil rights movement received the kind of media scrutiny that they received after 1960. From the Reverend Martin Luther King Jr.'s latest act of civil disobedience, to Malcom X's most eloquent statement against racism, the coverage of America's social revolution was more pervasive and culturally instrumental than ever before. In the 1940s and 1950s it would have been unthinkable for the media to report regularly on the words and deeds of NAACP executive secretary Walter White or black labor leader

A. Philip Randolph. However, by the 1960s it was almost taken for granted that, as well as seeing and hearing excerpts from the latest speeches by the Reverend King and Malcom X, James Baldwin's thoughts could be read in *Esquire*, Stokely Carmichael of the Student Non-Violent Coordinating Committee would be appearing on an evening talk show, and the opinions of African American intellectuals and political activists like Kenneth Clark, Bayard Rustin, Whitney Young, and others would be widely reviewed, analyzed, and discussed by the press.

Although African American-owned newspapers, magazines, and radio stations had always covered black issues, the 1960s (and its more entrepreneurial climate) ushered in a market-driven black press, with informational and cultural programming that was zealous in its race-based promotions. The African American media, often in concert with a powerful entertainment industry, supplied the news to "the community" (a popular euphemism for a fictitiously cohesive and monolithic black urban proletariat), as well as fostering a consumer culture of identities, goods, and services. Black pride and Black Power—at one time considered heretical ideas from the lunatic fringe—were now advocated in African American schools,

96 BELOW Andy Warhol, *Race Riot*, 1964
97 OPPOSITE Jeff Donaldson, *Aunt Jemima and the Pillsbury Doughboy*, 1963

churches, businesses, and media with the often combined goals of social freedom, economic gain, and self-affirmation. From the Afrocentric advertisements that plastered inner city billboards in the United States, to James Brown's declaration of cultural independence in his 1968 recording "Say It Loud, I'm Black and I'm Proud," black America's self-realization was just as much a marketing strategy as it was "the real thing."

Artistic responses to this media-saturated culture ranged from an empathy with the merging of art and society, to a suspicion of pop culture's infiltration into people's lives. When further compounded by the issue of race, these responses became even more complicated. For example, in Andy Warhol's
96 *Race Riot* (1964) the widely reported police-dog attacks on black demonstrators in Birmingham, Alabama in 1963 were transformed into radar blip-like graphics, drained of all emotional impact and details. In contrast, Jeff Donaldson's handling of a racial confrontation in *Aunt Jemima and the*
97 *Pillsbury Doughboy* (1963) interjected intense, opinionated

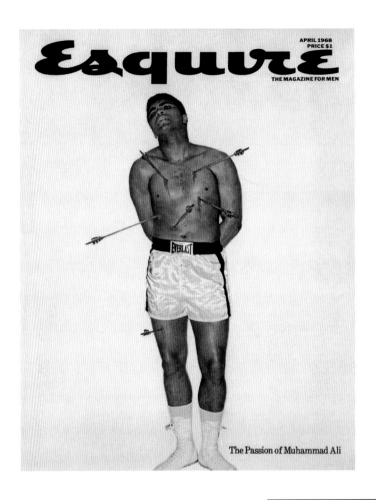

APRIL 1968
PRICE $1

THE MAGAZINE FOR MEN

The Passion of Muhammad Ali

98 ABOVE Carl Fischer and George
Lois "The Passion of Muhammad
Ali," cover of *Esquire*, April 1968
99 RIGHT Melvin Van Peebles,
*Sweet Sweetback's Baadasssss
Song*, 1971

sentiments on these racial clashes. Whereas Warhol rendered the scene via a detached photo-silkscreen transfer that obliterated specifics, Donaldson imposed on the image and incident a cast of ironic characterizations. Donaldson's self-defensive "Jemima," club-wielding "Doughboy," and swastika-like American flag contested Pop Art's love-hate relationship with American culture, while simultaneously making the African American struggle for civil rights a key component of it. Indeed, Donaldson's *The Civil Rights Yearbook* (1964)—a collection of satiric portraits drawn from an already commodified civil rights scene—continued this exploration of the movement's potential for appropriation and exploitation.

As Donaldson's book suggested, the media's power over the public's opinion on race was more than one-sided. Activists with public relations know-how frequently employed the media to promote their causes. In other instances, African American-related social issues conveyed enough universal appeal and human interest to attract many journalists, advertising agencies, and other media professionals to their cause. For example, when the US Boxing Commission stripped Muhammad Ali of the world heavyweight championship title because of his refusal on religious grounds to join the US armed forces and his opposition to the Vietnam war, the art director of *Esquire* magazine, George Lois, commissioned a photomontage of a bound Ali, riddled with arrows and mock anguish, in the manner of Andrea Mantegna's *St. Sebastian*. Boxing legend Ali, a master at self-promotion and "spin control," used such media images to publicize his cause and ultimately to succeed in his legal battle, winning back his former championship title.

With the 1971 release of the feature-length film *Sweet Sweetback's Baadasssss Song*, film producer, director, script writer, and featured actor Melvin Van Peebles provoked Hollywood into taking notice of a financially lucrative African American market. Van Peebles's cinematic "song" about a gigolo-turned-political outlaw was one of the year's most profitable films, grossing over four million dollars despite a limited number of rentals nationwide. What was surprising was that the picture's eclectic mix of genres—action movie, *cinema verité*, erotica, and "art film"—with its African American and overwhelmingly bleak urban setting, defied Hollywood's traditional formulae for artistic and commercial success. Van Peebles knew that after the 1968 assassination of Martin Luther King, a rash of urban riots, and the all-too-common instances of bloody, often fatal confrontations between black activists and governmental authorities, many African Americans

98

99

yearned for an escapist art that, as portrayed in his film, placed members of the black underclass in the role of unbridled, avenging anti-heroes.

Even when African American and other black diasporal tastes did not include Van Peebles's brazen images of a rebellious black underclass, the prevailing aesthetic called for other, equally distinctive, black visual markers. British fashion photographer Patrick Lichfield recorded one of the period's signifiers—a large, fluffy, combed-out, "Afro" hairstyle, worn by actor and model Marsha Hunt—for a 1969 issue of *Vogue*. African American printmaker Lev Mills, also working in London, portrayed himself as a grid- and photoscopic-enveloped dandy in *I'm Funky, But Clean* (1972). And New Yorker Anthony Barboza, in the "decisive moment" tradition of Henri Cartier-Bresson, captured the grace and rhythmic possibilities of black bodies in *Fadiouth, Senegal, West Africa* (1972).

These media-influenced artists equated a "black" style with self-confidence, beauty that was the antithesis of white supremist models, and "power." In the use of an ontologically inverted, black colloquialism like "I'm Funky, But Clean," Lev Mills proclaimed a cultural difference and even an aesthetic advantage over those

100 OPPOSITE Patrick Lichfield, *Marsha Hunt*, 1969
101 ABOVE Lev Mills, *I'm Funky, But Clean*, 1972

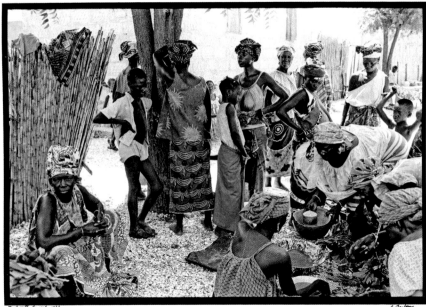

who not only lacked his particular fashion sense, but also those who, unlike him, were unable to communicate on both the vernacular and the standard levels. Although many blacks scoffed at the idea that a hairstyle, an attitude, or an alternative worldview could advance black people in the same way that political revolts had liberated oppressed peoples in the past, others believed that revolutions began with these metamorphoses of the self. The African Commune of Bad Relevant Artists, or AFRI-COBRA, was a Chicago-based group of black artists (founded in 1969 by Jeff Donaldson and Wadsworth Jarrell), who hoped to facilitate this self-transformation. A humanist orientation, design sensibilities that used African prototypes as reference, agendas that fostered liberation and solidarity throughout the African diaspora, and an art of "expressive awesomeness" were the philosophical concepts that AFRI-COBRA promoted. Among the original members of this black nationalist artists' group were three women—Jae Jarrell, Barbara Jones-Hogu, and Carolyn Lawrence—whose art (while sometimes eclipsed in discussions about the works of AFRI-COBRA's mostly male members) frequently revealed a countertype to AFRI-COBRA's often patriarchal view of black culture. For example, textile artist Jae Jarrell's inventive work *Revolutionary Suit* (1970) most certainly alluded to the aggressive position that black women could take in this revolution of the mind, body, and spirit.

103

102 OPPOSITE Anthony Barboza, *Fadiouth, Senegal, West Africa*, 1972
103 ABOVE Jae Jarrell, *Revolutionary Suit*, 1970

The Heirs of Olympia's Maid

I Like Olympia in Black Face (1970), created by the white American artist Larry Rivers, was originally commissioned by the Menil Foundation for "Some American History": the artist's 1971 exhibition on "the black experience." Although the exhibition (which also included works by Joe Overstreet, Frank Bowling, and others) received mixed reviews, works like this *tableau vivant* burlesque of *Olympia* (Edouard Manet's scandal-provoking painting shown at the Paris Salon of 1865) marked a historic detour in black cultural representations in American art. Unlike Rivers's other works in the exhibition (which dealt with Africa, slavery, contemporary issues in race relations, and important black cultural figures), *I Like Olympia in Black Face* redressed the peripheral and often negative place of blacks in Western art history. While blacks were certainly not invisible to artists prior to 1970, their sympathetic representations in Western art were rare. Although Rivers's juxtaposition of Manet's *Olympia* with a "black" version (like Picasso's 1901 rendition of a black *Olympia*) smacked of a tongue-in-cheek witticism, it also fearlessly ventured into a forbidden territory of black erotica that very few artists in the US had dared to enter.

Indeed very few American artists, black or white, concentrated on depicting black nudes prior to the 1970s. The exceptions included sculptor Richmond Barthé, painter Eldzier Cortor, and photographers F. Holland Day and Carl Van Vechten. Beyond the larger societal restrictions under which American artists had long operated (even when confronting the nude's widely accepted position in classical and Western art), the reactionary values of many African Americans prevented artists from depicting blacks in ways that departed from the conservative or Social-Realistic. This self-censorship emanated from artists who worked within black communities, as well as from artistic "outsiders," who feared that if they created sexually provocative images of blacks they would be perceived as racists or pornographers. All these factors, along with a history of assumptions by social scientists about pathology and moral depravity in black communities, discouraged artists from creating images that would have supplied visual fodder for these pernicious views. Not until the late 1960s—with the onslaught of a sexual and social revolution—would a few artists and select audiences feel comfortable enough to explore the formal and psychological implications of black nudes in art.

Of course, the artistic process of removing a human subject's clothing and focusing on his or her essentially biological, naked self, interjected a close and discomfiting element of objectification into representation. When this

104

104　Larry Rivers, *I Like Olympia in Black Face*, 1970

disrobing, deindividualizing, and sexualizing was imposed
on black subjects (who were already susceptible to erasures of
personhood), the visual results—even in a seemingly innocuous
image like Lichfield's nude photograph of *Vogue* model Marsha
Hunt—often meant that the individual was presented as both
artifact and sexual object.

　　For figurative artists whose aesthetics were shaped by
the period's various black nationalist ideologies, the nude
embodied a multiplicity of themes, ideas, and meanings. And,
depending on whether the nude was a black male or a black
female, these same themes, ideas, and meanings often carried
additional and, at times, conflicting messages. In the works of
painter Murry N. DePillars (who, with poet Gwendolyn Brooks,

editor Hoyt Fuller, and jazz musician Muhal Richard Abrams, helped shape Chicago's vibrant black arts scene in the late 1960s), images of black women fused traditional "feminine" qualities with the themes of omnipotence and physical potentiality. DePillars's *Queen Candace* (1989), produced after his initial Chicago period and under the utopian tenets of AFRI-COBRA, bespoke royalty and placed colorful, African-style designs on the silhouetted, pregnant, and virtually nude body of a black woman.

From the vantage point of New Yorker Faith Ringgold and her multi-paneled *Slave Rape* series (1972), the black female nude also conveyed multiple messages, concerning her union with and sanctuary in nature, as well as resistance and self-defense. Ringgold's visual black nationalism—prescribed by a feminist

105 OPPOSITE Murry N. DePillars,
Queen Candace, 1989
106 RIGHT Faith Ringgold, *Fight
to Save your Life*, 1972, from the
Slave Rape series

107

stance that constantly negotiated between a personal identity
and a political one—was in accord with Dana C. Chandler's
similarly conceptualized approach in his *Genocide* series (1971).
This Boston-based artist created his nude with the Black Power
movement's anxieties about sexual emasculation and political
violation uppermost in his mind, as seen in his agitprop image
of a jailed, chained, yet defiantly erect, black penis. Despite the
gendered demarcations here between the black female nude as
an object of desire and the black male nude as an objectified
desirer, in both works nakedness and the specter of sexuality
become icons of fear, imprisonment, and dislocation.

Ideologically placed between Rivers's art-historical
commentary on *Olympia*, and DePillars, Ringgold, and
Chandler's politically charged images of black naked bodies

were the African American nudes of the Philadelphia-born, Connecticut-based painter Barkley L. Hendricks. His portraits of the 1970s—black, beautiful, and suave—stood apart from the majority of black cultural representations produced during this period. The jarring combination of a droll, self-effacing humor with an unnerving naturalism that bordered on the profane was Hendricks's artistic trademark: a characteristic that even in a work like *Brilliantly Endowed (Self-Portrait)* of 1977 dominated the artist's dual discourse on blackness and masculinity. With an attitude that recalled Albrecht Dürer's nude *Self-Portrait* of c. 1518, Hendricks's *Brilliantly Endowed (Self-Portrait)* examined the myths of artistic greatness and black male sexual prowess, but within the context of his study of an African American *élan*—an investigation that informed his whole career as an artist.

108

Photographic studies of the black nude during this same period were often dismissed as pornographic, although they were capable of being as innovative and thematically complex as their painted counterparts. For example, in Adger Cowans's surrealistic *P.B.* (1974), his allusions to the folklore surrounding black steatopygia—here isolated and symmetrically viewed—introduced an ethnographic element into this particular work. In Robert Mapplethorpe's *Alistair Butler* (1980), the artist likened a homoerotic gaze on the black male body to the art of antiquity. In both, the black body as a photographed object of desire, while unquestionably nuanced, elicited what author Alice Walker pronounced in her novel *Meridian* (1976) as the

109

110

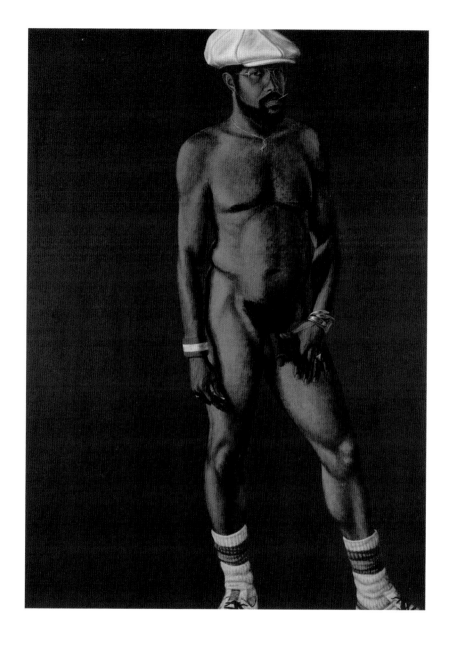

107 OPPOSITE Dana C. Chandler Jr., *American Penal System...Pan-African Concentration Camps and Death Houses,* from the *Genocide* series, 1971
108 ABOVE Barkley L. Hendricks, *Brilliantly Endowed (Self-Portrait),* 1977

109 ᴛᴏᴘ Adger Cowans, *P.B.*, 1974
110 ᴀʙᴏᴠᴇ Robert Mapplethorpe, *Alistair Butler*, 1980
111 ᴏᴘᴘᴏsɪᴛᴇ Bill Gunn, *Ganja & Hess*, 1973

ultimate sin: the turning of real, thinking and feeling people
into Art. Yet one could also argue that, at this moment of an
expanded black consciousness, it was precisely this sense
that blacks could be both objects of artistic contemplation
and actors in their own aesthetic discernment, that made
these works provocative and central to a revised art history
of transgressive, radical black images.

Conjure

If the 1960s was the decade when a new black cultural
consciousness came into existence, then the period of the 1970s
and early 1980s with its milieu of black art institutionalization
was certainly its watershed. Through a number of catalysts—
including the loud petitions for artistic equity, the Smithsonian
Institution's acquisition of works by black artists from the
recently closed Harmon Foundation, a series of "all-black" art
exhibitions at mainstream institutions, and the creation and
expansion of the National Endowment for the Arts—African

112 Betye Saar, *The Time Inbetween*, 1974

American artists, their works, and a loosely defined black aesthetic were focal points in the contemporary arts scene.

In addition to the reprinting of earlier art history "classics" by Locke, Porter, and Cedric Dover (the Anglo-Indian sociologist and author of the 1960 book *American Negro Art*), the 1970s ushered in a plethora of new "black art" publications, such as Samella Lewis and Ruth Waddy's *Black Artists on Art* (1969, 1971), Elton Fax's *Seventeen Black Artists* (1971), Romare Bearden and Harry Henderson's *Six Black Masters of American Art* (1972), Elsa Honig Fine's *The Afro-American Artist* (1973) and Samella Lewis's journal *Black Art: An International Quarterly*. These publications, with the catalogues and reviews that accompanied the flurry of solo and group exhibitions by African American artists, documented the earlier contributions of black artists, as well as the principal figures and icons of a concurrent black arts scene. Artist and curator David C. Driskell's accumulative achievement—the corporate-sponsored exhibition and publication *Two Centuries of Black American Art* (1976)—signaled a dramatic shift in the mainstream art world. This change in perception acknowledged not only individual black talent, but the idea of a collective artistic genius based on race, history, and a creative drive whose source was a spirituality that, in turn, sprang from the phenomenon of cultural connections throughout the African diaspora.

In 1973, filmmaker Bill Gunn attempted to visualize this spiritual, black essence in *Ganja & Hess*: his updated, African American version of the Hollywood vampire movie. But rather than depicting supernatural metamorphoses and horrific, murderous acts, Gunn, through the rituals and habits of sex, drug addiction, and religion, explored symbiosis and possession in Afro-America. At the same time, Betye Saar, a Los Angeles-based artist, was continuing to create her memory and spirit-conjuring assemblages made from discarded bric-a-brac, family mementos, and other ephemera. As representative of a different school of artists, who were plunging into a previously unexamined African American psyche, Saar regarded works like her own *The Time Inbetween* (1974) in spiritual and trans-racial terms, rather than in a purely secular or "black" way. In sharp contrast to the black nationalist references of activist Ron Karenga or the members of AFRI-COBRA, a group of artists emerged in the 1970s who, while conversant with the current discourse on black consciousness, devoted themselves to an art of symbolic accretions and altar-like settings, whose inspiration was just as likely to come from Latin American art, California Funk, or so-called folk arts, as from a traditional African or African American source.

With this emphasis on a blackness that was metaphysical and that derived its form not from painted or sculpted black humanity but, rather, from a marshaling of symbolic or conceptual strategies in visual communication, Betye Saar, with fellow Los Angeles artists Houston Conwill, David Hammons, Senga Nengudi, John Outterbridge, and Noah Purifoy, gradually began to redefine "black consciousness" in art. Of particular importance to this revisionist impulse was the work of David Hammons. Beginning with his "body prints" of the early 1970s, Hammons contested conventional black representations with works and performances that delved deeply into race, culture, class, and commodification in America. With his move to New York City in the mid-1970s, and his affiliation with the Just Above Midtown Gallery, Hammons established himself as a major presence in New York, creating installations with African American hair, food, and detritus, and producing outdoor environmental works that invoked black cultural metaphors that were often ironic, but with lyricism and empathy.

Although considered an imitator of the European avant-garde by critics sympathetic to black nationalist views, Hammons's utilization of materials and things that were once in direct, physical contact with black people (such as hair, foods, bottles)

113 BELOW Dawoud Bey, David Hammons constructing *Higher Goals* in Cadman Plaza, Brooklyn, New York, 1986
114 OPPOSITE Francis Griffith, *Untitled*, c. 1963–95

strongly resonated with similar artistic practices and religious beliefs among West and Central African peoples. Thus, as a creator of "African American power objects," Hammons inadvertently joined his more conservative black colleagues in their quest to recreate an African sensibility in American art. What made this artistic identification with Africa different from, say, the visual appropriations by artists aligned with the "New Negro" arts movement was, first, the timing of this aesthetic embrace with the era of colonial dismantlement and African independence, and second, a greater knowledge in Europe and the Americas of African peoples, cultures, and geography.

Beginning in the 1950s with the African American painter John Biggers and his "discovery" of a modernist impulse in West African art, European and American artists throughout the 1960s and 1970s went to Africa, reimagining the continent and reconceptualizing their work along the way. The idea that Africa was a cultural utopia and mecca (as visualized in a c. 1963–95 painting by the Barbadian artist Francis Griffith) was often put forward during this period by Jamaican and other English-speaking Caribbean intellectuals with a historic memory of Marcus Garvey and his "Back to Africa" movement. These millennial ideas, in conjunction with the myths and imagery surrounding the Ethiopian Emperor Haile Selassie and his symbolic stewardship of the black race, led to the rise in Jamaica of the Rastafarian movement, and its attendant black nationalist influence on Caribbean politics and art.

114

Among the many African American artists who experienced similar esoteric revelations as a result of their encounters with Africa were Elton Fax, Tom Feelings and, remarkably, James Lesesne Wells and Lois Mailou Jones: two sexagenarians and original participants in the "New Negro" arts movement of some forty years earlier. Following her tour of Africa in 1970, Jones embarked on a two-dimensional, brilliantly colored painting style that (as seen in her 1971 *Magic of Nigeria*) aligned itself with the African pattern paintings of AFRI-COBRA artists like Jeff Donaldson. As chairman of the US delegation for the Second World Black and African Festival of Arts and Culture in 1977, Donaldson led his African American emissaries to FESTAC's Nigerian headquarters with the conviction that, unlike the largely white-administered US delegation for the First World Festival of Negro Arts in 1966 (held in Dakar, Senegal), FESTAC was going to be a Black- and African-directed artistic undertaking.

Although FESTAC presented visual arts, theatrical performances, and literary readings by black artists from all over the world, music drew the Festival's disparate black peoples together more than any of the other featured art forms. For example, what other medium at FESTAC had the distinction of having assembled, in perfect artistic equality, the diverse sensibilities of a battery of Yoruba talking drums, Trinidadian steel bands, Cuban *conjuntos*, Brazilian *afoxé*, and such musical talents as Stevie Wonder, Miriam Makeba, Osibisa, and Sun Ra's Intergalactic Arkestra?

That the world's various black musics had an allure that crossed the boundaries of culture, nationality, and racial identity was something that many visual artists knew and attempted to recreate. In addition to the rhythmic abstractions and music-themed works of a whole range of artists in the 1970s, the Brooklyn painter Archie Rand summoned the performing energies of assorted African American-influenced singers in his series entitled *The Groups*. In a 1970 painting from this series (with the same name), Rand's hand-rendered, marquee-like invocation of various rock-and-roll singers was both a homage to African American popular music and a witty rejoinder to the period's reigning Art & Language Conceptualists.

Black music and art also found a common space to inhabit in the record industry's innovative packaging of long-playing albums during this period. Of special note was Columbia Records' eye-catching reproductions of the *Aleph Sanctuary* murals by artist Abdul Mati Klarwein for selected album covers of recordings by Carlos Santana, Jimi Hendrix, and Miles Davis. But even more popular than Klarwein's hallucinatory

115 Lois Mailou Jones, *Magic of Nigeria*, 1971

116 TOP Archie Rand, *The Groups*, 1970
117 ABOVE Ernie Barnes, *The Sugar Shack*, 1972–76

album covers was the football player-turned-artist Ernie Barnes's "Neo-Mannerist" treatment of ecstatic black dancers on the cover of singer Marvin Gaye's 1976 album, *I Want You*. If ever African American images coincided with African American sounds, then Barnes's *The Sugar Shack* was the visual equivalent to Gaye's percussive, multi-layered dance tracks.

This desire to visualize something racial and cultural, yet also conceptual and metaphysical, found the ideal subject in black religion. In New Orleans, the street evangelist and artist Sister Gertrude Morgan transformed her humble living quarters into a space for meditation and spiritual union by painting the walls, floors, and all her furnishings white. In *Come in my Room, Come on in the Prayer Room* (c. 1970) Sister Morgan portrayed herself within her literally white yet figuratively black and sanctified Everlasting Gospel Mission, surrounded by white angels, interracial groups of people tending to the sick and the children, and (on the right) her own painting of the all-seeing "Eye of God." The Divine Eye, identified by Sister Morgan as "the unseen host at every meal," also appeared at this time in several works by the Jamaican artist Brother Everald Brown. Like Sister Morgan, Brother Brown's religion—Rastafarianism and the Ethiopian Orthodox Church—shaped his entire cultural sphere, turning his self-built home in the hills of St. Ann Parish and even his decades-long series of hand-made musical instruments like *Dove Harp* (1996) into media for visual and spiritual fulfillment.

With these black visionaries as a source of inspiration, printmaker Margo Humphrey transformed one of Christianity's most venerated scenes—Jesus's last supper with his disciples—into a post-nationalist statement on community and syncretism. Like much of her work since the mid-1970s, *The Last Bar-B-Que* (1988–89) framed blackness

118

120

119

within an absurdist, yet penetrating and heartfelt view that ultimately reinvigorated and redeemed an often restrictive black nationalism. Humphrey's consciously naive treatment of this motley crew of disciples and their final feast of barbecued chicken, watermelons, and the standard liturgical fare perfectly represented what cultural critic Greg Tate described as "the impulse towards enmeshing self-criticism and celebration" found in the works of the more provocative black artists of the period. Moving beyond questions of nomenclature and vaulting beyond the choice between making either "abstractions" or "black figures," Humphrey and her cohorts set sail on uncharted waters that were perhaps more choppy and heterogeneous than any that had come before. And like the decorative facades that permeated *The Last Bar-B-Que*, representations of black culture in the future were likely to be placed against the contrasting rigs of the shifting racial paradigms of this period.

118 OPPOSITE ABOVE Sister Gertrude Morgan, *Come in my Room, Come on in the Prayer Room*, c. 1970
119 OPPOSITE BELOW Margo Humphrey, *The Last Bar-B-Que*, 1988–89
120 BELOW Everald Brown, *Dove Harp*, 1996

121 Lyle Ashton Harris, *For Cleopatra*, 1994

Chapter 6
Culture as Currency

Beyond Scarification

Lyle Ashton Harris's exhibition in the fall of 1994 of large format Polaroids, "The Good Life," received a remarkably wide coverage for a young artist presenting his first solo show in New York. In response to his self-portraits, one reviewer concluded that his work was "a rich and probing photographic autobiography" that stressed "issues of racial, gender, and sexual marginalization." Commenting on the other works in "The Good Life"—staged and impromptu photographs of family members and friends—another writer observed that Harris's photographic rejoicing and dominion over his subjects made him the "goad," "provocateur," and "locus of emotional catharsis" in these works.

What neither reviewer noted about "The Good Life" was Harris's complete subversion of various notions of identity—gender, sexual, and familial—which, ironically, caused another indicator of identity—blackness—to twist, snake, and splice itself into a complex yet irreducible ingredient. For many viewers, the anonymity of the person with scarifications, dreadlocked hair, and black nationalist tricolors in Harris's *For Cleopatra* (1994) confounded their basic assumptions about gender and beauty: an unease for which, surprisingly, blackness was a consoling presence. But instead of a 1960s or 1970s styled blackness with raised fists and neo-African figures, Harris's blackness was soft, ambiguous, mercurial, non-exclusionary, and completely unencumbered by racial doctrine or social conventions.

"Fertile Ground," Alison Saar's 1993–94 traveling exhibition, also presented protean concepts. In this collection of carved wooden figures, organic matter, and other manufactured and environmental elements, Saar attempted to give

121

three-dimensional form and allegorical meaning to a southern US landscape. This ambition of Saar's—to create certain moods, emotions, and states of consciousness in her work—not only resonated with her family's long involvement in the visual arts and spiritual dimensions of objects, but with her own acquired knowledge of non-Western religions, world art, and social history.

122   *Terra Rosa* (1993), one of seven sculptural components that made up the "Fertile Ground" installation, reflected Saar's intellectual complexity as much as it communicated her installation's multifaceted theme. As described by "Fertile Ground" curator Susan Krane, "The pregnant *Terra Rosa* consumes and is consumed by the soil—by red earth endowed with spiritual powers, as is cemetery earth throughout the African American South." This figure's attitude of charity and supplication moved freely between German Expressionist *angst*, Roman Catholic *pietas*, and Kongo/Angolan *kiyaala-mooko* ("she who holds out hands"), defying single interpretations, just as Saar's focus on the products and impact of an African diasporic culture has resisted glib categorization.

        The embracing of an artistic and intellectual plurality took other forms beyond Harris's multivocal portraiture and Saar's installations. The sculptor Martin Puryear engaged both three-dimensional form and suggested meaning while still maintaining a sense of artistic and thematic unity in his work.

123   In *His Eminence* (1993–95), the sculpture's solitary grandeur and anthropomorphic presence are matched by journeyman-like sawing, assembling, joining, bending, shaping, and finishing: lessons learned among the artists and craftsmen of West Africa, Northern Europe, the Far East, and the United States. Recalling the spatial witticisms of Constantin Brancusi and the monolithic sculptures of prehistory, *His Eminence* also conjures an icon that is distinctly American: akin to John Henry, Casey Jones, Stagger Lee, and a host of other mythological, strong, and enigmatic male personas.

124   Gary Simmons also employed vestiges of mythological figures in his work, but with irony and a legacy of racial misapprehension. From his large-scale drawings, diagrammatic images of footprints and blurred gestures, to the more intimate works from his *Erasure* series, Simmons drew on a whole archive of stereotypes. His fleeting images of the tap-dancing, shuffling, and grinning actions of clowns, athletes, and other black entertainers turned the watching of black performance into a multifaceted act of admiration, revulsion, and complicity.

        These late twentieth-century artists and their responses to culture and identity emerged at an odd moment in history.

122 RIGHT Alison Saar,
Terra Rosa, 1993
123 BELOW Martin Puryear,
His Eminence, 1993-95

124 Gary Simmons, *Black Chalkboard (Double Grin)*, 1993, from the *Erasure* series

While the 1980s and 1990s were a time of expanding opportunities, greater global awareness, and increasing public access to visual art, this period also saw cultural conservativism, a less enthusiastic support for the arts, de facto censorship, and an unstable art market.

Practitioners and supporters of black culture also experienced highs and lows during this period. In the US, the Civil Rights Act of 1965 and subsequent federal legislation for a more racially diverse workplace and educational system meant that African Americans entered into social, political, and economic arenas with a new-found confidence. Correspondingly, a black middle class grew and asserted itself in the economy. The black nationalist politics of the previous decades were transformed into a less authoritative philosophy, creating a renewed sense of black solidarity. The UK experienced its own black "renaissance" as seen in an outpouring of literary works, art exhibitions, and mass media products on the subject of a black cultural identity. Finally, the dismantling of apartheid in South Africa and the ascent of political activist Nelson Mandela were universal symbols of an acceptance of black self-determination and social justice.

In contrast to these milestones of progress, black culture during this period also suffered disillusionment, dislocation, and a moral vacuum. In spite of the growth of a black middle class, Americans in the 1980s and 1990s encountered even larger numbers of the black poor, unemployed, and homeless. The unfortunate reality in the success story of black America's new-found purchasing power was the collapse of inner cities and the subsequent demise of small, historically black businesses and social institutions. This black hopelessness— unimaginable in those heady years of the 1960s and 1970s— manifested itself in incidents ranging from drug-related acts of violence in countless African American communities, to the spiritual "deaths" and territorial violence that plagued the peoples of Haiti, Liberia, Somalia, Rwanda, and other centers of political unrest.

For visual artists, these conflicting signs—both within and beyond black culture—often resulted in analytic (though not always dispassionate) investigations in their work. For example, in Gary Simmons's drawings of racist caricatures and the telltale traces of black humanity, a major part of his cross-examination was the dismantling of black objectivity and (in Simmons's own words) the revealing of its structural "blue-print." In this way, many late-twentieth-century artists took their work beyond the racial and cultural "scarification" that identified previous generations and, instead of these "tribal markings," employed a multiplicity of conceptual mechanisms: analyzing socially rooted emblems, questioning traditional concepts of identity, utilizing testimony and scripted narrative, and, in general, dealing with culture and history as artistic currency.

Because of an omnipresent racial dimension in the works of these artists and others working with similar concepts, these postmodernist activities are seen as different. This ideological aligning of artworks with black history and culture—as seen in Harris's intimations of the slave master's lash in *For Cleopatra*, or Saar's allegories on race and nature in *Terra Rosa*, or even Puryear's allusions to the totemic potential of the abstract in *His Eminence*—has converted postmodernism into a far more lineage-conscious and, therefore, intriguing approach. The role of black culture in this period of ruin and reconfiguration has been to divest art of its current despair and create in its place a new optimism, an alternative worldview, and an unparalleled critical stance.

Icons and Signs

Like the allusions to a portentous sign in the old African American spiritual "Handwriting on the Wall," the graffiti that began to cover virtually everything in New York City in the late 1970s prophesied a sociological shift in this urban landscape, from an environment of suppressed disorder, to an atmosphere of virtual chaos and decline. But rather than being emblematic merely of society's ills, these ink marker scrawls and spray paint "tags"—produced mostly by Latino and African American youth—transmitted information, such as neighborhood boundaries, social rankings, artistic *noms de plume*, and even creativity itself.

One of the participants in this writing of names and claims, the African American painter Jean-Michel Basquiat, went through a rapid rise and fall in this period. Beginning with his 1980 debut in a widely reviewed group exhibition (held in a vacant building in New York City's Time Square district), Basquiat and his works were soon incorporated into the larger New York art scene, and then internationally celebrated, marketed, and imitated. During his relatively brief career and after his premature death in 1988, Basquiat's paintings were dismissed by some critics as having been promoted undeservedly by art dealers in the US and Europe who knew how to play the media, but their collective energy and, in many cases, their explorations of an African American psyche, entitle them to serious study. A frequent motif in Basquiat's work—the "see-through" man—not only responded metaphorically to this period's fascination with exposé and destroying people's facades, but also spoke to the notion that anatomy had a theatrical quality that, when paired with blackness, was a radical attack on society's superficiality and deep-seated racism.

125 The exposed lungs, sinew, and guts in Basquiat's *Flexible* (1984) convey this notion of the black-body-as-public-theater, while the entire piece recalls a white-washed wooden barrier, fit to be covered with urban hieroglyphs and prophetic black imagery.

Basquiat's invocations of blackness appeared both independently and correspondingly in the works of other artists, especially those who, like Basquiat, reacted to the cultural politics of race and racism during this period. For

126 example, in the London-based painter Tam Joseph's *Learning to Walk* (1988), action verbs and historically charged pictographs joined forces in a visual discourse about evolutionary,

127 revolutionary, and personal advancement. In his *Hip Hop Jazz Makoussa* (1994) the Côte d'Ivoire painter Ouattara Watts symbolically hinged together ancient and modern motifs from Africa with collaged friezes of album covers for jazz,

125 Jean-Michel Basquiat, *Flexible*, 1984

126 TOP Tam Joseph, *Learning to Walk*, 1988
127 ABOVE Ouattara Watts, *Hip-Hop Jazz Makoussa*, 1994
128 OPPOSITE Ras Ishi Butcher, *400 Years New World Order*, 1995

128

reggae, rock, rap, and traditional ethnic music. In this way
he communicated his adherence to a multilingual, though
commonly valued, spirituality from his native West Africa. The
paintings of the Barbadian artist Ras Ishi Butcher joined his
personal iconographies of slavery and rebellion in the West Indies
with chromatic, heavily textured surfaces (present, for example,
in his 1995 *400 Years New World Order*), which gave his Basquiat
brand of cultural analysis an international countenance.

Beyond the generic symbols of blackness, Butcher
incorporated into his compositions large anecdotal figures,
whose presence made a sociopolitical statement about human
agency and cultural intervention. Butcher, Basquiat, and other
iconographers used black subjects (and sometimes actual
figures) to revisit the cultural nationalist's goals of recognizing
and celebrating distinctiveness, but with a postmodern
difference. For example, in the assemblages by the Chicago

129 LEFT Mr. Imagination, *Portrait Head Paintbrush Tree*, 1991
130 OPPOSITE Philip Moore, *King Sparrow in Sacred Wonder Heart*, 1992

129   artist Mr. Imagination (formerly Gregory Warmack), the artist's humble, bricolage-like use of discarded paintbrushes and bottle caps deflated their allusions to royal effigies and finery.

      The Guyanese painter Philip Moore also displayed a visual atavism and reformulation of black consciousness in his work.

130   *King Sparrow in Sacred Wonder Heart* (1992)—Moore's "portrait" of the legendary West Indian calypso singer "the Mighty Sparrow"—replaced the naturalistic depictions of this cultural icon with a radiant, gestural, and pigment-laden image. By the 1990s, Moore believed that blacks needed "to reinterpret the Myths and Legends of life" that were imposed on them by whites; in addition, they had to be "bold enough to recreate [their] destinies" by assuming control over the processes of analysis and performance. As shown in *King Sparrow in Sacred Wonder Heart*, Moore's neo-nationalist call embraced experimentation, improvisation, and the opening of one's work as the conduit through which a spiritual rollcall of black culture could flow.

The tenacity of an aesthetic that dealt with old and new icons, and also recognized the inspiration in artistic media and human experience, made both cultural nationalism and postmodernism less demanding and divisive. This revisionist spirit reigned supreme in Martha Jackson Jarvis's *Last Rites: Sarcophagi II (Earth)* (1992–93) and Melvin Edwards's *Tambo* (1993), resulting in two highly idiosyncratic art objects that responded to several late-twentieth-century theoretical

132
131

131 BELOW Melvin Edwards, *Tambo*, 1993
132 OPPOSITE Martha Jackson Jarvis, *Last Rites: Sarcophagi II (Earth)*, 1992–93

concerns. Jarvis's rococo, ceramic reinterpretation of an ancient Greek form introduced a theatrical, festive and, therefore, black diasporal way of thinking about death. And Edwards's platter-like assembly of welded hardware and industrial parts—named after the late South African political activist Oliver Tambo, and closely related to other assemblages from Edwards's *Lynch Fragment* series—imposed a specific historical and political meaning on to this object's material reality.

No Place/Like Home

The concept of home figured prominently among the many cultural icons that artists explored toward the end of the twentieth century. But rather than a definition of home as an inviting and cozy domicile, or even as a figurative place of rest and comfort, home often took on an ironic character, having just as much to do with disconnectedness and annexation as with a sense of belonging in the world. No doubt the more visible presence of the urban homeless during this period, as well as the increased numbers of refugees internationally, forever shattered the image of the universal hearth. Whereas in previous times, black artists often waxed nostalgic about "the old homestead," "the community," or "the motherland," by the 1980s and 1990s a more sober and perhaps cynical view of "the hood" had entered into black cultural discourse, with multiple views of place and position emerging in literary works, visual arts, and popular culture. In her novel *The Bluest Eye* (1970), Toni Morrison deftly anticipated this fascination and dread in late twentieth-century black culture in having a home, as well as being homeless, describing the latter (being "put outdoors") as "the end of something, an irrevocable, physical fact, defining and complementing our metaphysical condition."

As an extension of this theme—and as part of a postmodernist rejection of conventional art practices—many artists in the 1980s and 1990s created installations: object-, image-, and concept-laden environments, manufactured either within the art gallery proper or in the world, with the intention (wrote Museum of Modern Art curator Robert Storr in 1991) of displacing, disorientating, re-placing, and re-orientating. Even when these inquiries into place and position were confined to just the art world and its inner sanctum of objects, galleries, curators, and audiences, there was a similar sense of domestic and familial disjuncture (as described in the passage from Morrison's *The Bluest Eye*).

New York artist Lorna Simpson, in collaboration with actor, singer, and composer Alva Rogers, created such an installation in Charleston, South Carolina, for the "Places With A Past" exhibition for the 1991 Spoleto Festival USA. In a vacant outbuilding of *c.* 1822 next to the Governor Thomas Bennett House, Simpson used Charleston's importance in the infamous transatlantic slave trade to explore "those things that connect you to your identity and those things (violence) that happen to you because of your identity." In Room One of the *Five Rooms*, she displayed dozens of large glass jugs, filled with water and labeled with the names of slave ships, the African and Caribbean countries from which their human cargoes originated, and the names of the South Carolina waterways that ultimately linked these disparate worlds. On one wall, Simpson's four-part photographic image of two, virtually identical black women, linked by a long, chain-like braid, continued this exegesis on perpetuity and dislocation in black culture.

For Beverly Buchanan, Sue Williamson, and Kerry James Marshall, the unadorned realities of a contemporary black existence inspired each of them to incorporate aspects of those received realities into their work: art objects that channeled both the experiential "truths" of their respective

133

133 Lorna Simpson, *Five Rooms* (detail of Room One). Installation at Spoleto Festival USA, Charleston, South Carolina, 1991

134 TOP Beverly Buchanan, *Red Shack*, c. 1990
135 ABOVE RIGHT Sue Williamson, *Mementoes of District Six*, 1993
136 OPPOSITE Kerry James Marshall, *Better Homes Better Gardens*, 1994–95

subjects, as well as the artifices and imaginings of the artists involved. Georgia-based artist Beverly Buchanan's miniature reconstructions of the homes of an African American, southern, and rural poor (as in *Red Shack* of *c.* 1990), possessed a diminutive yet emphatic power, communicating an ingenuity and spiritual presence where society usually sees offensive poverty and underdevelopment. On an altogether different scale and level of intent, the Cape Town artist Sue Williamson envisioned a monument to South Africa's black dispossessed in her *Mementoes of District Six* (1993), with its lucite bricks of encased rubble from an annexed (and demolished) "non-White" community and amplified interviews with its former residents. Chicagoan Kerry James Marshall's interplay between perspectival cityscape and graffiti-covered signs in *Better Homes Better Gardens* (1994–95) avoided the essentialist trap of turning this visual essay on public housing into either an indictment of, or an apology for, these failed urban experiments in living. Rather, Marshall's loving, colloquial "homeboy" and "homegirl" (like Buchanan's *Red Shack* and Williamson's disembodied black voices) converted these humble lodgings into sites of miraculous, restorative possibilities.

137 TOP Fred Wilson, *Insight: In Site: In Sight: Incite: Memory*. Installation in
St Philip's Church, Old Salem, Winston-Salem, North Carolina, 1994
138 ABOVE Sonia Boyce, *Peep*. Installation view, intervention in Cultures Gallery,
Brighton Museum and Art Gallery, Sussex, 1995

Simpson's use of plastic exhibition labels mocked the museum world's often unsatisfactory efforts to educate audiences, and also exposed the sexist and racist ways in which the English language is used. This critical stance— directed toward museum practices and display strategies— was also the theoretical locus for several other artists
137 engaged in site-specific installations. New Yorker Fred Wilson achieved similar objectives with his 1994 art installation in the eighteenth-century Moravian village of Old Salem (in Winston-Salem, North Carolina). His re-positioning of historical objects and manipulation of exhibition labels, lighting, and other display techniques helped reveal aspects of the site's tragic African American past that (because of the conspiratorial forces of time, ignorance, and racism) had largely become invisible.
138 Similarly, London artist Sonia Boyce papered over the glass of the display cases in Brighton Museum's diminutive "Cultures" gallery (where art objects by the world's black, brown, and yellow peoples were exhibited) transforming them into a series of translucent vitrines: a few strategically placed "peep holes" allowed glimpses of the exhibits, which included Boyce's own faux ethnographic creations. In both instances, voyeurism and disclosure of the cultural crimes that were perpetrated against blacks and other colonized peoples framed the artist's and audience's relationship to the "official" history on exhibition.

Installations that addressed the entire conceptual basis of past black lives—from the axiomatic womb to the proverbial tomb—took center stage in site-specific works by the collaborative artists' team of Houston Conwill, Joseph de Pace, and Estella Conwill Majozo. Their floor-level cosmogram
139 *The New Ring Shout* (1995) was situated in a lower Manhattan office built on the site of a long-forgotten, eighteenth-century African burial ground. Related to Houston Conwill's marked and ritualized art spaces of the 1970s and 1980s, *The New Ring Shout* used assorted texts, lexicons, and ideograms to reveal history and a spiritual "mapping" of the universe. Although removed from Conwill, De Pace, and Majozo's aesthetics of black space and spirituality, the Chilean-born artist
140 Alfredo Jaar achieved similar ends in his gallery installation of 1995, addressing the genocide in the central African nation of Rwanda following the assassination of its president in 1994. Jaar's "cemetery of images"—boxed (that is, unseen) and stacked photographs of Rwanda's dead and dying—changed the often intrusive act of documentary photography into a procedure that supported a bigger and more consequential enterprise: a conceptual art of social contrition and humanitarianism.

139 ABOVE Houston Conwill, Joseph de Pace, Estella Conwill Majozo,
The New Ring Shout, 1995. Central rotunda of Federal Office Building built
over an excavated African burial ground, New York
140 OPPOSITE Alfredo Jaar, *Real Pictures*, installation at Museum of
Contemporary Photography, Columbia College, Chicago, 1995

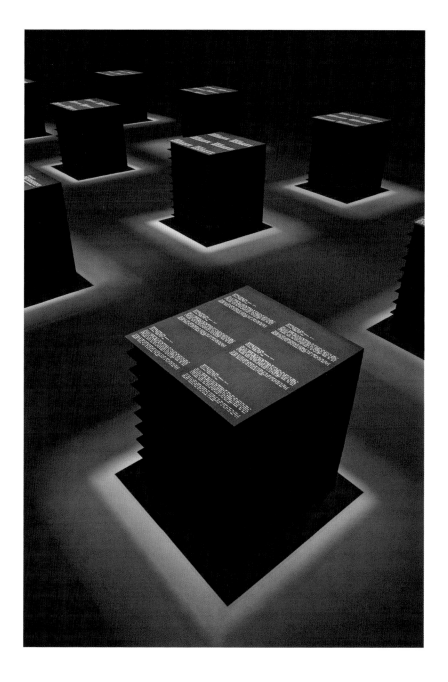

Virtual Realities

The Ghanaian philosopher Kwame Anthony Appiah wrote:

If an African identity is to empower us, what is required is not so much that we throw out falsehood but that we acknowledge first of all that race and history and metaphysics do not enforce an identity: that we can choose, within broad limits set by ecological, political, and economic realities what it will mean to be African in the coming years.

Almost simultaneously with this statement, the Ethiopian artist Achamyeleh Debela created *Artist Under A Mask* (1990–91): a computer-assisted "portrait" of his Euro-American teacher, the pioneering computer artist Charles Csuri. Debela's christening of Csuri with a "spirit" mask from the Punu peoples of Gabon, was a telling act, especially in the light of Appiah's statement, which rejected racial, historical, and spiritual determinants in an African consciousness, and, instead, embraced a deliberate, politically centered act of cultural identification. Appiah's stress on the political will toward self-definition and Debela's digital/spiritual license to Africanize the "uninitiated" were, in fact, components of one comprehensive mindset in the 1990s: namely cultural empowerment through image processing, transmutation, and choice.

141

141 BELOW Achamyeleh Debela, *Artist Under a Mask*, 1990–91
142 OPPOSITE Philip Mallory Jones, *First World Order*, 1994

One example of how issues of racism and visual perception became linked in the 1990s was the controversy that arose in 1991 after the national screening of George Holliday's videotape of the beating of Rodney King, an African American, by several Los Angeles County police officers. Another example was the public outcry in 1994 over the darkened and duly demonized *Time* magazine cover of the African American Hollywood actor, ex-athlete, and murder suspect O.J. Simpson. These debates underscored how photographed, videographed, and filmed images of blacks became case studies in the United States on cultural slander, as well as public disputes over contested black realities and authenticities. Even in the world of advertising, the racially integrated—and frequently controversial—print and billboard advertisements set up by the Italian clothing manufacturer Benetton exploited perceived racial difference as a blatant, visual stop sign for its products.

In the 1980s and 1990s, the African American videographer Philip Mallory Jones created a series of short works that, using original music, animation and, occasionally, multichannel and synchronized monitors, visualized his notion of an interconnected black diaspora. Jones, attuned to the battles in the media over the representations of black people, eventually expanded upon these earlier works with his longer and more layered *First World Order* (1994): a part documentary/part impressionistic vision of creativity and spirituality in the

142

so-called Third World, which ambitiously cut across the presumed borders of these territories. With the use of computer-assisted image morphing in *First World Order* (where, for example, African and Pre-Columbian sculptures were digitally "transformed" into human beings) Jones succeeded in articulating the connections— transracial as well as intercultural—between group creativity and individual emotions and desires.

The Jamaican photographer Albert Chong, based in the US, 143 vied for similar effects in such works as his *Winged Desire* (1994), but the arresting and spiritually charged elements in his art curiously turned these photographs into timeless, iconographic documents. In Chong's solarized surfaces and darkroom manipulated layers of ritual artifacts (animal skulls, cowrie shells, feathers, and the artist's own body), a metamorphosis was more likely to issue from the mind's eye than from a filmic perspective, coalescing into a reality largely shaped by Caribbean, anthropological and syncretic factors.

For New York artists Lorraine O'Grady and Emma Amos, the fact that the photographic image can be altered redirected their shared theme of transformation into two distinct yet 144 related realms of intent. In Lorraine O'Grady's *The Strange Taxi: From Africa to Jamaica to Boston in 200 Years* (1991), the neo-Dadaist combining of old family photos with environmental and anatomical details presented viewers with an architectonic montage, whose black and female armature literally propelled viewers through pictorial space. On a somewhat different 145 path, Emma Amos in *Confederates* (1994) not only challenged the racist premise presented by the Confederate flag, but also photography's so-called objectivity.

Even when many artists relied on "direct" photographic techniques, it was important that they were able to reinvent and reinvigorate a black reality that "wouldn't fade in the light of day" (to paraphrase the African American pop songwriters Nickolas Ashford and Valerie Simpson). This was vital to counteract the visual assaults on black culture from both the wider society and scattered, spiritually impoverished pockets within black communities. One of those photographic "purists," New Yorker Coreen Simpson, responded in the 1980s to the one-dimensional and often negative representations of blacks with a series of larger-than-life, black-and-white studio photographs of the most maligned members of the culture. Especially provocative were Simpson's photographs of the institutionally "written-off," yet self-consciously visual, urban 146 black youth, as seen in her 1984 *Jamien*, from the *B-Boy* series. In the spirit of past portrait/social documentary photographers like Diane Arbus and Weegee, Simpson made no apologies for

143 Albert Chong, *Winged Desire*, 1994

144 ABOVE Lorraine O'Grady, *The Strange Taxi: From Africa to Jamaica to Boston in 200 Years*, 1991
145 OPPOSITE ABOVE Emma Amos, *Confederates*, 1994
146 OPPOSITE BELOW Coreen Simpson, *Jamien*, 1984, from the *B-Boy* series

147 Dawoud Bey, *Sara, Martin David and Tolani*, 1992

her fascination with and empathy for these young, black, social outcasts, describing them—and, in effect, captioning their portraits—with the honorific "the soul of our people."

147 Similarly, Dawoud Bey, another New Yorker, embarked on a series of photographic portraits in the early 1990s that (using the large-format Polaroid camera) revisited the theme of the formation of identity. His triptych of sociologist Sara Lawrence-Lightfoot and her children, Martin David and Tolani (1992), was imbued with color and the passage of time, and an example of what art historian Kellie Jones described in Bey's portraits as "testimonies to people always 'becoming,' to their being forever in the midst of transformation."

The time factor in Bey's work (like the long, exhaustive sittings that people endured in photography's early years) changed these portrait sessions into extended, interpersonal exchanges between Bey and his sitters. In her *Zabat* series (1989), the black Scottish artist Maud Sulter created a similar photographer–sitter relationship, but framed by a feminist, postmodern, and postcolonial vision of portraiture as "an occasion of power." Among the series' nine Cibachromes of black women (including novelist Alice Walker and Sweet Honey in the Rock group member and vocalist Ysaÿe Maria Barnwell)

148 was a portrait of Sulter as *Calliope*, the classical muse of heroic poetry. Like Debela's masking of Charles Csuri in *Artist Under A Mask*, Sulter's re-creation of Jeanne Duval, Charles Baudelaire's black mistress and muse—enshrouded in plush velvet, holding a daguerreotype, and reminiscent of a Nadar photograph from the 1860s—moved effortlessly between autobiography, fiction, *tableau vivant*, and spirit possession in this period of dismantled and refurbished realities.

148 Maud Sulter, *Calliope,* from the *Zabat* series, 1989

Testimony

Many artists in the 1980s and 1990s—in addition to making the theoretical leap from a fixed and racially circumscribed blackness to one that was conceptually rooted, culturally grounded, and complex in its subjectivity—turned to personal or political events for source material. What singled out these text- and narrative-driven creations from similar works in other traditions (Romare Bearden's folk medleys for instance, or Ernie Barnes's interpretations of a fabled black athleticism) was an acknowledgment of the pliancy and unreliability of texts, as well as an appreciation of the narrative's capacity for a visual elucidation.

Edouard Duval-Carrié's *Un Touriste chez lui* (1981)—inspired by the artist's return to his native Haiti—exemplified this unfettered and ingenious approach to the pictorial narrative. Haiti in the 1980s—fraught with coup d'états, public strikes, civil disobedience, and violence—was re-imagined by Duval-Carrié as an idyllic and luminous seascape in which a naked, brown angel watches over the artist. In this strange, almost sacred setting, an artist-in-exile can return home, but only as a tourist and only by imagining a deformed street-beggar from Port-au-Prince as his guardian spirit.

149

149 BELOW Edouard Duval-Carrié, *Un Touriste chez lui*, 1981
150 OPPOSITE Sue Coe, *Woman Shot in the Back*, 1985

Unlike Duval-Carrié's pastoral re-landscaping of a turbulent Haiti, Sue Coe's visual transcription of an incident that precipitated one of London's worst urban uprisings vaulted all conceptions of the ideal. The incident was the 1985 shooting of Mrs Cherry Groce, a black woman, by a white policeman. In the manner of George Grosz's caustic drawings of Weimar Berlin, Coe—ever alert to the inequities and atrocities in Britain in the time of Margaret Thatcher's government—drew *Woman Shot in the Back* (1985) with a journalistic immediacy comparable only to photography, but with her measured, dramatic application of chiaroscuro and line.

In 1986 conceptual artist Adrian Piper also created a linear, text-based art in the form of multiple, machine typeset business cards, for instance, *My Calling (Card) No. 2*, which she described as a "reactive guerilla performance (for dinners and cocktail parties)." As an African American who was often taken for

150

152

Culture as Currency

209

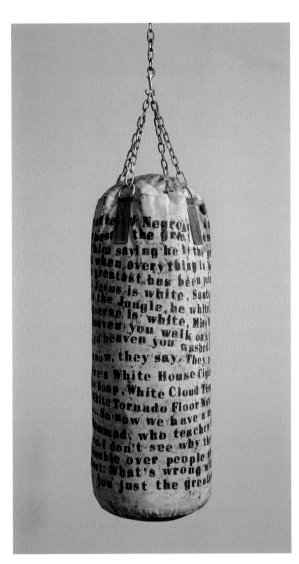

151 LEFT Byron Kim and Glenn
Ligon, *Rumble, Young Man,
Rumble (Version No. 2)*, 1993
152 BELOW Adrian Piper, *My
Calling (Card) No. 2*, 1986
153 OPPOSITE Howardena Pindell,
*Separate But Equal Genocide:
AIDS*, 1991–92

Dear Friend,
I am black.
I am sure you did not realize this when you made/laughed
at/agreed with that racist remark. In the past, I have attempted to
alert white people to my racial identity in advance. Unfortunately, this invariably causes them to react to me as pushy,
manipulative, or socially inappropriate. Therefore, my policy is to
assume that white people do not make these remarks, even when
they believe there are no black people present, and to distribute
this card when they do.
I regret any discomfort my presence is causing you, just as I
am sure you regret the discomfort your racism is causing me.

"white" in unfamiliar social settings, Piper's euphemistic
"calling" in art (apart from her postmodern interrogations of
artistic practices and definitions) was frequently a judgment
of American racism, as well as of racial categories as a whole.
Recalling literary critic Robert Stepto's theory of "narrative
control" in the nineteenth-century autobiographies of African
Americans, Piper's "narrative" interjected into the New York art
scene her identity and capacity (as an object-turned-subject) to
engage, interact and, if necessary, challenge racism on all fronts.

153   Howardena Pindell, another artist who was a critic of society's
shortcomings concerning racial justice, reconstituted the
stars and stripes of the American flag into two parallel black-
and-white fields in her mixed media work *Separate But Equal:
Genocide: AIDS* (1991–92). Pindell's juxtaposition of the two
sets of names—all of people who have died from the disease

AIDS—underscored (like Piper) the absurdity of racism, especially in the face of this late-twentieth-century plague and its power to mete out sickness and death indiscriminately.

Pindell—whose abstractions from the 1960s and 1970s employed relief and collage techniques comparable to works like her *Separate But Equal: Genocide: AIDS*—served as a role model for other formalists in the 1990s preoccupied with text and narrative. Korean American Byron Kim and African American Glenn Ligon collaborated on *Rumble, Young Man, Rumble (Version No. 2)* (1993): a suspended punchbag with statements by boxing legend Muhammad Ali stenciled on its canvas. Despite the awkwardness that audiences felt walking round this piece and trying to decipher Ali's words in their entirety, his repeated references to "white" people clearly stood out and, in effect, emphasized how concepts like "white" and "black" obstruct people's thinking, eventually forming inpenetrable barriers to understanding cultural differences beyond these abstractions.

In contrast to these text-based strategies for investigating blackness, whiteness, and all the racial categories and controversies packed between them, the African American figurative expressionist Robert Colescott painted *Lightening*

154 BELOW Robert Colescott, *Lightening Lipstick*, 1994
155 OPPOSITE Keith Morrison, *Chariot*, 1987

154   *Lipstick* (1994): a humorous and telling commentary on race, history, and society's prevailing illusions about them. Colescott's implied narrative was that a "Latina blanca," while applying her cosmetics, confronted a history of slavery, racial miscegenation, and the genealogical prospects of being "negrita". Color was therefore *Lightening Lipstick*'s primary subject and (like the Byron Kim/Glenn Ligon collaboration) placed viewers in the position of "sparring" with these unfounded but embedded racial assumptions.

    The idea of "color," an illusory concept yet with such a power to transform, was redeemed in *Lightening Lipstick* by placing it within the literal borders of culture and geography. In the

155   1987 painting *Chariot*, the Jamaica-born, Bay area artist Keith Morrison also saw culture (as opposed to race) as his conceptual point of departure. However, Morrison's irreverent consignment of civilization (including Piero della Francesca's *The Flagellation* and an African statue) to a fantastic, funerary cortege drawn by demons and horses, assigned culture to a less elevated station and made it into something ephemeral and mortal.

    This view of culture—as fleeting, narrative-generated, politically contentious, and impervious to single definitions or reductive categories—appeared in the works of numerous artists for whom language and image were partners in visual communication. The realization that labor and leisure in the

156 Stanley
Greaves, *The
Presentation No. 2,*
1992, from *There
is a Meeting Here
Tonight* series

culturally distinct yet marginalized communities throughout
the black diaspora could yield an abundance of information
led many artists into these margins, in search of artistic
models. These revelations from the periphery played an
important role in the work of Stanley Greaves, who was born
in Guyana and settled in Barbados. Although educated in
three, rather distinct, art institutions—Guyana's Working
People's Art Class, the University of Newcastle upon Tyne in
the UK, and Howard University in the US—Greaves combined
their divergent curricula with his own Caribbean sense of
156   a visual polemic. *The Presentation No. 2* (1992), one of three
paintings from his series *There is a Meeting Here Tonight*,
showed the porch, the alley, and their actors-in-residence
in a view reminiscent of Giorgio de Chirico, and therefore
emphasized the jostling for prestige and position that often
characterizes social and political behaviour in the Caribbean.
The ubiquitous "black dogs" in this series symbolized the

constant struggle in the postcolonial world for territory and power: an issue for which Greaves and other late twentieth-century commentators offered two fundamental questions: "How can I get what I want?" and "What methods am I prepared to use?" As mercenary as these questions—and these "mongrels"—might be, concealed within the shadows of *The Presentation* were a few life-affirming signs, as well as a colloquial pair of used but natty double-width shoes, waiting to be stepped into (by someone from this black diasporal "frontier") with all the answers.

Black Bodies

A language and imagery that objectified black bodies filtered through much of the cultural nationalist poetry, prose, and visual arts during the 1960s and 1970s. In the light of a long, tortured history of racist lampooning and devaluation of black people, one might argue that this emphasis on hair, skin, and black physicality was an understandable and even necessary strategy. Yet these tributes to the "black and beautiful" ones, especially when uncritically voiced or visualized, also contained their own special venom: the compulsion toward superficiality, reverse racism, and racial fetishism.

Around 1975–78 (coinciding with a major exodus of West Coast and Midwestern artists—musical, literary, and visual—to New York City), this fascination with black bodies in poetry and painting shifted to the conviction that this artistic idea could exist in time and space, proclaiming itself in both words and images, and realized by people of color. For example, in the Bay area (and a little later in New York) various poets and actors (including Ntozake Shange, Jayne Cortez, Jessica Hagedorn, Miguel Algarín) staged performances of their poetry and prose in jazz clubs and cafés (like those of the Beat poets of the 1950s and 1960s), while in other major cultural centers in the US, Europe, and Africa, musical performers like Sun Ra's Intergalactic Arkestra, the Art Ensemble of Chicago, and Fela Anikulapo Kuti and his "Africa '70" turned their concerts into multimedia spectacles, with costumes, makeup, and innovative staging. Among several New York- and Miami-based artists—many of whom were of Cuban and Puerto Rican descent—the rituals and regalia of *Santería*, *Vodun*, *Candomble*, and other African-derived New World religions also inspired a body-centered art.

These harbingers of a late-twentieth-century black performance art movement raised the stakes in their artistic identification with black peoples through explorations of black myths and religion, African masking traditions, and also through consciously playing off a long, often tangled, history of objectification and culturally encoded theatrics (or what art historian Lowery Stokes Sims has described in black women's performance art as "acting out"). These culture-specific theatrics with the artistic cues inherited from a mostly European and Euro-American tradition of "happenings," situationist and action art, and creative acts of a political and social dimension—influenced a whole new generation of performance artists, many of whom (like Adrian Piper, David Hammons, Houston Conwill, Faith Ringgold, and Lorraine O'Grady) would also make definitive statements about black culture through art objects.

In 1983, photographer Tseng Kwong Chi, painter Keith Haring, and the avant-garde dancer/choreographer Bill T. Jones collaborated in an art "happening," which illustrated the pivotal role that performance played in the blurring (and even the breakdown) of traditional art categories. Their collaboration merged their special talents under the thematic canopy of an articulated, culturally positioned, black male body. Critic Kobena Mercer perhaps captured the essence of this collaboration—the homoerotic implications of the black male body both as altar and as *tabula rasa*—in his discussion of similar collaborations between photographer Robert Mapplethorpe and his black male models when he described these projects as ambivalent products of the "political unconscious."

Mercer's reflections on Mapplethorpe's racial fetishism and on the challenges that filmmaker Isaac Julien, photographer Rotimi Fani-Kayode, and other artists imposed on these systems of seeing and representing black male bodies would have been further complicated had Mercer also analyzed the works of Ben Jones and Sherman Fleming. These are two African American artists for whom the black male body has long been the starting point, as well as the ultimate destination for theoretical and performing possibilities. Jones—whose painted plaster body casts of black faces and arms in the early 1970s signaled a dramatic step away from more conventional modes of black representation—used these past works as yet another stepping-stone for his 1994 *Shango* wall installation. The life-size paper cut-outs of stylized men and women, each painted differently and mounted on walls that enclosed an art gallery-cum-ritual space, functioned (like many black diasporal shrine settings) as both tracings of black corporeality and diagrams for spiritual action.

Sherman Fleming's 1995 performance in Amsterdam, *UN/SUB: De Jacht op Zwarte Piet* (*The Hunt for Black Peter*), was inspired by the Dutch myth of Zwarte Piet, who was St. Nicholas's black helper, and the African American story of Harriet

157

158

159

157 Tseng Kwong Chi and Keith Haring, *Bill T. Jones*, 1983

Tubman, the nineteenth-century escaped slave and liberator of slaves. Fleming played on the theme of slaves "stealing away," as well as on Zwarte Piet's dual nature (benevolent in dispensing sweets to well-behaved children, and malevolent in threatening to abduct the ill-mannered ones to a faraway, Moorish Spain). He first submerged his body, clad only in a G-string, for an hour in a vat of sugar and cinnamon, and then, after this "tub man's" dramatic emergence from the vat, stepped on to the gallery floor, removed his breathing tubes (and protection for eyes and nose), and shook off the excess confection. Finally, Fleming's two Dutch assistants licked the clinging "sugar and spice" off his body in patterns that (like the paintings on Bill T. Jones's body) resembled the body decorations in Leni Riefenstahl's photographs of the nomadic Nuba people of East Africa. As with all Fleming's performances, this merged the spectacle of a perceived racial difference with notions of desire, contagion, concealment, and emancipation, all within his theoretical construct of physical (as well as psychological) endurance.

Each of these "body-centric" works toyed with representations of black masculinity shaped to a great extent by a particular view, or rather impression, of the African body. Whether

158 BELOW Ben Jones, *Shango* wall installation (detail), 1994
159 OPPOSITE Sherman Fleming, *UN/SUB: De Jacht op Zwarte Piet*, 1995

specifically informed by Riefenstahl's photographs, or
inspired by the legions of other exotic (and often sexually
charged) photographic images of African men, women, and
children, they nonetheless fed into a common image of African
peoples that, ironically, was not perceptually different from
the primitivist attitudes about Africans that had long been
held by many Europeans and Americans.

    The works of two African women have provided an
interesting counterpoint to these racial and sexual images.
In Sokari Douglas Camp's *Gelede From Top to Toe* (1995),
the sculptor has shifted the emphasis of a traditional
masquerade (when males impersonate females) among
the Yoruba peoples of southwestern Nigeria. Constantly
balancing her Kalabari roots with her interest in Nigeria's
diverse cultures, her American and British art training, and
her London home, Douglas Camp created something here
that was no longer Yoruba, nor even Nigerian but, rather,
transnational, industrial, and postmodern. Similarly,
Werewere Liking, the Cameroon-born, Côte d'Ivoire-based
performance artist, used multimedia, ritual-based works
such as her 1992 *Un Touareg s'est marié à une pygmée* (*The
Marriage of a Touareg and a Pygmy*) as a catharsis for an
ailing, morally dissolute, African body politic. Ki-Yi Mbock

160

161

160 ABOVE Sokari Douglas Camp, *Gelede From Top to Toe*, 1995
161 OPPOSITE Werewere Liking, *Un Touareg s'est marié à une pygmée*, 1992

Théâtre (Liking's theatrical troupe and artists collective) performed her fantasy of a marriage between a North African nomadic man and a Central African hunting/gathering woman using an intertextual, black African aesthetic that, according to Liking, communicated "different kinds of emotions" and reached "different levels of language" from which "everything can be expressed." In both instances, Douglas Camp and Liking avoided stereotypical conceptions of Africans, while still engaged in an identity-conscious discourse on visual embodiments of culture.

In the US, artists Joyce J. Scott and Carrie Mae Weems were also creators of an alternative art of gendered and racialized bodies. But rather than a black-body-centered art whose image and thematic impetus resided in the realm of the erotic or exotic, Scott and Weems shifted their performances and figurative works in the direction of ethical and political questions. In her performance piece *Generic Interference/ Genetic Engineering* (1992), Scott leveled high-spirited critiques of racism and sexism, framed by the thorny and problematic presence in a post-industrial world of a striving for physical perfection, a revolution in reproductive technology, and a climate of moral absolutism. Scott's satirical yet emotionally

162

gripping characterizations—such as Gene 3000: the last, genetically untampered-with human being—emphasized that our fixations on idealized identities and social engineering have irrevocably complicated and even imperiled life as it was once known.

These fin-de-siècle misgivings about identity—especially related to culture and consciousness within various black diasporal experiences—encircled Carrie Mac Weems's *Ode to Affirmative Action* (1989). Like Scott's parodic character Gene 3000, Weems's black female singer, Dee Dee (performed and staged by Weems herself), challenged audiences with the hypothesis, "If You Should Lose Me": an assumption that, given Weems's allusions to the largely African American Mississippi Delta in her song "Clarksdale" and US policies of racial restitution in her song "Affirmative Action," revolved around questions of black inclusion, participation, and advantage in a world that, alas, resembled a mob-controlled

163

162 BELOW Joyce J. Scott, *Generic Interference, Genetic Engineering*, 1992
163 OPPOSITE Carrie Mae Weems, *Ode to Affirmative Action*, 1989

nightclub. The performative dimensions of art and black lives, encouraged these and other artists in the 1980s and 1990s not only to analyze and dissect a culture-in-process, but also to lay claim to those spirits and truths that, in this atmosphere of post-structuralist doubt, called for recognition.

Chapter 7
Through A Glass, Diasporally

Afterbirth

Most art historians have ignored the pivotal position of black cultural themes in the construction of a cinematic vision in the twentieth century, much less a black presence within the twenty-first century digital and online worlds. They have also slighted the important role that black actors, directors, cinematographers, and screenwriters have played in creating what could be described as a performative, vocal, and interactive "black art." Of course, those who could not fully appreciate the art of photography or the most expressionistic paintings by African American artists would not have been able to see the intrinsic visuality in Oscar Micheaux's early films, or the self-conscious artistry in films featuring the inimitable Paul Robeson. Not only were they incapable of seeing film (and later video) as art, but they maintained that the mass media was primarily a vehicle for commercial entertainment and propaganda. Considering the uphill struggle that black culture in general has faced, there was little possibility that black film and video would be considered of artistic value and historical worth.

Even with a proliferation of black images in the media arts, several fundamental questions arise: do blatantly racist, stereotype-wielding films like D.W. Griffith's *The Birth of a Nation* (1915) qualify for inclusion in a diasporally rooted art history? Do primitivist works like Jean Renoir's *Sur Un air de Charleston* (1926) deserve consideration in the context of studies of black subjectivity and identity in art? Are the "all-black" films by white directors like Vincente Minnelli or Marcel Camus more reflective of a white mindset, rather than of a black consciousness or cultural ethos?

In spite of the distorted characterizations of black culture in the works of filmmakers like D.W. Griffith and others, a study of these images educates people in racial and cultural stereotyping: visual assaults that have a historical precedent in eighteenth- and nineteenth-century representations of the proverbial Other. This visual data strengthens rather than disables scholars, allowing them to see critically what others see cursorily and naively. A study of specific racist mechanisms (for example, Griffith's sinister uses in *The Birth of a Nation* of black and white actors) ultimately politicizes the scholar, not through dismissing or censoring Griffith's work, but in revealing the film's underlying structure, evaluating its artistic strategies, and countering its white supremacist motives.

The value of examining white-directed films or videos with predominately black casts is a more difficult one to gauge—it is conceivable that they could be a product of a European or Euro-American cultural framework. Supporters of this view could point to Vincente Minnelli's *Cabin in the Sky* (1943), Otto Preminger's *Carmen Jones* (1954), or even Robert Downey's *Putney Swope* (1969) as examples of white accounts of black people. But one could also argue that a film or video with a black cast and a well-crafted screenplay, based on the experiences, narratives, and emotional states of black peoples (as seen, for example, in the 1976 US television series *Roots*), cannot be anything but a black cultural statement, regardless of the ethnicity of the directors involved. When white directors sacrifice, for example, the typical Hollywood approach to musicals for something more interactive, musically sophisticated, and structurally integrative (as in Perry Henzell's 1972 *The Harder They Come*, or George T. Nierenberg's 1983 *Say Amen, Somebody*), the result is often regarded as unquestionably black.

What then does make a film black, or, rather, what components of cinema make a film that has black characters and a black mise-en-scène an appropriate subject for exploring diasporal arts and aesthetics? A glance at Minnelli's 1943 *Cabin in the Sky*, and a close look at *The Blood of Jesus* (1941)—an independent film by the African American actor and director Spencer Williams—may provide some answers.

The plots for both films were derived from earlier works: the 1930 Broadway musical, and 1936 motion picture, *The Green Pastures* (Marc Connelly's folk-inspired fable about African American conceptions of the Old Testament), and the original 1940 Broadway version of *Cabin in the Sky* (also indebted to *The Green Pastures*). In *Cabin*, Minnelli's fascination with the contest between reality and illusion (rather than the script's surface battle between good and evil) was matched—and perhaps opposed—by Williams's unabashed sermon on redemption and resurrection in *The Blood of Jesus*. These distinctions—between a cinema of "smoke and mirrors" and a cinema about spiritual restoration—did not necessarily indicate an aesthetic schism between Minnelli's Hollywood and Williams's Harlem, so much as they represented two distinct views about African Americans' life around World War II. The scene in *Cabin* when femme fatale Georgia Brown (played by Lena Horne) plucks a magnolia blossom from a tree and fastens it to her hair (like Billie Holiday's trademark white gardenia) functioned as a subtle reminder to audiences of improvisation and the illusory nature of appearances. These were twin themes that haunted this film, from its beginnings in a rural, black Baptist church, to its conclusion in Little Joe and Petunia's bedroom. *Cabin*'s dream-within-a-fantasy premise—a narrative ploy straight out of Victor Fleming's *Wizard of Oz* (1939)—had a special resonance with black audiences, given the film's required mock belief in the integrity of waiting for one's hard-earned recompense in Heaven: an unlikely proposition that Minnelli, his cast of black urban sophisticates, and their cinematic deconstruction of Negro rectitude, could not accept.

    The Blood of Jesus (1941)—also about an out-of-the-body brush with divinity—differed from *Cabin in the Sky* in that its director, producer, writer, and featured actor, Spencer Williams, specifically created his film for African American audiences. His main message—that following a Christian path provided black people with not only their just rewards in the afterlife, but blessed assurances here on earth—diverged dramatically from *Cabin in the Sky*'s counterfeit "pie-in-the-sky" prescription. Where *Cabin* avoided the potentially estranging details of an authentic African American experience, *The Blood of Jesus* stepped head-on into a semi-documentary world of open-air baptisms, tawdry speakeasies, and "saints" falling into fits of religious ecstasy. Indeed, one could imagine the reactions of black filmgoers of 1941 when, toward the end of the film, they "witnessed" the blood of a crucified Jesus dripping on to the face of the female protagonist (played by Cathryn Caviness). This showed Williams's familiarity with an exaggerated theatricality in the African American church pageant tradition, as well as his willingness to experiment with the most provocative and visceral special effects in filmmaking.

    For Spencer Williams, the moral compass of Afro-America resisted co-option by the market forces that dictated the struttings of Vincente Minnelli's star-studded cast of pseudo-religious types. Of course, Williams limited his ambitions

164 Spencer Williams, *The Blood of Jesus*, 1941

to appealing to an already attuned, church-going black
audience. Thirteen years before *The Blood of Jesus*, in a period
of materialism and commodification, the filmmaker and actor
Richard D. Maurice also appealed to an African American
sense of morality. Maurice's *Eleven p.m.* (1928)—another
cinematic story within a story—explored the common literary
themes of moral incorrigibility, spiritual retribution, and
the city as a den of deception, but now situated among "New
Negro" types in Detroit. What singled out *Eleven p.m.* from
the stock silent productions of this period were Maurice's
abilities as both actor and auteur. His portrayal of the morally
upright, racially mixed protagonist, the street violinist
Sundaisy, elicited compassion, and his flirtation with the idea
of reincarnation—when a dog with the face of the deceased
Sundaisy attacked the film's villain—interjected a fantastic,
almost mystical element into what was otherwise an urban
melodrama. Although succeeded by dozens of other "all black"
films of various minds and motives, *Eleven p.m.* introduced
a decidedly visionary way of looking at black culture: a
vision that, with its allusions to hybridity and spirituality,

165

165 Richard D. Maurice, *Eleven p.m.*, 1928

and implanted tensions between the real and make-believe, suggested something on the order of a black cinematic imagination in the making.

Black Joy on Film

In *The Cinema as Art* (1965), Ralph Stephenson and J.R. Debrix discussed how cinema—from its beginnings as the twentieth century opened, to its New Wave ruminations in the early 1960s on the meaning of life after the atomic bomb—had a language and structure comparable to painting, sculpture, and other visual art forms. Among the many observations that Stephenson and Debrix made about cinema's intrinsic artistry was that an "objectively false" film universe asked viewers to suspend their disbelief, and that films as art first emerged within the context of this "false seeming." Stephenson and Debrix continued their examination with the view that, in spite of their artifice, films as works of art not only affected the senses and seized the imagination, but were "deliberately made to attack us, to force [their] way into our feelings and our beliefs." This anthropomorphic, confrontational view of film—an artistic entity capable of grasping, attacking, and forcing its way into one's mind and soul—summoned an alternative meaning for this art form in light of the cultural moment in which Stephenson and Debrix were writing and the artistic weight that three films from that period carried in redefining this vision, namely Jean-Luc Godard's *À Bout de souffle* (*Breathless*, 1959), Alain Resnais's *Hiroshima, Mon Amour* (*Hiroshima, My Love*, 1959), and François Truffaut's *Les Quatre cent coups* (*The 400 Blows*, 1959).

Absent from most studies of New Wave cinema was Marcel Camus's *Black Orpheus* (1958). Despite its inherently "false" film universe, it seduced the imagination and ingratiated itself rather than forcing itself on its audience. Despite winning the prestigious Palme d'Or at the 1959 Cannes Film Festival, the 1959 Academy Award (for best non-English language motion picture), as well as a commercial success in international film markets, *Black Orpheus* received mixed reviews. The most criticized features of the film were its travelogue-like footage of Rio de Janeiro, its dazzling (to the point of intoxicating) Afro-Brazilian soundtrack and color photography, and finally its highly stylized atmosphere. Although these criticisms of *Black Orpheus* were valid from the perspective of the majority of films being produced at that time, curiously missing from these discussions was the obvious: that Camus had placed not just a racial blackness, but also a cultural and discursive blackness, at the core of his retelling of an ancient Greek myth, and that this imposition fundamentally altered his New Wave aesthetics into something that dealt a sharp blow to the artistic consciousness.

Camus introduced this aesthetic rupture in the film's opening shot, where a colorless detail of a seemingly immovable Greek sculptural relief was visually shattered, giving way to four, colorfully dressed black people, dancing and promenading to the rhythms of African-sounding drums. In the establishing shots of Rio de Janeiro, black women negotiating steep slopes with burdens on their heads, wattle-and-daub houses, and barefoot children underlined that this rarely filmed world— black, humble, and teeming with life—had its own, visual allure.

Brazilian soccer player Breno Mello and African American dancer Marpessa Dawn played the ill-fated lovers with an athletic grace and a deep intelligence that converged into something far more abstract than usually communicated by black film characters up to that point. Cinematographer Jean Bourgoin's *plein air* medium shot near Orpheus's hillside shack—with Orpheus curled up beside Eurydice and resting his head on her hand, and she sitting upright with her back to the camera and facing a horizon across which a jet plane soars—

perfectly captured this abstract essence and the bittersweet refrain of one of *Black Orpheus*'s bossa nova anthems: "Sadness has no end, but happiness does."

This acknowledgment of fleeting pleasures—in spite of life's hardships and, ultimately, death—emerged not only in the film's music and screenplay, but in the documentary-like footage of black revelers (photographed by Bourgoin over several Carnival seasons). In a neo-realist gesture that unknowingly recalled Williams's crude but effective use of non-professional, black churchgoers in *The Blood of Jesus*. Camus's lingering, close pan shots of Rio de Janeiro's black peasants— as they clapped hands, moved to the rhythms of the drums, and threw back their heads and laughed with abandon—turned *Black Orpheus* into a diasporal document. Whether depicted as eighteenth-century European courtiers in their Carnival finery, or as possessed souls in a clandestine, Afro-Brazilian religious rite, these images of blacks embodied joy in the recognition of their own existence, survival, and capacity to love. In an amazing allusion to (as well as a stark departure from) a black minstrel tradition, Camus's final scene of three dancing children, photographed against Rio's harbor at sunrise— redefined the use of black music and dance in film. Beyond this scene's outdoor, impromptu setting, Camus's pairing of an exhilarating musical soundtrack with a trio of seemingly carefree children again stressed *Black Orpheus*'s paean to black pleasure: a joy, free of licentiousness and buffoonery that, despite cinema's artificiality, appeared to reflect reality.

Since *Black Orpheus*, the combined aesthetic forces of first a scenic verisimilitude and secondly a compelling audio and musical soundtrack, have provided other filmmakers working within a black cultural sphere with strategies for creating films that present an alternative worldview. Fred Padula and Edward Spriggs employed these devices effectively in *Ephesus* (1966). Filmed at the Ephesian Church of God in Christ in Berkeley, California, *Ephesus* compressed this African American church's revival services (and the farewell to their soon-to-be demolished building) into half-an-hour's worth of interior shots of the church, congregation, choir, and the church's spiritual leader, Elder James E. Cleveland. Although photographed in black-and-white, with a separately recorded soundtrack, *Ephesus* succeeded in capturing a colorful, black Pentecostal style of worship via a broad range of camera-to-subject distances, hand-held shots, and sophisticated editing techniques. By the end of *Ephesus*, the spirited singing, shouting, and exhorting had, in effect, transformed the camera—and therefore the film audience— into a similarly convulsive, prostrate, and "happy" convert.

166 Edward Spriggs and Fred Padula, *Ephesus*, 1966

99
167

Two very dissimilar cinematic works of art—Melvin Van Peebles's *Sweet Sweetback's Baadasssss Song* (1971) and Isaac Julien's *Looking for Langston* (1989)—shared this impulse to invoke an almost indescribable, transitory joy, largely through the devices of an audio/music soundtrack and what film critic Manthia Diawara described as a "cinema of the real." In Van Peebles's film, his unrelenting funky soundtrack dominated by keyboard and saxophone (by the progressive soul group Earth, Wind, and Fire) perfectly matched his hyper-edited exterior shots of Los Angeles, so much so that the results reinforced his twin themes of transgression and revolution. Almost twenty years later, the black British filmmaker Isaac Julien also employed hypnotic soundtracks and documentary footage to show a black gay presence in the world, and, once it was identified, to celebrate a beauty denied and a sexuality demonized. One sequence juxtaposed the electronically derived dance rhythms of "house music," the incantatory recitations of the African American poet Essex Hemphill, and a mélange of special effects, cross-cuts, and moving camera shots; here

167 TOP Isaac Julien, *Looking for Langston*, 1989
168 ABOVE Martina Attille, *Dreaming Rivers*, 1988

Julien attained an emotional pitch in *Looking for Langston* that, like Van Peebles's ode to the renegade in *Sweet Sweetback's Baadasssss Song*, fused style with rebellion, and the quest for cultural blueprints with a revolution-turned-carnival.

Dreaming in Color

In *Looking for Langston*, the mix of old documentary footage from the 1920s and 1930s with contemporary black-and-white photography by Nina Kellgren, Robert Mapplethorpe, and Sunil Gupta framed Julien's meditation on race, sexuality, and cultural regeneration within a historicized yet postmodern notion of beauty: images more akin to George Hurrell's (or, rather, Herb Ritts's) black-and-white celebrity portraits than to Kodachrome or Eastmancolor realities. The tensions that arose out of this interplay between documented, black gay lives, and fantasies (in black and white) about black gay lives, inevitably shifted the prevailing attitudes on black cinema. It was first suggested by literary critic Henry Louis Gates Jr., in his discussion of Julien and Kobena Mercer's film theories, that this shift marked an ideological tug-of-war between "representation as a practice of depicting" and "representation as a practice of delegation." In the context of late-twentieth-century film and video, a brief discussion on how color, optical effects, and mise-en-scène served the "black representation" debate will, it is hoped, add to an understanding of how these strategies influenced other black images.

111 As discussed earlier, Bill Gunn's *Ganja & Hess* (1973) reveled in a race-conscious yet abstract world of interpersonal rituals and doubts. Gunn's desired cinematic atmosphere—gothic tinged with contemporary race and class conflicts—was achieved when he cast Duane Jones, an actor featured in George Romero's horror classic of 1968, *Night of the Living Dead*, as the diseased Dr. Hess Green. Photographed mostly in shadows, with raking light, and against a fairly intense color scale, Gunn's study of contamination, addiction, and possession looked neither to ideal nor real depictions of black culture but, rather, to a collection of symbols (blood, Africa, and Christianity) that, through a postmodern lens, offered a flexible and metaphysical definition of blackness.

168 Perhaps even more than *Ganja & Hess*, Martina Attille's *Dreaming Rivers* (1988) used the symbolic possibilities of scenery, an actor's physical type, and the manner in which these elements were lit and framed, in order to visualize what Diawara called the "terrain of contestation" that occurred both between the characters and within their black selves. In this non-linear treatment of the story of Miss T, an older Caribbean

169 Camille Billops and James Hatch, *The KKK Boutique Ain't Just Rednecks*, 1994

woman in England, and her three young adult children who
were assimilated into British culture, questions of identity and
lineage were raised in close, painstakingly arranged shots of
this family, as well as in extreme close-ups and tracking shots
of the deceased Miss T's bedroom, where a dressing-table,
photographs, religious artifacts, books, flowers, and candles
introduced other cultural markers.

Attille, aided by her set designer, fellow black British artist
Sonia Boyce, transformed the insular bedroom world of a
culturally dislocated Caribbean mother into a theory-free
zone of self-representation. In a related vein, New York artists
and filmmakers Camille Billops and James Hatch turned
the racialized trappings of life in the United States into a
comedic excursion through an imagined underworld in *The
KKK Boutique Ain't Just Rednecks* (1994). Sculptor and graphic
artist Billops, in addition to co-directing, co-writing, and co-
producing, designed its costumes and sets; she constructed
this part cinéma verité, part scripted story line around her
conviction that "hatred does not deliver." In a scene that
recalled the ecclesiastical "fashions" in Federico Fellini's
Roma (1972), Billops staged (among other spectacles) a "racist

169

170 Spike Lee, *School Daze*, 1988

fashion show," in which shots of models wearing a Klansman's white hooded robe and neo-Nazis "goose-stepping" down a stage-lit runway were intercut with "real people" recounting past encounters with hate groups. In instances such as these, Billops's juxtaposition of a scripted theatricality with personal testimony was accentuated by her scenic (and, by association, chromatic) reimagining of a filmed space.

170   Two other films that relied upon color to address issues of difference, dissension, and cultural expressivity were Spike Lee's *School Daze* (1988) and Felix de Rooy's *Ava & Gabriel: A Love Story* (1990). Riding on the critical and commercial success of his 1986 sex comedy *She's Gotta Have It*, Lee turned in *School Daze* to the class and color antagonisms found among African Americans at historically black colleges and universities. To underline these tensions, as well as to highlight their absurdist, almost surreal dimensions, cinematographer Ernest Dickerson photographed Lee's script in vivid colors, and also processed certain scenes in jarring, expressionistic hues. These techniques—especially in tandem with the Broadway-styled set and music of Lee's fantasy "challenge dance" scene between two "camps" of black women (the stylistically "Euro-centric" versus the stylistically

"Afro-centric")—pushed what was otherwise a heavy-handed race/class polemic into something operatic and visual.

Shortly after *School Daze*, Ernest Dickerson again explored the possibilities of color and light in *Ava & Gabriel: A Love Story* (1990): a film by the Dutch Antillean director and visual artist Felix de Rooy from a screenplay by Norman de Palm. De Rooy's film revolved around the controversies that arose when in Curaçao in the late 1940s the Roman Catholic Church commissioned a Surinamese artist to paint a mural of the Virgin Mary. Unlike *School Daze*, *Ava & Gabriel*'s compelling and inflammatory narrative about race and representation, along with Dickerson's luxurious color cinematography, anchored the film's multiple messages on colonialism, censorship, and illicit love, and, simultaneously, moved de Rooy's social consciousness into the realm of the visually seductive.

In response to curator Roger Malbert's observation that "the mix is what defines de Rooy," the artist/filmmaker offered this:

...a vision born—a colonial orgasm torn from historical hypocrisy—cultural schizophrenia—religious insanity with the delicate balance of sexual duality—a universal identity set free....

Although referring to his own art, de Rooy's evocation described the cinematic works of several other black diasporal filmmakers before him, especially in regard to the impact of the colonial experience on their films. The "Father of African Cinema," Senegalese filmmaker Ousmane Sembène, brought colonialism, history, and religion to the forefront of his critically acclaimed 1976 film epic *Ceddo* (which, figuratively translated from the Wolof language, means "the common people who resist religious and/or cultural expropriation"). Mixing Western dramatization, modern film techniques, and traditional West African story-telling and oratory, *Ceddo* confronted the often suppressed history of Islamic and Christian expansionism in West Africa, and its damaging effects on indigenous African societies. If Sembène's fusion of stylistic approaches and cultural subjects was not sufficient evidence for viewing *Ceddo* (in de Rooy's words) as "an identity set free," then the jazz-influenced soundtrack by the Cameroonian musician Manu Dibango and the film's assertive black heroine, played by Senegalese actress Tabata N'Diaye, made *Ceddo* a truly diasporal work about cultural "conversion" and "resistance."

Euzhan Palcy's film *Rue Cases-Nègres* (*Sugar Cane Alley*, 1983), set in French-dominated Martinique around 1930, also negotiated the treacherous divide between a soul-sustaining

171 TOP Felix de Rooy, *Ava & Gabriel: A Love Story*, 1990
172 ABOVE Ousmane Sembène, *Ceddo*, 1976

173 Euzhan Palcy, *Rue Cases-Nègres* (*Sugar Cane Alley*), 1983

African identity and an equally essential mastery of Western discourse. Palcy's photographic close-ups—on the inquisitive faces of children, as well as on the gnarled hands and feet of the aged and infirm—communicated a cultural philosophy that prevented either "black" traditions or a "white" education from being the only options: the film's child protagonist, José (played by Garry Cadenet), seemed to have an intuitive understanding of this philosophical premise. One of the most powerful scenes is a fireside exchange at night between José and an elder, Mdouze (played by Senegalese actor Douta Seck). It was used by Palcy as an opportunity to examine black narratives and histories not just as occasions for verbal artistry and free interpretations of the past, but, more importantly, also as vehicles for grassroots education, a personal code of ethics, and political action.

Sembène and Palcy's art—defined by differences with former French colonialists and, paradoxically, collaborations with the French film industry—brought to filmmaking the recounting of black diasporal experiences and historical narratives. They constructed small, intimate worlds in which history unfolded through the simple actions, language, and images of black peoples. *Ceddo* and *Sugar Cane Alley* featured a specifically African mode of storytelling that avoided a fact-bound, structural linearity for a collaged, rhythmic, and prophetic testimony.

174   Julie Dash's *Daughters of the Dust* (1991) and Haile Gerima's *Sankofa* (1993) had intellectual investments in black history comparable to *Ceddo* and *Sugar Cane Alley*, although Dash and Gerima's works—both informed by a Los Angeles-based "school" of black filmmakers in the 1970s, and a general boom in films by and about African Americans in the early 1990s—expressed more expansive views of a black universe. The core narrative in *Daughters of the Dust* concerned a large, turn-of-the-century black family, living on one of the isolated Sea Islands off the coast of South Carolina, and struggling with the decision by several of its members to migrate to the mainland and eventually north. But interestingly, there was a visual subtext running through *Daughters of the Dust* that came through more strongly. This dealt with black modes of self-presentation and metaphysical perspectives on the natural environment, articulated from a black feminist perspective

174 Julie Dash, *Daughters of the Dust*, 1991

that had not before been encountered on such a scale in film. The contributions of artist and production designer Kerry James Marshall, cinematographer Arthur Jafa, and hair stylist Pamela Ferrell especially helped shape Dash's vision.

In *Sankofa*, the veteran Ethiopian filmmaker Haile Gerima continued the sweeping, cinematic explorations of black landscapes, identities, and anxieties that *Daughters of the Dust* had inaugurated; it was independently released about a year after Dash's film. The screenplay revolved around an African American fashion model who, while on assignment in an old Ghanaian fort and slave dungeon, experienced a flashback that for the majority of the film turned her into human chattel and transported her back to colonial Jamaica during the period of the transatlantic slave trade. Although as surrealistically conceived and beautifully photographed (by Augustin Cubano) as *Daughters of the Dust*, *Sankofa* (which, in the Akan language, means "to go back and retrieve") was more emphatic with its principal narrative, its prevailing theme of black remembrance, and the pain that remembering often brings. Both films used impressionistic, outdoor color photography that, with poignant close-ups and long shots from the sea and sky, turned bodies of water, expanses of land, and black faces into translucent pools of memory, mirroring the beauty and anguish in a past recollected and reimagined.

Moving from cinema to video, the merging of a meaningful and artistic representation of blackness suffered not so much from the medium itself as from the fact that the portable video camera was not used for artistic projects until around 1968: until then it was confined to commercial ventures. From the early (and rare) appearances by black entertainers during television's infancy, to the post-1971 flood of black-casted sitcoms, dramas, and musicals, a broadcast and videographed image of black culture has usually been for entertainment and advertising.

In the US, the first signs of a black artistic life in this vast television wasteland occurred in the late 1960s and early 1970s when (following Martin Luther King's assassination and a rise in black urban unrest) several television producers broached the idea of black cultural programming to their local educational channels: these were eventually syndicated nationally on public television stations. Pioneering television programs like Maya Angelou's *Blacks, Blues, Black!* (1967–68), William Greaves's *Black Journal* (1968–70), and Ellis Haizlip's *Soul!* (1968–75) introduced the possibilities of broadcasting serious (and often challenging) African American poetry, theater, dance, visual arts, cultural criticism, and a range of black musical styles that were absent from the commercial

175 Haile Gerima, *Sankofa*, 1993

stations. Ironically, by the 1980s and 1990s in a period of cable, direct broadcast satellite, and public access television—most black cultural programming in the US (with the exception of the occasional specials, documentaries, or independent video art productions like Philip Mallory Jones's *First World Order* of 1994) recalled a conservative agenda that, even with the advent of Music Television, Black Entertainment Television, and a profusion of black music videos, was often without an artistic, experimental, and political perspective.

Since the arrival of music videos in the early 1980s, artists have been limited mostly to making marketing tools for record companies. All the same, many have excelled in their respective genres with interesting story lines, innovative art direction, unusual camera work, and sophisticated imaging technology. The collaborations, for example, between performing legend Michael Jackson and director John Landis for the 1983 video *Thriller*, or between rap group Black Sheep and director Charles S. Stone III for the 1992 video *The Choice is Yours*, were recognized as artistic and commercial successes in black music video production. But one of the earliest examples of a visually stunning black music video was the 1982 feature-length work, *A One Man Show*, created by the Jamaican American fashion model, singer, and actor Grace Jones and the French photographer, graphic designer, and video director Jean-Paul Goude. In contrast to the hyper-edited concert-stage approaches of many music videos of the time, *A One Man Show*, according to film historian Raymond Durgnat, relied on what Russian filmmaker Sergei Eisenstein called "dynamic montage." Goude's postmodernist yet enamored video manipulations of Grace Jones's face and figure—recalling the Josephine Baker and Paul Colin collaborations of almost sixty years earlier—selected from a whole range of historical black images. Minstrels, l'art nègre, Carmen Miranda, and Harlem zoot suits were interpolated with 1980s exhibitionism and examination of identity. In their follow-up music video, *A State of Grace* (1986), Jones and Goude continued their assault on black representational conventions with, again, a series of video "sound paintings" that projected a persona whose very voice and posture confounded mainstream expectations of black popular culture.

176

As in the US after the 1968 riots, a black cultural presence in the British media followed civil disturbances in Brixton in south London during the spring of 1981. This emerging black British consciousness, which happened to coincide with the advent of Channel 4 (the country's alternative, cultural television channel), encouraged British television to diversify staffs, to expand cultural programming, and (following the leads of such organizations as the British Film Institute and the Greater London Council) to give financial and technical assistance to various black media initiatives. It was out of this mix that several black independent media organizations emerged—Black Audio Film Collective, Ceddo Film/Video Workshop, Retake Film and Video Collective, and Sankofa Film and Video Collective, among others. This resulted in the creation of an important, London-based, black media arts scene in the 1980s and 1990s: a scene whose roots in the race politics and in the ideologies of postmodernism and cultural studies have produced films (such as *Dreaming Rivers* and *Looking for Langston)* and videos that reinvigorated an artistic cross-examination of identity, culture, and history.

The difference, however, between this group of black filmmakers and videographers and a mostly white, European and North American-based group of media (and, increasingly, computer) artists, was the realization that, in spite of the so-called "worldwide webs" and "networks," the majority

GRACE JONES

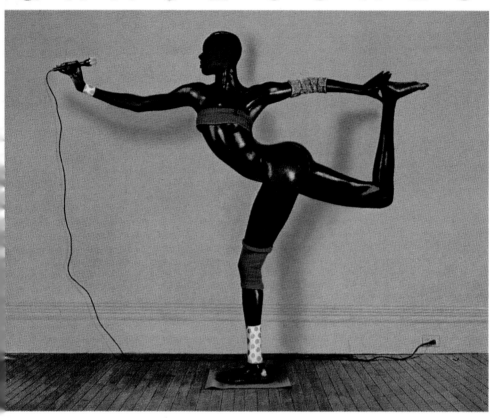

ISLAND LIFE

176 Jean-Paul Goude, album cover for *Island Life*, Grace Jones, 1985 of peoples of color in the world were neither connected nor allowed any power over how they were represented in these new technologies. This recognition that they had little input on "the information highway" gave black media artists a sense of trailblazing, as well as of political insurgency and anti-utopianism in their work.

177   Keith Piper's *Reckless Eyeballing* (1995) was a video and laser disk installation activated by spectators as they stepped up to one of three lecterns in an art gallery. This explored the very question of black participation in the acts of seeing, of being seen and, more pointedly, of being seen seeing. The title of this installation was taken from the 1950s American euphemism about the then fatal, black male act of merely looking at white women (as in the notorious Emmett Till murder case of 1955). Its relationship to Piper's succession of projected black images and amplified sounds nevertheless leapt beyond any historically documented incident of white-on-black violence, or of individual spectatorship. Rather, in the context of a late twentieth-century black British renaissance in the arts, this installation advanced Keith Piper's notion of "true interactivity"—an experience that, via computers, videography, and black cultural interventions such as "call and response," aural "cutting and mixing," and "polyphony," allowed for "an unpredictable and intuitive interaction between presenter and spectator." Emphasizing histories (both remote and recent) of exclusion and subjugation, Piper's *Reckless Eyeballing* suggested an alternative way of moving through cyberspace and through the more conventional art world that, in spite of the prominence of the forbidden look, balanced this with messages of empowerment for both the artist and the viewer.

Sites and Sounds

Keith Piper's indictment in *Reckless Eyeballing* and Haile Gerima's oppressive yet beautiful black world in *Sankofa*
178   were pushed to their extreme in Jonathan Demme's *Beloved* (1998). Adapted for the screen from the acclaimed novel of the same name by Toni Morrison, it was based on an actual 1856 incident when a runaway slave, rather than see her children taken from her and returned to slavery, killed one of them. Ironically, it suffered in the view of most film critics and audiences from having brought these horrific truths to the cinema screen. *Beloved*, however, arguably succeeded in doing what no other film had done before: it turned a very psychologically complex work of literature based on a true event in African American history into a film of major artistic importance.

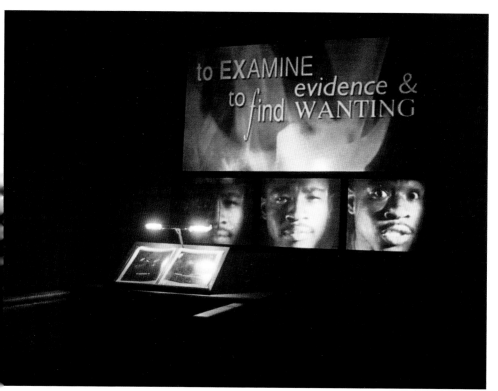

177 Keith Piper, *Reckless Eyeballing*. Installation, Ferens Art Gallery, Hull, UK, June–July 1995

The film's cinematography, innovative uses of color-saturation in film stock, historic sets, and period costume designs transformed this ersatz commercial product into art. The story of the spirits of the past who re-emerge and cause havoc among ex-slaves required the creation of an historically accurate, atmospheric place that both amazed and terrified. Cinematographer Tak Fujimoto's close-ups of water, woodland, and black skin—the latter often disfigured and bloodied—made it a far cry from typical cinematic experience.

A large part of Demme's conjuration in *Beloved*—apart from Toni Morrison's word magic and Oprah Winfrey's bewitching performance—was his use of Haitian imagery in this tale of horror and redemption. "On an unconscious level," Demme acknowledged while filming *Beloved*, "[Haitian art] has affected my work enormously." Although set in Kentucky and Ohio in the 1870s, the film contained vestiges of a Haitian world view, where Creole is miraculously spoken

178 Jonathan Demme, *Beloved*, 1998

and unsuspecting individuals are "mounted" by the spirits (or *loas*). From Demme's opening shot of graveyard tombstones to the film's hallucinatory house-party (reminiscent of streamer-festooned, *Vodun* temples), *Beloved* drew much of its visual and aesthetic strength from Haiti and its symbolic image of the *zombi*. Morrison's incarnated slave/child/ghost shared many of the attributes of the *zombi*—an oppressed being denied a decent death and trapped in a world it should have left—and it was Demme who made this diasporic connection.

Not all film and video artists in the 1990s, and later, followed Demme's use of black diasporic imagery. As with their counterparts in the art world, many film, video, and computer artists made no explicit reference to either racial or cultural blackness in their work. Instead, media artists like Oladélé Ajiboyé Bamgboyé, Rico Gaston, and others disguised this blackness inside abstract passages, experimental film and video techniques, distorted soundtracks, and other manipulations—methods of expression that, while synonymous with "hip-hop" music and other forms of black urban art, were sufficiently postmodernist and self-critical to be perceived as "universal."

This "sometimes I am, sometimes I'm not, sometimes I forget" sense of the racial self at the end of the twentieth century was exemplified in British filmmaker Steve McQueen. He became a pivotal figure in the black British art scene of the 1990s—an artist who made "beautifully composed ciphers out of human existence and its wants," wrote one reviewer. From his earliest experimental film *Bear* (1993), which featured two nude male wrestlers (one of them himself), to his acclaimed *Deadpan* (1997), in which the facade of a wooden building falls around McQueen, this time clothed (reminiscent of Buster Keaton's famous scene from Hollywood's silent era), McQueen's "heartfelt immersion in his chosen medium...to speak to the mechanics and history of cinema itself" distinguished him. *12 Years a Slave* (2013), a subsequent feature film based on the 1853 autobiography of Solomon Northrup, a free black man who was kidnapped and thrust into enslavement in Louisiana, earned McQueen the Best Picture Award from the Academy of Motion Picture Arts and Sciences, and countless other film industry accolades. The fact that in *12 Years a Slave* and in other selected works McQueen's protagonists are black, while of secondary importance to the greater artistic vision, was undoubtedly a part of their narrative allure, and inseparable from McQueen's visual imagination.

Another black filmmaker, Charles S. Stone III, stood on the opposite end of the spectrum from McQueen. Stone had been noticed himself as an auteur and maker of distinctive music videos in the short history of this genre. By the end of the 1990s Stone had expanded his repertoire to include short experimental films, one of which, entitled *True* (1998), was a series of deftly edited cross-cuts between five African American men who chat with one another by phone in a hilarious coded language; this was sold to a national advertising agency and repackaged as the "Whassup True" television campaign for Budweiser Beer. This TV commercial—which Stone had conceived, directed, co-written, and acted in—received many awards worldwide, and soon brought his work to the attention of Hollywood.

But prior to this mainstream acceptance, Stone (with several innovative urban musicians) had already pushed the music video genre to comparable heights. Stone's *You Got Me* (1998), performed by The Roots, Eve, and Erykah Badu, introduced a more tender and conceptually poignant perspective on black identity than most music videos of the time. The words of *You Got Me*—about love, emotional neglect, jealousy, and reassurance—were translated by Stone into a surreal urban reverie: the city's sidewalks, playgrounds, and buses are filled with reclining, comatose people, who are roused only toward the

179

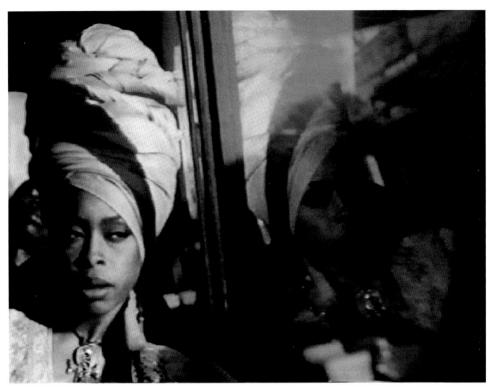

179 Charles S. Stone III, *You Got Me*, 1998

end of the video, and replaced with the death-like recumbency of Black Thought, The Roots's lead voice on this piece.

The push-and-pull between, on one hand, the conventions of communication in film and video production and, on the other, the high-art means of expression was constantly being put into play by fin-de-siècle black artists. This creative dialogue was evident in many projects, ranging from Thomas Allen Harris's films, which bridged fictional scriptwriting with documentary, to Jean-Pierre Bekolo's films, which seemed to luxuriate in an often fractured succession of mise-en-scènes. Even music videos were subjected to artistic analysis and occasional derision, as seen in the work of Susan Smith-Pinelo and several of Charles S. Stone III's satires of the genre. Similarly, meticulously splicing footage from obscure films into a rhythmic montage of sensory unease and social commentary was taken to a heightened level of intensity by Raphael Montañez Ortiz, Fatimah Tuggar, Sanford Biggers, and other media artists of color.

Describing this aesthetic, which combines postmodernism and an African American "cut-and-mix" sensibility, conceptual artist Paul D. Miller, a.k.a. DJ Spooky, wrote:

... the sense here is one of prolonging the formal implications of the expressive act—move into the frame, get the picture, re-invent your name. Movement, flow, flux: the nomad takes on the sedentary qualities of the urban dweller. Movement on the screen becomes an omnipresent quality. Absolute time becomes dream machine flicker. The eyes move. The body stays still. Travel. Big picture, small frame.

He recalled a hundred years of technological innovations in film, video, and digital imaging: a century that, unacknowledged by most critics, owed a part of its language to black diasporal concepts of time and space. From filmed and theorized "ritual time" in Haitian *Vodun* to a multimedia language of hip-hop, Miller included these contributions in a set of acknowledged creative acts, thoughts, and players. He constantly revisited the metaphor of a record-spinning, sound-and-light controlling, sensibility-fragmenting disk jockey. In this way he was not

180 DJ Spooky, (a.k.a. Paul D. Miller) *Rebirth of a Nation*, 2002

only reminding readers of his own artistic persona and alter ego, but also of the conceptual reach of this deconstructing aesthetic, and of how largely this cultural contingent figures in a virtual world.

Paul Miller's own artistic forays into what he called a "prosthetic realism"—under the name DJ Spooky—drew from a whole universe of sensory data. He constructed soundtracks for experimental films and videos from snippets of pre-recorded music, monologues, and static, repeated and "scratched" (replayed in quick flutters of the reverse mode). But such aural and visual samplings did not seem chaotic, and audiences found wholeness and continuity in this work. *Rebirth of a Nation* (2002), for example, DJ Spooky's retort to D.W. Griffith, paired an elegiac synthesizer soundtrack with a sequence of grayscale-altered, split-screened frames from the 1915 original. Mindful of how *The Birth of a Nation* employed sophisticated editing to develop an alternative US history that promoted white supremacy and advocated black subjugation, DJ Spooky also used advanced technologies to transform Griffith's transformative film: a politically inspired interference where, according to the artist, "echo meets alias in the coded exchange of glances."

Projections for A New Millennium

For all of the paradigm-shifting, media-based works that artists of African descent produced at the end of the twentieth century, the first two decades of the twenty-first century ushered in an even more extraordinary group of black films, videos, and digital works. Many channeling Paul D. Miller's "cut-and-mix" model, these media-based artworks radically altered the motion picture and "small screen" genres, incorporating, like in no previous era, a broad array of black images. From Spike Lee's bitterly acerbic *Bamboozled* (2000) to Ryan Coogler's imagistically spectacular *Black Panther* (2017), Hollywood deviated from its tried and true formulae and incorporated entirely different stories, characters and, most significantly, atmospheres and moods, much of this bringing black truths and fantasies into an expanded cinematic consciousness.

Although miniscule in comparison to Hollywood, France's film industry also reflected these changes by portraying the peoples, plots, and states of play within the African diaspora in atypical ways, frequently in co-productions with filmmakers from predominately French-speaking Africa and the Caribbean. In the wake of the trailblazing French Caribbean auteurs Euzhan Palcy and Raoul Peck, filmmaker Gilles Elie-Dit-Cosaque created *Twinkl / Zétwal* (2008), a beguiling mockumentary that revolved around the story of Robert Saint-Rose, a Martiniquan who,

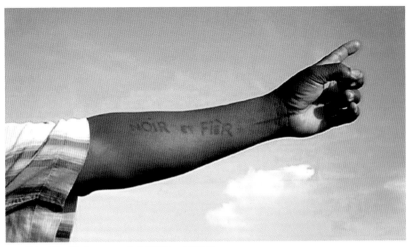

181 Gilles Elie-Dit-Cosaque, *Twinkl/Zétwal*, 2008

according to local legend, built an interplanetary capsule in the 1970s in which he launched himself into outer space, the first person from that Caribbean island to do so. Enlisting everyday citizens/actors from Martinique to expound upon Saint-Rose (who was featured intermittently in faux-archival, semi-degraded, black-and-white outtakes), Elie-Dit-Cosaque maintained an illusion of reality in *Twinkl* while interjecting a magical and mystical dimension by repeatedly referencing the real-life twentieth-century poet, politician, and famous Martiniquan, Aimé Césaire. "The poetry of Césaire is energy," Elie-Dit-Cosaque said about Saint-Rose's catalyst (and the film's metaphorical engine). "It's 'action poetry.' It pushes the reader to take action, to move, to create...to build a spaceship and to go beyond him or herself."

What also pushed cinema to reinvent itself—often utilizing a black diasporal ambience and alternative modes of visual storytelling—was the competition the film industry faced, beginning in the late 1990s, from newly formed media-streaming outlets and their digital providers. These entertainment networks—recognizing a previously unfilled niche for cutting-edge programs geared toward a much broader demographic than the conventional film and television offerings— circumvented the major film studios and created their own made-for-cable and online programming, for which they hired emerging artists of color, whose products drew audiences far beyond the usual pools of subscribers. For example, video sharing platforms like YouTube and Vimeo introduced the performances of innovative black musicians like Childish Gambino (Donald Glover): videos that precipitated Glover's critically acclaimed, comedic and dramatic television series *Atlanta* (2015–present) on the FX channel. It was also on YouTube where the public fully absorbed the artistic range of fin-de-siècle pop artist Beyoncé, which ultimately led to her three most popular video presentations toward the end of the first quarter of the twenty-first century, *Lemonade: A Visual Album* (2016), *Homecoming* (2019), and *Black is King* (2020), premiering respectively on the media-service providers HBO, Netflix, and Disney+.

Many of these new black television shows and long-form music videos carried the unmistakable imprint of Arthur Jafa, a cinematographer whose critically acclaimed work on Julie Dash's *Daughters of the Dust* (1991) and Spike Lee's *Crooklyn* (1994) brought a heretofore absent, refreshing cinematic afterglow to black and brown bodies. Under Jafa's directorial aegis, this same attention to lighting and vividly capturing peoples of color on film was augmented by a circumspect position on black subject matter: a viewpoint that, in spite of an appreciation for the rich complexities of African American life, was counterbalanced by a profound gravity and subtext of mortality. A film by
Jafa in this milieu was *Dreams are Colder than Death* (2013): a documentary that interrogated the meanings of blackness— and the consequences of Martin Luther King Jr.'s proverbial dream—at a moment when disappointments and anxieties in black communities proliferated. Soliciting the insights of a virtual who's who of contemporary black artists and intellectuals (such as Charles Burnett, Nicole Fleetwood, Saidiya Hartman, Fred Moten, Hortense Spillers, and Kara Walker), Jafa placed the absorbing words of these pundits alongside black history photographs, filmed highways and crashing ocean surf, and

182 Arthur Jafa, *Dreams are Colder than Death*, 2013

183 Sondra Perry, *IT'S IN THE GAME '17 or Mirror Gag for Vitrine and Projection*, 2017

evocative, slowed down footage of ordinary black people going about their everyday activities, the latter underscoring the disconnect between the experiences and ideas of cultural critics, King's platitudes, and the fatality-shaped realities of the black quotidian.

Well into the twenty-first century, many black artists had become cynical about the contemporary social circumstances and future prospects of peoples of African descent (a topic that will be discussed at greater length in Chapter 9). That works like Arthur Jafa's *Dreams are Colder than Death* and other artists' films, videos, and computer-generated artworks contained a significant measure of pessimism, or at least distrust and foreboding in matters of racial equity and inclusion, was also present in media artist Sondra Perry's *IT'S IN THE GAME '17 or Mirror Gag for Vitrine and Projection* (2017), an immersive sculpture and video installation examining how digital technology was frequently implicated in incapacitating synopses of peoples of African descent. During this work's exhibition during the 10th Berlin Biennale, gallery visitors moving through *IT'S IN THE GAME '17* were compelled to pause at several critical junctures: opposite a projection of Perry and her twin brother, Sandy, a college basketball player, viewing 3-D depictions of African sculptures in New York and London museums; before Perry's animations of Sandy (whose image had been sold years earlier to a collegiate basketball video game developer without

183

his consent); and in front of several small video screens, affixed to metal basketball shot trainers, each showing grisly 3-D medical renderings of Sandy's head from the interiors of his eye sockets and nasal cavity. The soundtrack for much of this imagery—a slowed-down version of "You Are Everything" by the 1970s soul group The Stylistics—subliminally conveyed Perry's concerns about the contemporary co-opting of black identities and narratives, and about the uneasy relationship between identity and the latest imaging technologies, or what she described as the "abstraction of subjecthood" in digital representations of black people.

More than a hundred years after D.W. Griffith and his followers branded "with lightning" their version of history, Keith Piper, DJ Spooky, Sondra Perry and other new media artists challenged those accounts with their own, digitally enriched works. By invoking the storytelling and prophesying of the West African griot, embellishing the narratives with cultural representations informed by the media and cyberspace, and adding reinterpretations of the past and present, they not only raised the perception of black diasporal arts but, more importantly, they changed their function. These modes of image-making—demarcated by what Paul Miller called a "geographic and temporal simultaneity"—revealed contemporary conditions and, like the futuristic rays in an Aaron Douglas painting, they illuminated today's sites and sounds and tomorrow's projections, as seen through a glass, diasporally.

Chapter 8
Fin-de-Siècle Blues

Subverting the "B" Word

Unlike the European artistic dominance of the early twentieth century, the late 1990s and early years of the twenty-first century were full of a black cultural consciousness that was especially strong in the visual arts. Previously it had been a disadvantage for one's art to be too closely associated with black cultural concerns, but in the late 1990s it was acceptable, even fashionable, to be a black artist, or to interrogate black identity in one's work. This was an era that saw several major exhibitions and international biennials featuring exciting new work by artists from Africa, the Caribbean, and throughout the black diaspora. Johannesburg, Dakar, and Havana joined New York, London, and Paris as meeting grounds for serious art collectors and other observers of contemporary art. From "Seven Stories about Modern Art in Africa" (1995) at London's Whitechapel Gallery to "Freestyle" (2001) at New York's Studio Museum in Harlem, exhibitions put black artists under the spotlight, and they and their works became the subjects of widespread critical interest.

As with the black literary flowerings of the 1920s and 1960s, the 1990s saw art historians, theoreticians, and critics embracing the once-marginalized black artist, and examining racially encoded signs and images. A general interest in the artistic manifestations of racial identities, postcolonialism, the politics of difference, and the impact of globalization on the world's communities was clearly communicated by the flood of artists' monographs, critical studies, exhibition catalogues, articles, and websites.

Yet this was also a period when some artists built their reputations on works that clearly turned away from the current constructs of racial identity and, instead, undermined historical representations of racial and cultural difference. Beneficiaries of a more inclusive attitude as well as saboteurs of anything redolent of postcolonial complacency, "political correctness", or a celebration of the era of civil rights, these artists subverted the "b" word—black—and, like no generation before them, experienced critical and financial success through their artistic advocacy of a questionable racial and cultural identity.

Certain critics and curators at the start of the twenty-first century also foretold the end of the "black" label in contemporary culture, arguing that it could no longer effectively describe a racially hybrid people of cultural diversity, social complexity, and broad-based political alliances. While acknowledging the socially constructed realities of race and the lingering effects of racial discrimination for large segments of the world's population, they called for a critical discourse to cut through, like the works of art themselves, a cultural and racial clarity too often assumed by commentators. The descriptive term black did not make sense anymore.

These fin-de-siècle anxieties were echoed by sociologist Paul Gilroy in *Against Race: Imagining Political Culture Beyond the Color Line* (2000). Although written as an historical critique of racism and fascism, much of Gilroy's complaint was against those perpetrators of racist and fascist acts, past and present, who have more or less operated under the programs and designs of an "Afrocentric" or "black" cause. For Gilroy no amount of racial and cultural redress for past injustices justified black supremacism, especially when this implied segregation and resounded with overwhelmingly misogynist and racial myth-making tendencies.

The representative artist for the critical successes and conceptual limitations of a "black art" at this time was Kara Walker. While studying for a Master of Fine Arts degree at the Rhode Island School of Design in the early 1990s, Walker had discovered the old-fashioned and genteel technique of mounting black paper silhouettes of sentimental scenes on white backgrounds. With postmodern irony and an unapologetic ambivalence toward what Gilroy has described as a burdensome "black particularity," Walker skillfully gave her black silhouettes the trappings of an antebellum Southern melodrama, but they are large, the size of murals, and depict horrific acts of sexual assault and violence. Even in works not tied to a nightmarish master-slave narrative (like Walker's large-scale print *African/American*, 1998), her meticulous delineations of physical characteristics and costumes are fearlessly propelled into the viewer's inner maelstrom of racial, cultural, and sexual clichés. Walker stated:

184

184 Kara Walker, *African/American*, 1998

*...the power [of these images], for me, comes from...[my] all-
encompassing sense of blackness, an all-encompassing kind of
awareness that I didn't know I had. So like it's an acknowledgment
of a naiveté on the one hand, and a really heavy acknowledgment
that I think I'm getting to a point where I understand not just what
it means to be black, but what blackness means in our culture, and
how, as a thing disembodied from myself or ourselves, it goes about
making itself known in the world, in the culture.*

Walker's description of an illusory yet phenomenological
blackness may explain why such images are particularly
incendiary for many African Americans, who also sense the
false nature of this version of blackness, but cannot tolerate its
physical portrayal.

Fin-de-Siècle Blues

185 David Levinthal, *Blackface*, 1995

David Levinthal produced a series of photographs in the mid-1990s that, like Kara Walker's cut-outs, embraced the racial underside. Acknowledging that "race is probably one of the rawest nerves in our society," Levinthal used this truth in a close scrutiny of the black stereotype, resulting in *Blackface* (1995). His close-up, dramatically lit color photographs of racist, mass-produced ephemera against black velvet transformed rather ordinary mechanical toys, cookie jars, tins, dolls, and figurines into rarified treasures. Levinthal's *Blackface*, Michael Ray Charles's paintings, which revamped black stereotypes with a controversial edge, and *Without Sanctuary*, a collection of postcards documenting lynchings, which was exhibited and published, all intentionally blurred the historical boundaries between the evidence of racism and the desirable art object.

What's So Funny About Being Black?

Thelma Golden, who curated "Freestyle," the Studio Museum in Harlem's exhibition, wrote in her catalogue essay that the artists "live in a world where their particular cultural specificity is marketed to the planet and sold back to them." Her undisguised sarcasm for a kind of black "free-trade agreement" is only equalled by the absurdity of the phenomenon itself: that of mass marketers, in a media-saturated, fantasy-inducing society, selling people's identities back to them in the form of popular culture, although in a repackaged and often degraded version. Paul Gilroy also noted in *Against Race* how the already problematic condition of blackness is further mired and cheapened "amid the gloss of cultural industries and their insatiable machinery of commodification." As perceived by Golden and Gilroy, this global marketing of black cultures is an undeniable fact of the early twenty-first century, fueling social schizophrenia, ethical debates and, remarkably, contemporary art.

The work of Renée Cox is especially preoccupied with a perceived progression toward a market-driven blackness. Throughout the 1990s this artist exhumed (and frequently laid bare) society's racial, sexual, and gender-informed stereotypes in her large photographs, sometimes studio-based, sometimes digitally manipulated. Often using her own nude body as the vehicle for these social critiques (as in *Yo Mama*, 1992–94), Cox's sardonic and rather unconventional approach to self-portraiture made her photographs ironic rather than exploitative. This was most evident in her *Rajé Superhero* series: a collection of computer-altered photo-narratives featuring the artist as an Afrocentric Wonder Woman avenger. In a work from this series, subtitled *The Liberation of Lady J. and U.B.* (1998),

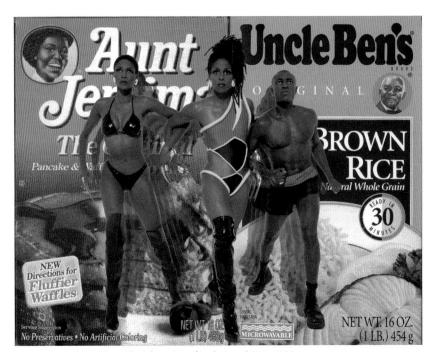

186 Renée Cox, *The Liberation of Lady J. and U. B.*, 1998

Cox has her Rajé Superhero character escort two fashion
models out of two food packages that feature the most familiar
and commercially successful black characters in modern
advertising history: Aunt Jemima and Uncle Ben. By staging
such a fantastic escape, Cox comments on the "thin line"
between stereotypic characterizations and idealized depictions.
186 *The Liberation of Lady J. and U.B.* appeared in the wake of
comparable works by artists Jeff Donaldson, Joe Overstreet,
Faith Ringgold, Betye Saar, and Robert Colescott, who also
redeployed the inscrutable Aunt Jemima character in service
to a satirical, countervailing artistic statement.

But as transformative as Renée Cox's and these other artists'
works were, the Quaker Oats Company's decision in 2020 to
remove the Aunt Jemima character from its highly profitable,
130-year-old product was more surprising and even more
significant. The Company's executive-level call proved that even
corporate America eventually realized the long-term deficits in
holding onto such racist relics and, as seen in other, subsequent
post-black satires, how such works might themselves become
ensnared in what the cultural critic Tavia Nyong'o described as
"the unhappy dynamic of disseminating an iconography that

[they] cannot stop destroying, and which [they] therefore cannot stop producing."

Huey Freeman, the wise-cracking main character in Aaron McGruder's comic strip *The Boondocks*, shared Cox's bemusement with the absurdities of racial representations and role models, as seen in his Afrocentric critique of the X-Men comics. McGruder fuses the popular Japanese anime style with a personal graphic shorthand, but his biting commentaries on mass media and African American affairs are entirely American.

Chris Ofili's *Afrodizzia (2nd Version)* (1996) raises similar questions. Like so many of this British artist's paintings, it operates on multiple levels of seeing and believing. At a distance one marvels at the swirling, paisley-like patterns made from colorful map pins and textured pigments, and a strident underpainting of multicolored scallops and circular shapes. Close-up, one discerns balls of elephant dung, strategically placed over and under the stretched canvas, many with map pins spelling out the names of famous black performing artists (like rapper LL Cool J) and sports heroes (like boxing impresario Don King). Closer still one can see hundreds of little black faces, cut from assorted magazines, adorned with crudely painted "Afro" hairstyles, and dispersed over the entire painting surface.

One school of thought views works like *Afrodizzia (2nd Version)* as an artistic variation on 1990s hip-hop music— the aural layering and musical quotations akin to Chris Ofili's layers of paint, collage, and cultural references. Other interpretations focus on Ofili's ironic yet decidedly critical stance toward contemporary black culture, disparaging the necessity or efficacy of identity markers, sartorial and individual. Like Renée Cox's Rajé Superhero, Ofili here

187 Aaron McGruder, strip from *The Boondocks*, 2000

THE BOONDOCKS   **BY AARON McGRUDER**

188 Chris Ofili, *Afrodizzia (second version)*, 1996

uses satire to pose a serious question: at what social cost in historical ignorance and cultural disintegration are people "free" from the psychological shackles of racism in an era of media saturation and cultural commodification? Although the answer (as sensed from Ofili's preoccupation with excrement and ephemera) is at a tremendous social cost, both he and Cox have chosen to respond with humor and ambiguity, rather than a solemn denunciation. In both instances, the wit in imagining a completely transformed or exaggerated sign of blackness (Cox's Lady J. and U. B. and Ofili's "Afros," respectively) only underscores how ineffectual and even counterproductive are many racial conventions in today's world.

That humor and visual irony are adopted to communicate this identity-conundrum in turn-of-the-century art is no surprise given the prominence in mass culture since the early 1990s of such black humorists as the US's Eddie Murphy and the UK's Lenny Henry. Although seemingly light-years removed from the raucous joking of a "Def Comedy Jam," the works of Cox, Ofili and others all rely on a comic premise: that being black, an active participant in contemporary culture, and ideologically wedged between a "Negro past" and a "post-black" present—regardless of how far society has progressed in terms of racial and economic parity—often invites an astonished recognition of laughable human folly. In 2000 the *New York Times Magazine* rhetorically posed the question, "What's so funny about being black?" The answer is: inherently nothing— and, in terms of a paradoxical position regarding race and self in the twenty-first century—plenty.

Another Form of Identification

There was a similar resistance to one-dimensional art categorizations based on race and ethnicity among African artists and curators at the end of the twentieth century. In 1999 Okwui Enwezor, the Nigerian-born artistic director of the 2nd Johannesburg Biennale (1997) and the former director of the Haus der Kunst, Munich (2011–18), wrote: "This practice of ratification, which postmodernism processes, reproduces, and fashions into 'difference' denies African artists a claim to subjectivity and self-narration." According to Enwezor, many forces—both from the traditional cultural factions and current art regimes—were implicated in limiting the ways in which many contemporary African artists' works were understood. The fact that African artists were practising in the metropolises of the West made it problematical to use difference as a "determining criterion for their inclusion within the pantheon of contemporary cultural producers." Even within the context of so-called inclusive categories of contemporary art concerned with difference, globalization, or identity, African artists rarely received informed assessments of their works that did not succumb to a stock anthropological response to peoples and things African. Many critics were unable to accept that African artists could be culturally conversant across national and linguistic boundaries, and that their reply to contemporary conditions was a sophisticated deployment of conceptual, performance, and other postmodern art-making strategies.

The works of Yinka Shonibare were emblematic of a fin-de-siècle art that disrupted conventional as well as non-conventional notions of what it meant to be African, British, black, postmodern, or any combination of these. Shonibare's visual dialogue between, on one hand, his installations of mannequins wearing tailored clothes made from so-called "African" printed fabrics—taken to unearthly heights in his *Cloud 9* (1999/2000)—and, on the other, his photo-serializations of historical costume dramas featuring himself, challenged those critics who might have categorized him as just a sculptor, a photographer, or a performance artist. In his installations his masterful assortment of historical allusion, postcolonial critique, and craftsmanship thrust his examinations of the authenticity of art, himself, and the artistic vocation straight

189

189 Yinka Shonibare, *Cloud 9*, 1999–2000

190 Yinka Shonibare, *Dorian Gray*, Scene 7, 2001

190

into the heart of visual meaning. Similarly, his highly theatrical
photographs, fusing a visualization of the English literary
tradition (as in a Merchant/Ivory film) with a meditation on
the history of blacks in Great Britain, have generated much
discussion on the black persona. Works from Shonibare's *Dorian
Gray* series (2001), with their moody cinematic atmosphere and
Shonibare's portrayal of Oscar Wilde's narcissistic protagonist,
revealed a conceptual link to his mannequin-and-printed-fabric
installations through their shared investigation of fashion as a
marker of distinction and disjuncture.

It was in this scrutiny of European/African cultural relations
that many African artists at the end of the twentieth century
found an abundance of visual information. In urban centers
both on the continent of Africa and in the West, they grappled
with the contradictions of "first-world" surplus and "third-
world" poverty, a sustained white entitlement and interminable
black derogation, as well as US cultural dominance and
disregard for all things non-Western. These contradictions,
with the end of racial apartheid in South Africa still recent,
encouraged several to employ a mix of theory, practice, and
morality in their investigations of this new social reality.

191 ABOVE Johannes Phokela, *Pantomime Act Trilogy*, 1999
192 OPPOSITE Minnette Vári, *Self-Portrait 2*, 1995

The South African artist Johannes Phokela quoted sixteenth- and seventeenth-century Dutch art in a series of ironic paintings. *Pantomime Act Trilogy* (1999) was partly inspired by the 1599 Jacob de Gheyn II drawing *Allegory of Death*, and continued its moralizing tenor. Phokela's iconography— diagrammatic grids and an armed and clownish African cherub/ child soldier—reflects the desire for a systemic understanding of an often fatal and tenuous postmodern existence.

Minnette Vári, another South African artist, also made works that frequently probed a traumatized and marginalized psyche. Her controversial *Self Portrait 2* (1995), a digitally altered and conscious affectation of the artist as a primordial black woman, fueled the indignation of even the most indulgent critics of contemporary African art. "Here we may not find hate necessarily," wrote the Nigerian artist and art historian Olu Oguibe, "but we do find racial disregard and license alright." Vári's *Self Portrait 2* intentionally elicited a critique of the limitations of a postmodern and post-apartheid "self-portrait" in South Africa: a place weighted down with racial and political baggage too pervasive to ignore.

Another conceptual work by a South African artist that roused a barrage of criticism was Tracey Rose's *Span II* (1997): a performance for the 2nd Johannesburg Biennale that featured the artist—nude and sheared of all scalp and body hair—within a large glass case. Knotting the strands of her shorn hair

191

192

193

and seated on a video monitor that simultaneously zoomed
in on her handiwork, Rose offered a whole litany of cultural
references—Europe's former practice of exhibiting peoples
of color, women's fundamental role in cottage industries
worldwide—and themes: feminism and racial difference.
In this work she was also proffering her allegiance to what
curator Gerardo Mosquera described in 2001 as the unstable
"international language" of contemporary art.

Mosquera's thoughts on a growing lack of interest in
identity were largely directed toward contemporary art and
artists from Latin America, yet these same observations
strongly resonated with other artworks and artists. In other
words, African artists like Yinka Shonibare, Johannes Phokela,
and others show an Africanity in their art not through
folk, religious, or historical references but, rather, through
artistic practices and critical discourses that, in different
ways, establish open channels of communication between
continents, cultural zones, and communities.

193 OPPOSITE Tracey Rose,
Span II, 1997
194 RIGHT Oumou Sy,
Cyberdress, 1997

194   Further evidence of this subtle but distinct shift at the
turn of the century—from an ethnically or racially emblematic
art, to an internalized or profound African/black/postmodern
art—can be seen in the work of the Senegalese fashion
designer and performance artist Oumou Sy. In her *Cyberdress*
(1997), for instance, the juxtaposition of costly hand-dyed
fabrics and recyclable CD-ROMs made it more concept than
artifact, a work worthy to be considered in a contemporary,
cosmopolitan context.

These sites of new African art—London, Johannesburg,
Dakar, Paris, New York, cyberspace, and all—have exploded
the assumption that ethnic and geographic demarcations
define and authenticate the genre. Similarly, artists like Tracey
Rose and Oumou Sy (and Sokari Douglas Camp and Werewere
Liking before them) have further questioned the images of the
African craftswoman and the cosmopolitan African male artist,
bringing radical ideas, including those of gender, to an African
artistic identity.

Finally, South Africa's multiracial makeup, its history of struggle, and its post-apartheid entry into the world community in 1991 have given African artists a new racial significance. Some have seen this as an unfortunate imposition on more inclusive views of modern culture in Africa, but others have acknowledged how impossible it is for African artists, curators, and intellectuals to deny racial oppression and discrimination.

Shonibare, Phokela, Vári, Rose, Sy, and others have abandoned the expectation that they will "show their passports" (Gerardo Mosquera), replacing this with something more conceptual in their quest for individual recognition. The message for other artists of African nationalities and descent is that by coming to terms with the act of declaring one's genealogy and repudiating historic injustices they, too, can transcend the distorted versions of race and place, participate in an international conversation in the visual arts and, paradoxically, also take part in an African diasporal and black postmodern dialogue.

Recuperations

Writing in 1990, Adrian Piper argued that the linguistic latitude of post-structuralism and the historical relativism of postmodernism were ideal "if you want to co-opt women and people of color and deny them access to the potent tools of rationality and objectivity." Well known for her denunciations of institutional and individual racism through conceptual art, Adrian Piper surprised many when she admonished the reigning cultural theorists (who were, like Piper, among the art world élite) for undermining the very real struggle by African Americans for recognition.

In 1997 philosopher Patricia Huntington substantially added to Piper's arguments, but within a larger study of an "Africana philosophy of existence." In her essay entitled "Fragmentation, Race, and Gender: Building Solidarity in the Postmodern Era," Huntington negotiated the theoretical expanse between W. E. B. Du Bois's premise that racial problems lie at the center of modern social issues, and the opposite position upheld by the French feminist Luce Irigaray that sexual difference is "the burning issue." Huntington, critical of both absolutes, prescribed "unlearning racial myopia" and cultivating "the ability to grasp any social event or phenomenon in terms of its multiple dimensions and its disjunctive and conflicting impact on various groups and individuals."

There were also several artists who attempted to bring a degree of moral purpose and conceptual wholeness to black art. Chakaia Booker's *Wrench (Wench) II* (2001), an undulating

195

195 Chakaia Booker, *Wrench (Wench) II*, 2001

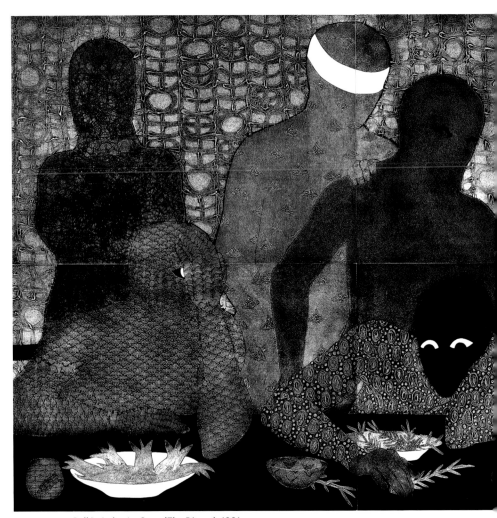

196 Belkis Ayón, *La Cena* (*The Dinner*), 1991

column of twisted rubber tires on a solid armature, brought a refreshing immediacy to the art scene. Its reference to earlier Modernist sculptures was respectful, and its invocation of former instruments of labor—both inanimate and human, the latter demarcated by race and gender—introduced a significant theoretical layer and, by association, a modicum of the postmodern. Several artists at this time opposed postmodernism's emotional distance with a spiritual, racially charged vision, in which black histories and mythologies were paramount. The Cuban artist Belkis Ayón, from the late 1980s

until her untimely death in 1999, introduced bold yet
enigmatic black-and-white depictions of the ceremonies of
the Afro-Cuban Secret Society known as Abakuá. Although
she used the demanding technique of collagraphy (a melding
of relief and intaglio printmaking from a combination of
collaged and hand-engraved plates), Ayón created elaborate,
graphically dense, and often multi-paneled scenes like *La Cena*
(*The Dinner*) (1991) featuring faceless human figures with
staring eyes and a serpent's skin, engaged in mysterious,
anguished rituals.

196

197 Pope.L, *Eating the Wall Street Journal*, at The Sculpture Center, New York, 2000

In *The Dinner*, the "brotherhood" at a ritual meal served as a visual metaphor not just for a symbolic Afro-Cuban covenant, but also for the possibility of a universal banquet where all humanity would be present, regardless of cultural distinctions. There was some evidence toward the end of Ayón's life and later that African diasporal arts and black artists were, indeed, becoming a recognized part of this new art world. During these years, awards and important art commissions were given to such black artists as Robert Colescott, Jacob Lawrence, Kerry James Marshall, Steve McQueen, Chris Ofili, Kara Walker, and artist and critic Deborah Willis. Belkis Ayón herself was honored with a purchase by MoMA, New York, and an art retrospective at the 7th Havana Bienal in Cuba. The Studio Museum in Harlem, the world's leading institution for African diasporal arts, also flourished during this period with new facilities, and the dynamic leadership of Lowery Stokes Sims and Thelma Golden.

For another example of a fin-de-siècle "ritual meal," the performance artist Pope.L installed a ten-foot pyramidal wooden armature in New York's Sculpture Center, on top of which he mounted a porcelain toilet bowl where he sat naked while reading, chewing, and spitting out chunks of the *Wall Street Journal*. First performed in 1991, this latest iteration of *Eating the Wall Street Journal* (2000) reflected Pope.L's interest in linguistic structures, social categories, and socio-economic stratifications, here all filtered through a reenactment of informational consumption and elimination. In *Eat Notes* (2000), the accompanying publication for this performance, Pope.L writes:

...Consuming is not just about

taking in. No. It's also about
being taken in. A kind of
inebriation. Delusion. Pleasure.
Terror. An Analgesic. All
simultaneous. **Yet broken and
jumbled. Note. Go ask Alice.**

Obliquely referring at the end of this passage to the protagonist of Lewis Carroll's *Alice's Adventures in Wonderland* (1865), who accidentally falls into an alternative universe and struggles to comprehend that world's arcane syntaxes and social systems, Pope.L sarcastically likened the *Wall Street Journal* to an edible manna, or a palliative, dropped from a capitalism-driven heaven. But as suggested in Pope.L's elevated throne and its

197

lifeguard-tower form, these symbolic acts of consumption, expectoration, and defecation were envisaged from a perspicacious yet hallucinatory place.

In another citation from *Alice's Adventures in Wonderland*, Pope.L told Lowery Stokes Sims that "Blackness has always been a kind of a rabbit's hole—an uncertainty of someone else's making." This "hole of disenfranchisement," and the fact of seeing one's destiny "at the bottom of the political and ideological hierarchy," offered Pope.L the fresh prospect of analyzing and politicizing this unstable position and, like many other black artists at this historic juncture, of entering the twenty-first century wholly cognizant of the preconceptions, contradictions, and absurdities that blackness navigated within the larger culture. *Blackness for Sale* (2001), one of several media works created at the dawn of the new millennium by artists Mendi and Keith Obadike, followed Pope.L's example in creating a conceptual work that troubled an unreflected engagement with racial identity. Utilizing the online auction preference on the website for the electronic commerce company eBay, Keith Obadike composed an advertisement that allowed prospective buyers to bid on his blackness (as if race was an article of trade), satirically guaranteeing "a certificate of authenticity" and glibly acknowledging its "benefits" (as well as its handicaps). Obadike's "sale," despite its eventual cancelation by eBay, initiated much philosophical rumination around what constituted blackness, and raised important questions concerning the commercializing of culture and the objectification of people: musings and forebodings that persisted well into the new century.

Among the benefits and warnings in Keith Obadike's auction notice were two, somewhat curious, irreconcilable disclosures, the first that "this Blackness may be used for creating black art," and the second that "the Seller does not recommend that this Blackness be used in the process of making or selling 'serious' art." On the one hand flippant and on the other hand cautionary, the two commendations insinuated, as with much of the art produced at this point in time, a markedly dissimilar attitude from previous art-historical moments. Substituting irony for optimism and scepticism for pride, Obadike's *Blackness for Sale* and other doubt-generating art—from Kara Walker's silhouettes to Pope.L's portrayals—were, for all of their despair and abjectness, purposeful and political. They shared a commitment to an ethic whose part-ecstatic, part-diagnostic temperament was characteristic of a modern African American "blues aesthetic," and whose main mission was enabling an intersectional approach to creative exchanges and engagements across geographical and political borders. As especially seen in the works of artists from Africa and the Caribbean, the other unspoken debts were artistic themes and narratives that, on the cusp of a new century with unsure and often unsettling outlooks, touched on a range of timely issues, such as nationalism, migration, homelessness, global violence, and environmental destruction. With these questions at the forefront of many artistic strategies throughout the African diaspora, a work like Belkis Ayón's *The Dinner* reads more like an Afro-Cuban version of Leonardo da Vinci's *The Last Supper* (1495–98), its guests forever suspended in an indeterminacy, or an extreme dread, about the future.

Chapter 9
The Price of Blackness

Introduction: After the Deluge

Among the commissioned works and special projects for Prospect.1, New Orleans (2008)—a sprawling, citywide art event envisioned to revitalize New Orleans, Louisiana in the aftermath of Hurricane Katrina (2005)—artist Mark Bradford's *Mithra* attracted throngs of admirers and, relatedly, elicited a surplus of emotions. Bradford's sculpture —three vertically stacked, forty-foot-long steel shipping containers encased in a plywood facade that evoked a ship's hull, and covered with torn and peeling posters and advertising circulars—referenced inner-city decay and migratory transience: societal concerns and geo-political circumstances that proliferated during the first decades of the new century. Seemingly moored in the Crescent City's still-decimated Lower Ninth Ward, *Mithra* was Bradford's grand materialization of an impoverished but resourceful urban milieu and, conversely, a wry commentary on displacement and abandonment—exigencies emanating from environmental malfeasance and social inequities on a global scale. That peoples of African descent were the most likely victims of these catastrophes was not lost on *Mithra*'s audience and, factoring in the human costs of infrastructural neglect and economic underdevelopment, one might conclude that, to paraphrase Zora Neale Hurston in her Depression-era novel *Their Eyes Were Watching God*, vessels (such as *Mithra)* that have humanity's hopes on board too often "sail forever on the horizon,...never landing until the Watcher turns his eyes away in resignation, his dreams mocked to death by Time."

Lost Americans (2008), a mixed-media painting by artist Thornton Dial, conveyed a similar fatalism as Mark Bradford's *Mithra*, but materialized in a murky accumulation of debris comprising the dregs of post-industrial black lives. Discovering his artistic talents and succeeding in the mainstream art world after many years as a laborer in a railroad car manufacturing plant in Bessemer, Alabama, Dial was intimately familiar with the dispossessed worlds from which he drew inspiration, assembling composite abstractions that, whether through their visual components or titles, acknowledged the grim realities that so many peoples of African descent faced. These two artworks obliquely addressed a pervading cultural melancholy that, despite a heightened visibility for artists of African descent, put into action art about black trauma and, in tandem, set the tone for debates about the perceived social worth of black lives.

Paradoxically, the 2008 election of US President Barack Obama, the first African American to hold such a pre-eminent office, inspired countless black Americans and others of African descent and, on the face of it, signified a shift toward greater racial inclusivity in the public sphere. However, as suggested in the aforementioned works by Bradford and Dial and their grave sentiments, this expanded racial purview was joined by cynicism on the part of many black observers, and a frank admission to a not-quite-transformed racial consciousness. Deadly and violent encounters between black people and the police fueled these misgivings and, under the rallying cry of "Black Lives Matter" by community activists and other concerned citizens, the world's "watchers" channeled this articulated anguish in remedial legislation, social media, and, most pertinent to black culture, in arts and letters.

A parallel disquiet and sense of loss that permeated many African and African-descended communities revolved around issues of migration to the US and industrialized countries in Europe. Fleeing political, social, and economic collapse in the developing world and, in many instances, facing lethal threats, black and brown asylum seekers made harrowing journeys across land and sea, only to encounter antipathy and inhumaneness at international borders, or worse, perishing en route. This growth in migrants, especially from North and sub-Saharan Africa, Central America, and the Caribbean, became a topic for numerous artists and, like the aforementioned art projects concerned with the perils and pitfalls of simply being black, art about peoples of color moving through an often hostile and strange world appreciably contributed to an early twenty-first century art scene.

Foremost among those artists whose work explored racial and cultural dislodgment, albeit through abstraction, was the Ghanaian-born, Nigeria-based sculptor El Anatsui. With massive, intermittently clustered, and draped assemblages created from thousands of flattened aluminum liquor bottle

Mark Bradford, *Mithra*, 2008

caps fastened with copper wire, El Anatsui indirectly alluded to those millions of African refugees making their way across the Sahara and Mediterranean in search of improved lives. Works like *In the World But Don't Know the World* (2009) employed the environment-friendly practice of recycling inorganic waste but, reminiscent of fellow artistic bricoleurs David Hammons and Mr. Imagination, El Anatsui generated these corporeal insinuations through the art languages of surface embellishment and multi-pattern design.

But not all abstract art by black sculptors and painters in these years alluded to trauma, nor did this work necessarily draw on design systems and aesthetic sensibilities from the black diaspora. In 2007 Julie Mehretu, an Ethiopian American painter, was commissioned by the Goldman Sachs Group. Inc., an American multinational investment bank and financial services company, to create a painting for the firm's lobby of its recently built lower Manhattan headquarters. *Mural* (2009), comparable to Mehretu's other large-scale paintings, incorporated geometric, boldly colored forms, fractional schematics of architecture, and free-form linear markings that, in an illusionistic way, moved in, out, and across the canvas's approximately 21 × 80 foot apportioned white field. Described as containing elements that refer to "the history of finance capitalism—maps, trade routes, population shifts, financial institutions, the growth of cities"—Mehretu's *Mural* fearlessly employed the precepts of an abstract graphic language to realize these economic and diagrammatic modes of representation.

Often mistaken as panoramas or map-like, paintings like Julie Mehretu's *Mural* contained the conceptual, palimpsestic substructures present in all of her work and, as seen in *Mural*'s prominence in New York's public art cityscape, exemplified the novel and elevated stature many young black artists achieved at the outset of the new millennium. Oddly, these years brought both black exceptionalism and black vulnerability—a layering of realities not dissimilar from the strata in Mehretu's *Mural*—and would be a contradiction that, from the sky-rocketing auction prices attained by works by Jean-Michel Basquiat, Mark Bradford, David Hammons, and Kerry James Marshall, to the ignoble number of African American homicides by law enforcement, characterized contemporary black art and life just before and after the deluge.

199 OPPOSITE ABOVE Thornton Dial, *Lost Americans*, 2008
200 OPPOSITE BELOW El Anatsui, *In the World But Don't Know the World*, 2009

201 Julie Mehretu, *Mural*, 2009

Precarity and Portraiture
A harbinger of this artistic perturbation concerning black
perceptibility, transience, and suffering surfaced earlier in two
notable publications: Deborah Willis's *Reflections in Black: A
History of Black Photographers from 1840 to the Present* (2000)
and James Allen's *Without Sanctuary: Lynching Photography
in America* (2000). Despite each book's respective editorial
tenor and emotional distance from the other, they shared
an acknowledgment of the importance of the photographic
medium to an emergent, modern black identity, and an
appreciation for the body's pivotal place in a dialectical
meditation on black freedom. These themes and their
formulations through photography (already introduced by
innumerable media-based image makers in the 1990s) were
recurrent departure points for many artists at the beginning
of the century, especially those whose works focused on
racialized subjects, the intersectional roles of gender and
sexuality, the underlying function and affect of images, and
the all-too-familiar occurrence of the marketable-turned-
disposable being.
    One of the earliest artistic benchmarks for this moment,
203   Hank Willis Thomas's *Branded Head* (2003), exposed the
uncomfortable parallels between the contemporary culture's
obsession with black bodies—commonly manifested in

sports—and Western civilization's sanctioning of black subjugation, captured in the digitized image of an anonymous black man's cranial scar in the shape of the athletic apparel company Nike's "swoosh" logo (or "brand"). Taking Andy Warhol's mid-twentieth-century critique of mass media further than a Pop Art commentary and into visual dissimulation, Thomas's photography puts a plethora of pre-existing media images on trial for various crimes and misdemeanors. Along with a cohort of recombinant artists (Terry Adkins, Sanford Biggers, Leslie Hewitt, Ellen Gallagher, et al.), Thomas placed the aides-mémoires and castoffs from the archives into service for an interrogation of African American identities, with the photograph performing a distinctive and critical role.

Although one of these artists, Rashid Johnson, would adopt a multidisciplinary practice of mixing media and utilizing unconventional materials (shea butter, wax, and soap), he began the century with a set of photographic self-portraits that introduced the idea of racial occlusion (in terms of the impenetrability, despite the repetition, of black images), while simultaneously and whimsically conversing with the past. One of those likenesses, *Self-Portrait Laying on Jack Johnson's Grave* (2006), performed double duty, not just depicting the artist and paying homage to Jack Johnson, the world's first black heavyweight boxing champion, but re-enacting a corpse that,

202

202 Rashid Johnson, *Self-Portrait Laying on Jack Johnson's Grave*, 2006

alas, was too common a sight on the streets of poorer African American neighborhoods.

With these earlier inroads into photographic images that, whether digitally altered or staged, forged a pattern in which peoples of African descent became the principal characters in a tale of weighted objecthood, photographers, and other media-based artists in the century's second decade embarked on an analogous, part thematic, part stylistic path. Whether taking cues from the documentary tradition (as seen in LaToya Ruby Frazier's photographs of communities in existential crises), or re-imagining studio portrait photography (for example, Paul Mpagi Sepuya's refracted and fragmented nudes), the camera and its operator portrayed not just the black subject at the proverbial crossroads, but actual people and their artistic surrogates standing on the precipice of a universal tragedy.

The mythic contours of black narratives and their sundry protagonists were boldly foregrounded in Deana Lawson's *The Garden, Gemena, DR Congo* (2015), whose subjects, rather than being one-dimensional vehicles for narrow, pictorial objectives,

203 Hank Willis Thomas, *Branded Head,* from the series *B®anded,* 2003

204 TOP Deana Lawson, *The Garden, Gemena, DR Congo,* 2015
205 ABOVE John Akomfrah, *Precarity,* 2017

portrayed both themselves and adopted personas, and whose blackness, rather than polemical, was both matter-of-fact and visually potent. Extending the photograph's narrative reach so as to plumb history, the present, perception, and the self, contributed to the medium's increased critical and popular appeal well into the twenty-first century, enabling it to exert its influences beyond the photograph proper and, conspicuously, into film, video, and painting.

Artist and filmmaker John Akomfrah used the mystery surrounding the music and life of the legendary New Orleans jazz cornetist Buddy Bolden to create *Precarity* (2017): a three-channel video installation that, with its redolent soundtrack, long takes of taciturn actors, and filmed details of faded photographs and manuscripts—the latter submerged in a flowing stream—laid bare *Precarity*'s partial debt to philosopher Roland Barthes's elegiac meditations in *Camera Lucida*. Akomfrah, a founding member of the Black Audio Film Collective (which in the 1980s examined issues of Black British identity through film and media, most notably his 1986 film *Handsworth Songs*), was also motivated by the historical gaps, lost voices, and other "unknowables" missing from institutional archives and family albums in the African diaspora. Entitling this work of art *Precarity* not only connected it to Bolden's precipitous descent from musical innovator to state mental hospital patient, but to the insecurities and life-threatening incidents that many black people experienced in the 2010s, from police and vigilante excessive force against unarmed African Americans, to health disparities, government neglect, and environmental racism in black communities worldwide. Photography brought viewers into a subliminal tête-à-tête with the figure in art, and in an era of suspect African American fatalities such as Trayvon Martin, Eric Garner, Laquan McDonald, Sandra Bland, Freddie Gray, and Breonna Taylor, all black faces in media-based artworks were kindred spirits to these contemporary martyrs. The media's role in raising the specter of a contemporary danse macabre with black people— in 2020 glaringly demonstrated in the filmed and widely broadcasted suffocation death of George Floyd by a Minneapolis police officer—would haunt the collective consciousness and, along with the crimes themselves, be broadly viewed as accidental accessories.

The portrait-conscious impulse in these and other photography-based artworks prompted, ironically, painters to reassert the predominance of their chosen medium in the portrait genre, but in ways that diverged significantly from camera-produced figurative art. In addition, with predecessors

205

such as painters Alice Neel and Barkley L. Hendricks providing roadmaps, the factors of racial blackness and a heretical subject diverted many twenty-first century portraitists along markedly different artistic paths. One direction (as seen in the works of Beverly McIver, Henry Taylor, and Jordan Casteel) was work created in a painterly mode where likeness was subordinate to a highly idiosyncratic and empathetic preconception. Lynette Yiadom-Boakye's loosely executed canvases in subdued palettes and with black subjects created from composite figures were representative of this gestural subjectivity. For example, her *8am Cadiz* (2017), while not strictly a "portrait," impersonated the genre's formal and psychological characteristics to the extent that these attributes, along with the painting's central, animated black man, co-opted the art of verisimilitude to advance an expressive and boundless Africanity.

The other direction in contemporary black portraiture—a revamped academism—upended photography's representational authority and turned black subjects into incarnations of, again, precarity and, on the other hand, a vaunted pre-eminence. The myriad ways in which painters like Meleko Mokgosi, Toyin Ojih

206 BELOW Lynette Yiadom-Boakye, *8am Cadiz*, 2017
207 OPPOSITE Kehinde Wiley, *President Barack Obama*, 2018

Odutola, Robert Pruitt, and Amy Sherald pictorially vaulted realism and, instead, conceived their "sitters" in contemporary painting idioms spoke to a greater acceptance of non-literal conceptions of black bodies. Kehinde Wiley, a forerunner in this regard, made his mark by placing his subjects—initially African American men but, eventually, assorted youth of color—within vivid, highly decorative backgrounds, and having them assume exaggerated poses derived from Old Master paintings. In Wiley's acclaimed portrait of the 44th US President, Barack Obama, the artist tempered his characteristic figural

207

flamboyance and substituted it with a gravitas and "urban cool" befitting the first African American in this esteemed position. And yet this official portrait, for all its propitious vegetation and bodily candor, incorporated Wiley's melancholic specter and atmosphere of memento mori when depicting black subjects.

#BLACKWOMENREMIX

In 2004 the Spelman College Museum of Fine Art—an exhibition space in Atlanta, Georgia devoted to presenting art by and about women of African descent—featured for the first time the work of an "emerging woman artist," Iona Rozeal Brown. In sharp contrast to the museum's previous exhibitions, for example, of works by women quilters or legendary artists like Elizabeth Catlett, Rozeal's show, entitled "(afro-asiatic allegory)...black on both sides," was *au courant*, channeling African American cultural sensibilities, but filtered through Ukiyo-e, the traditional Japanese woodcut style, and the fashions of contemporary Japanese youth who emulated black urban culture. Iona Rozeal Brown's *Whoshi (ANA.ROGU-The Sender), (After Yoshitoshi's 'The Ghost Of Taira No Tomomori Appears At Diamotsu Bay')* (2008) was very much a creation of its times, when black artists embraced the mixed tape techniques of DJs, MCs, and rap musicians, and black women artists embarked on alternative feminist trajectories that probed beauty culture, queer identities, and society's assessments of the female body. Through her painting's main title, Brown playfully and rhetorically posed a question to which the painting's subject— a part-cyborg, part-black woman stepping through tidal waves and exhaling Takashi Murakami-like figures—artistically answered: an idiosyncratic, active entity, unconstrained by cultural norms and boundaries, and yet at ease in her own skin.

Around this same time, artist Mickalene Thomas also painted black women in non-illusionistic, visually embellished settings and, like Iona Rozeal Brown (and Kehinde Wiley), compositions that made references to the art of the past. But what distinguished Thomas's *Le déjeuner sur l'herbe: Les Trois Femmes Noires* (2010) from Édouard Manet's similarly composed and titled 1862–63 painting was an emphatic two-dimensionality, a mixed-media format, and an assertive black female presence, all conceived on a monumental scale, with alternating touches of sarcasm and sincerity. It is this last characteristic—an emotional stance that swings between pride and defiance, and an eye-rolling admission of disproportionate theatricality and surface excess—that thrust Thomas's paintings into what the poet and essayist Alexis Pauline Gumbs

208 Iona Rozeal Brown, *Whoshi (ANA.ROGU-The Sender), (After Yoshitoshi's "The Ghost Of Taira No Tomomori Appears At Diamotsu Bay")*, 2008

described as the world of the "uncontainable," in work that "[defies]...the oppressive interlocking set of narratives that entrap Black women every day."

An especially restrictive narrative that black women contested in these years was a presumptive heterosexuality. Much of the work by the South African photographer Zanele Muholi challenged the heteronormative scenario, foregrounding the humanity of lesbians, gay men, and transgender individuals in conventional, midrange-to-close-up poses. Photographic self-portraiture was also carefully composed, but in a more dramatic and purposely orchestrated fashion than Muholi's portraits of others. In *ZaVa, Amsterdam* (2014)—taken in a hotel room with a former partner—Muholi captured a moment of intimacy and tenderness. In portraying a relationship that in many places in the world provoked scorn, isolation, or physical attacks, the artist thus conveyed both "a sense of loss" through their depicted avoidances and glares, and a sense of inner strength.

The works of Brown, Thomas, and Muholi were responses to the out of proportion visuality that black women faced in an era of Facebook, Instagram, and intensified media scrutiny. From popular culture's fascination with the music and images of pop stars Rihanna and Beyoncé, to the media's fixations on the bodies, clothing, and hairstyles of the United States' First Lady Michelle Obama and the United Kingdom's Duchess of Sussex Meghan Markle, black women bore a spectatorial burden in these years. But rather than creating black female images that receded and disappeared from center stage, black women artists spot-lit their sisters, investing them with a distinction and social significance that, while reminiscent of earlier forays into the black female subject by artists

210 Zanele Muholi, *ZaVa, Amsterdam*, 2014

Elizabeth Catlett, Faith Ringgold, and Betye Saar, expanded
the representational possibilities.

Simone Leigh, a sculptor conversant in traditional African
art and architecture as well as in modern sculptural overtures
to a reductive abstraction, brought these lineages together in
Brick House (2019), a sixteen-foot-high bronze statue of a stylized
black woman's head atop a dome-like base. Temporarily
installed on New York's High Line—a linear park/greenway
on an inactive/elevated railroad branch line—*Brick House*
loomed over the congested traffic beneath it like a postmodern,
Afrocentric effigy, evoking an ancient herm with the power to
ward off evil. For a work of art to successfully compete for the
public's attention amidst midtown Manhattan's visual noise
required it to have both architectonic and denotative audacity,
all contained in Leigh's bold, black female form.

Simone Leigh's *Brick House* and its open-air interrogation
of black female imagery at a moment of high apperception
and public debate had a thematic antecedent five years prior,
in artist Kara Walker's temporary sculptural installation in

Brooklyn, New York, titled *A Subtlety, or the Marvelous Sugar Baby, an Homage to the unpaid and overworked Artisans who have refined our Sweet tastes from the cane fields to the Kitchens of the New World on the Occasion of the demolition of the Domino Sugar Refining Plant* (2014). Walker's phalanx of sugar-fabricated, anthropomorphic forms—most prominent among them, a thirty-five-foot-tall, sphinx-like female figure with distinct African facial features, an unclothed body and, in the manner of a stereotypic Aunt Jemima character, a handkerchief-bound head—drew thousands of viewers to the installation's site and, predictably, elicited far-reaching kudos and criticism. Known for her provocative, two-dimensional works that conceptually probed and re-imagined African American stereotypes, master–slave dynamics, and suppressed memories of sexual abuse and racial trauma, Walker turned here to the ultimate symbol of American racism—the romanticized, subservient southern US "mammy"—and by way of her figure's ancient Egyptian form, saccharine-addictive allusions, and symbolic whiteness, confounded a superficial construal of the black female stereotype. Walker's *A Subtlety...* was an enigma on par with Frantz Fanon's *Black Skin, White Masks* metaphor, and a satire in which the stereotype's patent fallacy and irrepressible, maddening dreamwork artfully coexisted.

211 Simone Leigh, *Brick House*, 2019

212 Kara Walker, *A Subtlety, or the Marvelous Sugar Baby, an Homage to the unpaid and overworked Artisans who have refined our Sweet tastes from the cane fields to the Kitchens of the New World on the Occasion of the demolition of the Domino Sugar Refining Plant*, 2014

Tomorrow's Temples

After years of congressional bills, presidential commissions, and bureaucratic false starts, at the end of 2003 the 108th Congress of the United States of America enacted legislation to establish in Washington, DC a new, free-standing museum of African American history and culture. In January 2006, an unoccupied site near the Washington Monument was selected as the museum's location and, three years later, a team— consisting of the Freelon Group of Durham, North Carolina, the London-based Adjaye Associates, New York City's Davis Brody Bond architecture firm, and the Detroit-based SmithGroup —was selected from twenty-two competing groups to design this museum.

Sir David Adjaye OBE RA, Principal of Adjaye Associates and the lead designer on this project, imagined a building that would "establish both a meaningful relationship to this unique site, as well as a strong conceptual resonance with America's deep and longstanding African heritage." By most critical standards, Adjaye's design for the National Museum of African American History and Culture (2016) succeeded in fulfilling these objectives, notably in the building's iconic, overall configuration: a three-tiered rectangle "crown" motif

213 Freelon/Adjaye/Bond/SmithGroup, National Museum of African American History and Culture, Smithsonian Institution, Washington, DC, 2016

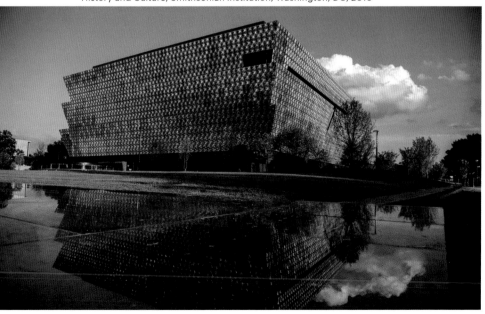

of inverted half-pyramids—inspired by works by the early twentieth-century Nigerian sculptor Olowe of Ise—matching the seventeen-degree angle of the Washington Monument's pointed capstone. The entire building was wrapped in 3,600 bronze-colored, cast-aluminum panels, filigreed in an abstract pattern based on the intricate ironwork created by black craftsmen in Charleston, South Carolina and New Orleans, Louisiana. An enormous roof over the museum's south entrance formed an expansive portico, extending the building out onto the National Mall and covering a shallow pool of water that cools bystanders during Washington's sweltering summers. These distinct design elements, along with 400,000-square feet of exhibition spaces, public areas, and the accompanying educational programs, immediately made the National Museum of African American History and Culture one of the most popular museums in the United States, on average attracting 2.4 million visitors annually.

A month prior to the opening of the museum, Bryan Stevenson, the director of the Equal Justice Initiative (a non-profit in Montgomery, Alabama, that provides legal aid to wrongly convicted and poorly represented prisoners), announced plans to build a memorial to the thousands of victims of racial lynchings in the US. The idea for the national memorial—the first of its kind to honor the casualties of extra-judicial killings—arose in 2010 when the Equal Justice Initiative (EJI) began a comprehensive investigation into this seventy-years plus history of racial terrorism, much of which had never been documented.

Set on an elevated, six-acre site in a residential neighborhood in Montgomery, the National Memorial for Peace and Justice (2018), at first glance, recalled other well-known memorials wrestling with difficult histories of genocide, apartheid, and horrific human losses (Washington, DC's Vietnam Veterans Memorial, Johannesburg's Apartheid Museum, Berlin's Holocaust Memorial, and Kigali, Rwanda's Genocide Memorial). But unlike these projects, the National Memorial for Peace and Justice—conceived and designed by Stevenson and his colleagues in collaboration with the Boston-based, non-profit architectural firm MASS Design Group, Ltd.—was conceptually bound to very specific, regional histories. The hillside memorial—a square, International-style, canopy/temple structure with a large peristyle, adjacent to a compact, above ground cemetery—features over 800 weathering steel rectangle boxes each six feet in height, hanging from the structure's ceiling, one for every US county where lynchings took place, and each bearing victims' names—more than 4,000—and the dates

214

214 MASS Design Group, Ltd/Equal Justice Initiative, National Memorial for Peace and Justice, Montgomery, Alabama, 2018

of their deaths. Upon entering the memorial, visitors encounter the suspended steel boxes at eye level but soon, thereafter, the floor gradually descends into the structure's concrete base, creating the effect of the boxes slowly rising over visitor's heads, like hanging, lynched bodies. Visitors exit the structure toward an open air, morgue-like area. There, duplicates of the hanging boxes are horizontally arranged on the ground and in alphabetical order by state, aiding visitors who are seeking out specific locations and victims. Stevenson's concept for the memorial factored in the possibility that individual counties would claim these duplicate steel boxes and properly bury them, and that the municipalities that refused would be shamed by their presence on the grounds of the memorial.

Stevenson's vision—to honor the dead, reflect upon the present-day meaning of lynching and racial injustice, and educate the public about these suppressed facts of US history—required a memorial that, despite the painful subject matter, aimed to heal. Similarly, the Freelon/Adjaye/Bond/SmithGroup's design for the African American museum required architectural citations that would counter the orthodox and hierarchical aspects of Washington, DC's federal core. Both structures—coming into existence at an uncertain, anxiety-filled moment for many African Americans and other marginalized US communities—enacted spatial rejoinders to historic discrimination and endangerment. These sites were conceived as cultural termini that, rather than imitating neoclassical preserves, fashioned themselves as ethically inspired spaces. Reasserting the Harlem Renaissance poet Langston Hughes's 1926 proclamation, "we build our temples for tomorrow," the National Museum of African American History and Culture and the National Memorial for Peace and Justice did not realize their respective institutional callings with white marble columns but, instead, with Corten steel, burnished aluminum, and a combination modern/hand-crafted aesthetic charged with recounting unvarnished histories as a call for restoration and political action.

Remarkably, these two testaments to African American history came into being at the same time as the widespread despoliation and purging of dozens of public monuments commemorating the Civil War-era Confederate States of America, European colonialism, and Western civilization's subjugation and annihilation of black and brown indigenous peoples. Grassroots activists have long petitioned for the removal of these mostly pre-1950s symbols of America's and Europe's dishonorable past pertaining to peoples of color, but it was not until the second decade of the twenty-first century that local governments and organized protesters rejected bureaucratic procedures and took matters into their own hands, attacking and tearing down these embodiments of racism and imperialism. Although many of these iconoclastic outbreaks followed highly publicized, incendiary incidents of unlawful black deaths, the global economic downturn, racial pessimism, and a pervasive social malaise certainly fueled and helped ignite these far-reaching, retributive actions.

Afrofutures

Despite on-again, off-again efforts as early as the 1990s, in 2005 the Marvel Studios film production company announced that a forthcoming motion picture would be based on the Black Panther, the first superhero of African descent to appear in a mainstream American comic book series. Theatrically released in 2018, the film *Black Panther*, directed by Ryan Coogler, mixed comic-book action sequences, dramatic special effects, science fiction, and an African diasporal mise-en-scène to reap broad critical accolades and commercial success, earning over $1.3 billion worldwide and becoming the ninth-highest grossing film of all time.

Apart from its melodramatic storyline of royal succession, leadership rivalry, and global revolution, *Black Panther* spectacularly illustrated Afrofuturism: a ubiquitous concept that re-examined the lived realities of black people through science fiction, speculative interpretations, and theories of racial othering and social alienation. In a 2003 essay, the British-Ghanaian writer and filmmaker Kodwo Eshun contended that Afrofuturism was a "chronopolitical act" for many contemporary African artists, whose historically informed and theoretically plotted conceptions of blackness demonstrated "the possibilities for intervention within the dimension of the predictive, the projected, the proleptic, the envisioned, the virtual, the anticipatory and the future conditional." As with Coogler's *Black Panther* and its allusions to real-life prejudices and Third World disparities, Afrofuturism used extraterrestriality as an analogy for Black Atlantic subjectivity—a condition that, especially through the popular novels of the science fiction writer Octavia E. Butler, was often associated with black women who have historically withstood and strategically seized the stigma of alienation to their advantage. This otherworldly view by the proponents of Afrofuturism—aspiring toward hybridity and a bionic identity or, at the very least, modeling the black self beyond a white, heterosexual, and male exemplar—seemed to be the underlying message in sculptor/performance artist Nick Cave's

215 contemporaneous *Soundsuits*: wearable fabric sculptures that,
with their improbable proportions and surface energies evoked
extraterrestrial African masks and space inhabitants.
  The aberrant yet striking figures that Cave's *Soundsuits*
conjured (comparable to the black superheroes and astronauts
that artists Belkis Ayón and Yinka Shonibare created at the
turn of the twenty-first century) aligned with Afrofuturism's
inclinations toward a nonconforming black aesthetic—a
criterion that, as the decade progressed, expanded and
morphed into a disembodied, semiotic blackness. An artist
who succinctly captured this reductive, cypher-like potential,
much of it emanating out of the tenets of Afrofuturism,
was Nina Chanel Abney. With their bright, saturated colors,
trapezoidal figural elements, and millennia-traversing
overtures to hieroglyphs and techno-symbols, paintings like
217 Abney's *Untitled* (2017) situated their narratives of social rupture
and racial impasse in a meta-language legible to admirers of
hard-edge abstraction as well as technophiles conversant in
computer-generated imagery.
  Unabashedly embracing the illusory nature of a black
Atlantic imaginary (and, relatedly, Afrofuturism's basis in
speculation and theory), beginning in 2011 artist Kapwani
216 Kiwanga launched *AFROGALACTICA* (2011–ongoing) which,

215 OPPOSITE Kapwani Kiwanga, *AFROGALACTICA: A brief history of the future*, 2015
216 ABOVE Nick Cave, *Soundsuits*, 2013

217 Nina Chanel Abney, *Untitled*, 2017

The Price of Blackness

218 Wangechi Mutu, *The Seated II*, from *The newOnes, will free Us*, 2019

via audio and video projections, public readings, and role-playing, analyzed and enacted the tenets of Afrofuturism. Taking on the role of an anthropologist from the future, Kiwanga used historical chronicles, mythology, pop culture, and scientific protocols to provide alternative histories of the African diaspora, to challenge and undermine hegemonic Western discourses and, ultimately, to envisage the future. By combining different genres and forms of knowledge related to Afrofuturism (including memorable quotes from the celebrated jazz musician Sun Ra, a mid-to-late twentieth-century promoter of space travel and interplanetary refuge for black people), Kiwanga put *AFROGALACTICA* in furtherance of this theory's adherence to simulation and prognostication.

If science fiction's emphasis on worlds-to-come fulfills its mission by concurrently scrutinizing the present alongside the past, as a parallel genre Afrofuturism bridged speculative narration with a black diasporal ethos, cognizant of its philosophical locus in ancient Africa, as well as its contemporary investitures and prerogatives. In another temporary installation—this one for the Corinthian column-accented facade of New York's Metropolitan Museum of Art—

artist Wangechi Mutu conjoined these various theoretical strains to create four bronze sculptures that, with nineteenth-century architect Richard Morris Hunt's building as a backdrop, realized what social scientist and cultural theorist Alondra Nelson described as Afrofuturism's quest to find artistic models that "transform spaces of alienation into novel forms of creative potential." The four sculptures, collectively titled *The newOnes, will free Us*, and individually subtitled *The Seated I, II, III,* and *IV* (2019), depicted their hieratic, stylized female subjects enveloped, from chin to toe, in serpentine coils, and each sporting on its head a highly polished bronze disk. Mutu's previous work in paintings, collages, assemblages, and video animation frequently included female figures that, rather than naturalistic, gave viewers the impressions of part-human/part-animal monstrosities and androids, not so expressly malevolent as unearthly and mystical, and similar to *The Seated* quartet. Complementary to the Met's exterior architecture, and yet refreshingly dissonant in their eccentricity and luminosity, Mutu's enthroned "newOnes"—amphibious, African, and astral—provided a visual and speculative antidote (to again paraphrase Nelson's description of Afrofuturism) to an "unbridled, raceless future-lust."

At different moments throughout a bright Manhattan day, several of the sculptures comprising *The newOnes, will free Us* capture the sun in their upraised bronze plates and, reflecting the radiance back, activate the Metropolitan Museum's austere, Beaux-Arts exterior. Wangechi Mutu's futuristic public works express the promise and ensuing light of these intelligent life-forms and their earthly counterparts, even in the context of the 2020 worldwide pandemic and its human costs. One can only speculate, after two decades of phenomenal achievements and social disasters, what the black cultural conditions will be for the rest of the twenty-first century, and whether the price of blackness—as the conceptual artist Keith Obadike first broached in 2001—holds its value, or reaps the consequences of gauges and frames of critical reference beyond its already expansive, cosmic breadth.

Biographical Notes

Associates and lead designer of the National Museum of African American History and Culture, Washington, DC. Other notable buildings are the Nobel Peace Centre in Oslo (2005), the Ruby City contemporary art center in San Antonio (2019), and the future new home for The Studio Museum in Harlem, New York. Adjaye's sculptural sensibilities and ingenious use of materials have established him as a visionary architect, whose buildings offer a rich civic experience.

Akomfrah, John (1957–)
British Ghanaian filmmaker. A founding member of the Black Audio Film Collective. Akomfrah's *Handsworth Songs* (1986) explored the events surrounding the 1985 riots in Birmingham and London through archival footage and still photos. Subsequent films, many utilizing multi-channel formats and rich color film stock, are characterized by their investigations of memory and post-colonialism, and often explore the experiences of migrants globally.

Compiled by Alexander X. Byrd and Richard J. Powell
These notes include those artists whose work is illustrated and discussed.
* = cross-reference
AFRI-COBRA = African Commune of Bad Relevant Artists, Chicago-based, founded 1969.
WPA/FAP = Works Progress Administration/ Federal Arts Project, USA 1935–43, state-funded artistic projects in the job creation scheme under the Roosevelt administration.

Amos, Emma (1938–2020)
African American painter. Most acclaimed work explores individual freedom and fear through the imaginative arrangement of human figures— often as falling or floating—on flat planes.

Anatsui, El (1944–)
Ghanaian sculptor active for much of his career in Nigeria. In 1975 began teaching at the University of Nigeria, Nsukka, where he was affiliated with a circle known for incorporating traditional African symbols in their work. El Anatsui gained recognition for his monumental wall hangings, composed of countless, shimmering liquor bottle caps. A cross between tapestry and sculpture, these hangings draw connections between consumption, colonialism, waste, and the environment, but are also deeply engaged with a unique formal language.

Abney, Nina Chanel (1982–)
African American painter. At the forefront of a generation revitalizing narrative art. Informed by cartoons, video games, Twitter feeds, and text messaging, Abney's early works explored interracial violence and biases, and were prophetic about escalating deaths of African Americans in the new millennium. Her paintings are commentaries on inequality as well as contemporary genre scenes punctuated by bold colors and an original figurative shorthand.

Attille, Martina (1959–)
St. Lucia-born filmmaker. Co-founder of the London-based film and video collective Sankofa, and director or producer for several of its influential features. As evinced in her work on *The Passion of Remembrance* (1986), and *Dreaming Rivers* (1988), especially concerned with the cultural politics of contemporary Britain—their historical roots and contemporary manifestations.

Adams, John Henry Jr. (c. 1880, fl. 1910s)
African American graphic artist and arts educator. Based in Atlanta, and a contributor to *Voice of the Negro* and *The Crisis*.

Adede, Sosa (fl. late 19th C)
Dahomey sculptor also known as Sosa Adede Likohe. Called "Da Atinkpato" or Lord Woodcarver for the imposing royal figures he carved for Dahomey kings Guezo and Glele.

Adjaye, David (1966–)
British Ghanaian architect. Principal at Adjaye

Ayón, Belkis (1967–1999)
Cuban artist whose enigmatic, spiritually

infused, multi-paneled prints raised the profile not only of Afro-Caribbean religious traditions internationally, but also of late twentieth-century Cuban art and culture in general.

Barboza, Anthony (1944–)
African American photographer. In the 1960s, active in New York's pace-setting Kamoinge Workshop of black photographers. Since the mid-1970s has worked in fashion, documentary, and editorial photography. Produced a highly acclaimed portrait series on black musicians, literati, and visual artists.

Barnes, Ernie (1939–2009)
African American painter and former professional football player. In the 1970s, and with some commercial success, depicted black social life and recreation.

Barthé, Richmond (1901–1989)
African American artist. Began his career as a painter, but mature work and present reputation stem from his remarkable talent as a sculptor—especially his long, lithe figures of black workers, dancers, and Broadway notables.

Basquiat, Jean-Michel (1960–1988)
American painter of Haitian and Puerto Rican parentage. In the 1980s achieved meteoric fame in the US and Europe for his crayon-and-paint drawings, graffiti art, and assemblages. In 1984–85 he collaborated with *Andy Warhol on a series of paintings.

Bearden, Romare (1911–1988)
African American painter and collagist. His work, rich in historical references, employs dazzling technique. He was an outspoken advocate for African American arts and artists.

Bey, Dawoud (1953–)
African American photographer. His patient, immensely contemplative portraits survey the attitudes and aspirations of black urbanites.

Biggers, John (1924–2001)
African American painter, sculptor, and muralist. Celebrated for the potent realism and painterly rhythm evident in his depiction of West African and African American life. Founded and chaired the art department at Texas Southern University.

Billops, Camille (1933–2019)
African American sculptor, painter, and filmmaker. Thought-provoking satires of contemporary racial imagery prevail in all three of her chosen media. Frequently collaborated with her husband James Hatch.

Boghossian, Alexander "Skunder" (1937–2003)
Recognized together with Gebre Kristos Desta as one of the main progenitors of contemporary Ethiopian art. His paintings and assemblages reflect a deep and strong basis in the ancient culture and symbolism of his homeland.

Booker, Chakaia (1953–)
African American sculptor. Proponent of a latter-day school of abstraction, this artist invests found materials, such as discarded automobile tires and machine parts with a dynamic, culturally suggestive character in her sculptural assemblages.

Bowling, Frank (1934–)
Guyanese painter working in London and New York since the late 1950s. Experimented with Pop Art subjects and techniques in 1960s, but moved on to thickly encrusted abstracts executed through various paint-pouring techniques.

Boyce, Sonia (1962–)
Black British painter and installation artist of Barbadian and Guyanese parentage. Issues relating to domesticity, sexual abuse, and the myriad cultural complexities of contemporary Britain permeate her work.

Bradford, Mark (1961–)
African American painter. Bradford transforms materials from the streets—billboard posters, advertisements, and commercial packaging—into wall-size collages that respond to the impromptu networks within cities. Bradford's videos and paintings refer not only to urban planning, but also to aerial images of crowds, from 1960s demonstrations to 2010s protests concerning immigration. His installation at the 2017 Venice Biennale turned the US pavilion into a post-Palladian gallery examining both painterly abstraction and social inequities.

Broodhagen, Karl (1909–2002)
Guyana-born sculptor, raised and working in Barbados. Recognized for finely executed busts of Barbadian notables and plain folk, as well as for trailblazing work as a Caribbean-wide arts educator.

Brown, Everald (1917–2003)
Jamaican carpenter, sculptor, and self-taught painter. Considered one of the Caribbean's outstanding folk artists. Work inspired by religious visions and often incorporates the iconography of Rastafarianism and the Ethiopian Orthodox Church.

Brown, Iona Rozeal (1966–)
African American painter. Best known for her use of traditional ukiyo-e design principles to meld Japanese folklore, geisha, *kabuki*, and *ganguro* fashions (the latter, an affected mode in young Japanese women's cosmetics and hairstyles) with hip hop themes and African American cultural references. Brown's work as a DJ also informs her art.

Buchanan, Beverly (1940–2015)
African American painter and sculptor. Her representations of Southern living space—paintings, drawings, assemblages, and full-sized installations—explored black rural life, past and present.

Burra, Edward (1905–1976)
White British painter, stage designer and draughtsman. Significant here for watercolors of Marseilles and Harlem street life, executed in the late 1920s and early 1930s respectively.

Butcher, Ras Ishi (1960–)
Barbadian painter. Informed by a Pan-Caribbean iconography and cultural impetus, his canvases are brightly colored contributions to the region's long-thriving and traditionally frank discourse on island history, culture, and politics.

Camus, Marcel (1912–1982)
French filmmaker. From the late 1950s to the late 1970s directed a series of haunting, exotic, location-films of which *Orfeu Negro* (*Black Orpheus*) of 1959 was the most celebrated, and remains the best known.

Catlett, Elizabeth (1915–2012)
African American sculptor whose work dealt masterfully with the struggles and triumphs of people of color throughout the hemisphere. Based in Mexico from the late 1940s, she remained, nonetheless, a celebrated interpreter of black life on both sides of the border.

Cave, Nick (1959–)
African American fabric sculptor, dancer, and performance artist. Prior to his art career, Cave created department store displays, worked as a fashion designer, and studied dance with the Alvin Ailey American Dance Theater. Cave is well known for his *Soundsuits*, sculptural forms layered in metal, plastic, fiber, and objects, and designed to resonate with the movement of the wearer, usually Cave himself.

Chandler, Dana C. Jr. (1941–)
African American painter and muralist, with a prominent place and vocal presence in the black arts movement of the late 1960s and early 1970s. Work explores themes of racial exploitation, uplift, and comparative race relations in the United States and South Africa. As an instructor at Northeastern University, was also a principal in the artist-in-residence movement during the 1970s.

Chase-Riboud, Barbara (1939–)
African American writer and sculptor. In the 1960s and 1970s, her enigmatic abstract sculpture—primarily in bronze—ensconced her among the leading lights of contemporary art. In 1979, her fictionalized account of Thomas Jefferson's affair with his slave, *Sally Hemings*, was a cause célèbre.

Chong, Albert (1958–)
Jamaican photographer. Acclaimed for prints capturing the complexes of identity in multi-ethnic Jamaica, and honoring the contours and consequences of African American spirituality and ritual—especially Rastafarianism, *Obeah*, *Santería*, and *Candomble*.

Clark, Edward (1926–2019)
African American painter. Expatriate in Paris from 1951–56, and during late 1960s. An eclectic abstractionist, he experimented with and mastered a range of non-representational techniques during his career—gestural and hard-edge abstraction, and color-field painting among them.

Coe, Sue (1951–)
White British political activist, illustrator, and painter working in New York. Since the mid-1970s, her protest art has caricatured and critiqued social antagonists from racial terrorists to the meat industry.

Colescott, Robert (1925–2009)
African American painter and arts educator. Distinguished since the late 1970s for dense, brightly colored montages reconnoitering the

social maze of race and sexuality in American life—especially the contemporary and historical exigencies of interracial sex.

Colin, Paul (1892–1985)
French graphic artist, set designer, and lithographer, famous in the 1920s and 1930s for his poster and theater designs. Image maker to Josephine Baker and to the equivalent of the "New Negro" ideal of 1920s Paris.

Conwill, Houston (1947–2016)
African American conceptual and installation artist, whose work focuses on transformations, marrying symbolism with a subtle irony. In some 1990s projects he collaborated with architect Joseph de Pace and writer Estella Conwill Majozo.

Cortor, Eldzier (1916–2015)
African American painter and printmaker. Gained national attention in the mid-1940s for his statuesque black nudes, some published in *Life* magazine. His work dealt prominently with representations of black femininity and beauty.

Covarrubias, Miguel (1904–1957)
Mexican draughtsman, painter, and stage designer. Working in New York in the 1920s and 1930s, he committed himself, for a time, to illustrating various "Negro types." Later deeply involved in anthropology and archaeology, and co-founder of Mexico's Ballet Bellas Artes.

Cowans, Adger (1936–)
African American photographer. Pioneer in the movement of American photography from craft to fine art. In the 1960s, he documented the civil rights movement—capturing critical moments in the history of the Student Non-Violent Coordinating Committee (SNCC) and the Congress of Racial Equality (CORE). A member of AFRI-COBRA.

Cox, Renée (1960–)
Jamaican-born, New York-based photographer. Best known—and, in some critical circles, considered notorious—for her at times sexually charged, often humorous *tableau/vivant* satires of racism and sexism.

Crichlow, Ernest (1914–2005)
African American painter and arts educator. In the late 1930s was among the cadre of black artists nurtured under Harlem's first WPA/FAP arts projects. Achieved commercial success as an illustrator of children's books and exhibited extensively. Co-founder—with *Romare Bearden and Norman Lewis—of New York's Cinque Gallery.

Cruz, Emilio (1938–2004)
African American artist. Recognized for his use of vibrant colors, symbolism, and highly stylized human figures. He shared a studio with *Bob Thompson in the late 1950s, and exhibited in New York, Dakar, and Chicago in the 1960s.

Dash, Julie (1952–)
African American, independent filmmaker. Acclaimed for her literate, non-linear, historical dramas such as *Illusions* (1982) and *Daughters of the Dust* (1991).

Davis, Stuart (1892–1964)
White American painter and art theorist. Until the 1950s, his studied, bold Cubism distinguished him as America's pre-eminent Modernist. In the 1910s, he composed a series of saloon and dance hall portraits of blacks—some featured in the radical periodical *The Masses*.

Dawson, Charles C. (1889–1982)
African American painter and illustrator. In the 1920s and 1930s he worked in product advertising, and illustrated publications on race—among them his 1933 *ABC of Great Negroes*. Also served as curator of the Tuskegee Institute Museum.

Debela, Achamyeleh (1947–)
Ethiopian media artist, noted for his cutting-edge recourse to arts technology, and as a curator for his efforts to maintain an Ethiopian presence in American and black diasporal arts.

Delaney, Beauford (1901–1979)
African American painter. His search for a satisfying, individual aesthetic led him to experiment in the early 1940s with non-representational abstract forms. He studied and worked in Harlem during the Depression, and from the 1950s as an expatriate in Paris. Closely associated in New York and Paris with the eminent African American writer James Baldwin.

Demme, Jonathan (1944–2017)
White American film director. In addition to *Beloved* (1998), this Academy Award-winning director's most notable film credits include *Melvin and Howard* (1980), *Stop Making Sense* (1984), *The Silence of the Lambs* (1991), and *Philadelphia* (1993).

DePillars, Murry N. (1938–2008)
African American painter, educator, and arts
administrator. Renowned for using the canvas
to explode stereotypical images of black
culture; heralded as an educator for his efforts
to integrate black artists into the modern
canon. Member of AFRI-COBRA, and, with *Jeff
Donaldson, shepherded the black arts movement
in Chicago in the 1960s and 1970s.

de Rooy, Felix (1952–)
Curaçao-born artist and filmmaker. From the
mid-1980s, his Comic Illusion Productions
delivered a number of astute historical dramas—
among them, *Almacita di Desolato* (1986), and
Ava & Gabriel (1990).

Dial, Thornton (1928–2016)
African American painter. Born into rural poverty,
Dial spent much of his life doing construction
work, while making junk assemblages that
he came to think of as art only years later. His
assemblages and paintings told the story of black
struggle in the American South, melding history,
racism, and politics. Dial was one of a few self-
taught artists who, since the 1980s, began making
art beyond the mainstream art world, but would
eventually gain cultural acclaim within it.

DJ Spooky, a.k.a. Paul D. Miller (1972–)
African American musician, conceptual artist,
and writer who uses a variety of digitally created
sounds as key elements in his work. Based in
New York City, he is widely acknowledged for
his insightful cultural criticism as well as for his
innovative art.

Donaldson, Jeff (1932–2004)
African American printmaker, painter, and
educator. Intent on the recovery and exhibition
of a distinctly black aesthetic linking and
encompassing visual traditions from Ancient
Egypt to the contemporary art of Africa and its
diaspora. Co-founder, with Wadsworth Jarrell,
of AFRI-COBRA.

Douglas, Aaron (1899–1979)
African American painter, muralist, and
illustrator. Prominent in the 1920s and 1930s,
his drawing style featured highly stylized
silhouettes, earthy, soft colors, and sharp angles.
His subject matter ranged from moments in
African American history to contemporary
motifs of jazz culture. Reached large audiences
because his illustrations were featured in

The Crisis—the organ of the NAACP—and in
several quintessential "New Negro" publications,
including James Weldon Johnson's *God's
Trombones: Seven Negro Sermons in Verse.*

Douglas Camp, Sokari (1958–)
Nigerian-born sculptor trained in California and
London. Her kinetic assemblages of wood, steel,
and cloth engage and re-present the cultural
practices of the Niger Delta.

Drummond, Arthur (1871–1951)
White British genre and figure painter. Exhibited
at the Royal Academy and other London galleries
from the 1890s.

Dunkley, John (c. 1891–1947)
Jamaican barber and self-taught painter. Work
depicted the Jamaican landscape and natural
environment. Exhibited in Jamaica, England,
and Canada in the 1930s and 1940s.

Duval-Carrié, Edouard (1954–)
Haitian painter, based in south Florida. Takes
as his subject the culture and history of his
birthplace—often concentrating on *Vodun*,
and the absurdity and tragedy of Haitian politics.

Edmondson, William (1874–1951)
African American sculptor. The first black artist
to have a one-man exhibition at the Museum of
Modern Art in New York. He had no formal art
training, worked only in limestone using a few
basic tools, and sculpted mainly religious and
Biblical figures—the crucifixion, angels, and
preachers among them.

Edwards, Melvin (1937–)
African American sculptor. His studio pieces and
large-scale public works in metal and stainless
steel are often executed and deployed to evoke
significant themes and episodes in African
American cultural politics, such as his celebrated
series *Lynch Fragments.*

Egonu, Uzo (1931– 1996)
Nigerian-born printmaker and painter residing
in London from the late 1940s. His work—always
showing a strong sense of design and often
flirting with abstraction—drew on African
religious themes, Igbo oral traditions, and motifs
from contemporary Nigerian life.

Elie-Dit-Cosaque, Gilles (1968–)
French filmmaker of Martiniquan ancestry.

Began as an art director for a French advertising agency. Since 1993 Elie-Dit-Cosaque has been a freelance art and film director, in 2003 forming his own production company. His films and videos—often set in the French West Indies—play with fact and fiction, obfuscating confession in favor of more open-ended narratives and inviting audiences to construct their own meaning.

Evans, Minnie (1892–1987)
Self-trained African American painter. Began sketching her religious visions in the mid-1930s, but did not show her work publicly until 1961. Acclaimed as a folk artist.

Evans, Walker (1903–1975)
White American documentary photographer. His Depression-era depiction of the American South—its people, its architecture, and its social convulsions—have earned him a place among the great photographers of the twentieth century. Collaborated with James Agee on *Let Us Now Praise Famous Men* (1939).

Fleming, Sherman (1953–)
African American visual and performance artist. From 1976 to 1988 his performances provocatively concentrated on issues relating to black masculinity, eroticism, and representations of them in society at large. Subsequently—often in collaboration with art historian Kristine Stiles—has focused his attention on issues of race and gender.

Fuller, Meta Warrick (1877–1968)
African American sculptor. Best known for work during the first and second decades of the century prefiguring themes amid styles of "New Negro" arts movement. Working predominantly in bronze and plaster, she explored the African heritage of black art, and condemned—through faithful depiction—the political and social tragedies of contemporary African American life.

Gerima, Haile (1946–)
Award winning Ethiopian filmmaker. Renowned for his cinematic critiques of "modernization" and the resulting class relations in contemporary Africa in films such as *Harvest, 3000 Years* (1974), *Bush Mama* (1975), and *Ashes and Embers* (1982).

Gilliam, Sam (1933–)
African American painter who came to prominence in late 1960s with stained, unsupported canvases draped or suspended from walls and ceiling. Since the late 1970s celebrated for his jazz-influenced collage and thickly painted canvases reminiscent of patchwork quilts.

Goude, Jean-Paul (1940–)
Commercial artist of French and Irish American parentage. Celebrated for his advertising campaigns, for Chanel fragrances Egoïste and Coco. Decried for his fascination with racial typing (apparent in his image-making for pop singer Grace Jones and model Toukie Smith).

Greaves, Stanley (1934–)
Guyana-born painter working and living in Barbados. Work interrogates political and social machinations in the post-colonial Caribbean. Founder of the Department of Creative Arts at the University of Guyana.

Griffith, D.W. (David Wark) (1875–1948)
White American screenwriter and director. A pioneer in the technical and dramatic development of US film. Revered and reviled for his epic, *The Birth of a Nation* (1915).

Griffith, Francis (1916–2001)
Barbadian painter. In the 1960s his portrayals of the African landscape informed and reflected a revived black nationalist impulse in Caribbean and American arts.

Gunn, Bill (1934–1989)
African American director and screenwriter, born William Harrison Gunn. Best known for his direction of the award-winning *Ganja & Hess* (1973). Wrote the screenplay for *The Landlord* (1970) and *The Greatest: The Muhammad Ali Story* (1977).

Gwathmey, Robert (1903–1988)
White American painter and arts educator. From the late 1930s through the early 1970s—against the grain of Abstract Expressionism—the racial politics of the American South remained his prime subject matter.

Hammons, David (1943–)
Avant-garde African American artist. His body prints, installations, and assemblages explore the problematic relationship between the stark material reality of contemporary black life, and the consumerism and political mythology of American society at large.

Hampton, James (1909–1964)
African American millenarian. Gained

posthumous recognition as a folk artist for the sprawling testament to his religious faith that he constructed and installed in a rented Washington, DC garage: *Throne of the Third Heaven of the Nations Millennium General Assembly.*

Haring, Keith (1958–1990)
White American artist whose graffiti-like drawings and commercial inroads into the market-driven art world made him one of the art celebrities of the 1980s.

Harleston, Edwin A. (1882–1931)
African American painter characterized as a Romantic Realist for his portraits, executed during the first third of the twentieth century, of African American rural folk and élite.

Harrington, Ollie (1912–1995)
African American journalist and political cartoonist. From the 1930s best known for his satirical anti-racist panels—*Dark Laughter* and *Jive Gray* among them. Branded a subversive, in 1951 he left the US for Europe, where he continued his searing critiques of American race-relations.

Harris, Lyle Ashton (1965–)
African American photographer. His self-portraits interrogate the social processes of gender construction, and confront stereotyped, heterosexual notions of black masculinity.

Hathaway, Isaac Scott (1872–1967)
African American sculptor, ceramist, and arts educator. At mid-century, referred to among race men and women as "the dean of Negro ceramists," for having executed busts and death masks of numerous African American notables, and for introducing ceramics education to several black colleges.

Hayden, Palmer C. (1890–1973)
African American painter renowned for work incorporating black folk hero John Henry, as well as for bright, action-packed scenes of African American life in the 1920s and 1930s (though also notorious for those that verged on stereotypes). In 1926, Hayden won the first Harmon Foundation prize for black achievement in fine arts.

Hendricks, Barkley L. (1945–2017)
African American painter. The self-assured, naturally rendered black men and women of his portraits reflected and informed the black consciousness movement of the 1970s.

Humphrey, Margo (1942–)
African American printmaker. She brings a refreshing irreverence to issues of race and class in American life—subjects often considered from an over-somber distance. Her arrangement of incongruous combinations of symbols and signs gives her work a disarming surrealism.

Hunt, Richard (1935–)
African American sculptor. His abstract and surrealist manipulations of welded metal, steel, aluminium, copper, and bronze have made him a leading US artist. Since the 1960s regularly awarded commissions for large public outdoor sculptures in the US.

Hyppolite, Hector (1894–1948)
House painter, *Vodun* priest, and internationally acclaimed, self-taught Haitian painter. In the late 1940s his interpretations of the *Vodun* pantheon intrigued Surrealist artists and theorists.

Jaar, Alfredo (1956–)
Chilean-born photographer. His installations—often photographs accompanied with light-boxes, mirrors, and transparencies—document and explore the exploitative links between the developed and developing worlds.

Jackson, Harlan (1918–1993)
African American painter. Following a trip to Haiti in the late 1940s (with *Eldzier Cortor), he developed a semi-abstract approach to art that continued into the late 1960s.

Jackson Jarvis, Martha (1952–)
African American ceramic sculptor and installation artist. Her abstract, ceramic accretions emote a concern with familial traditions—especially processes and rituals of cultural regeneration.

Jafa, Arthur (1960–)
African American filmmaker and mixed media artist. Cinematographer on films for *Julie Dash, *Spike Lee, and Stanley Kubrick, Jafa's own films shift from dazzlingly edited montages featuring iconic bodies and ambient imagery to profound, narrative-driven documentaries exploring black culture. He has also collaborated with Beyoncé, Solange, and Jay-Z, creating videos

that represent peoples of African descent in all of their visual and aural complexities.

Janniot, Alfred (1889–1969)
French sculptor. Commissions that he completed in the 1930s reflected the primitivist fascination with things African then coursing through European and American arts.

Jarrell, Jae (1935–)
African American textile artist and fashion designer. Works primarily in leather and suede, with hand-painted appliqué and silk screens. From the 1970s—first in Atlanta and now in New York—has designed for men, women, and children. Member of AFRI-COBRA.

Johnson, Rashid (1977–)
African American mixed-media artist. Explores themes of history and literature, frequently referencing African American intellectual history and cultural identity. Johnson has incorporated elements as diverse as CB radios, shea butter, books, record covers, black soap, and tropical plants in his work. Although his practice had its beginnings in photography, Johnson is equally interested in abstract visual languages to communicate across cultural boundaries.

Johnson, Sargent (1887–1967)
African American sculptor, ceramist, and printmaker especially active in the 1920s and 1930s. Working in wood and clay, he sculpted stylized African American figures of great dignity.

Johnson, William H. (1901–1970)
African American artist now considered one of the most important of his generation. He lived and worked in the US, Europe, and North Africa, and the subject matter and style of his paintings were as wide-ranging as his wanderings. He is best known for a series of brightly colored, narrative panels and portraits executed from the late 1930s to the mid-1940s depicting historical images as well as scenes from everyday African American life.

Jones, Ben (1942–)
African American mixed-media artist and printmaker. Combines African and Afro-American cultural symbolism—from Cuba and Brazil especially—with American political iconography, from the civil rights and gay rights movements in particular, to present black men as positive subject matter.

Jones, Lois Mailou (1905–1998)
African American painter who worked extensively in the French-speaking world, especially in France, Haiti, and Senegal. Known for her Cubist incorporation of African imagery. Recognized as a teacher for her prodigious influence on a generation of African American artists.

Jones, Philip Mallory (1947–)
African American video artist. Work attempts to capture the physicality and aesthetic of African, and diasporal, performance. Among his projects are *Soldiers of a Recent and Forgotten War* (1981), *Ghosts and Demons* (1987), *Footprints* (1988), and *First World Order* (1994).

Joseph, Tam (1947–)
Dominican-born painter of Nigerian descent, based first in London, later in France. Appreciated for his eclectic subject matter, and understated treatment of race and nation, and known for his use of acrylic paints on sand.

Julien, Isaac (1960–)
Black British critic and filmmaker. His productions—*Looking for Langston* (1989) and *Young Soul Rebels* (1991) among them—address issues concerning race, nation, and sexuality. A co-founder of the London-based film and video collective Sankofa.

Kim, Byron (1961–)
Asian American painter. Explores contemporary representations of race and the body through thought-provoking use of color and text. His paintings, though often non-figurative, inveigh against monolithic, homogenizing notions of race and ethnicity.

Kirchner, Ernst Ludwig (1880–1938)
German painter. A co-founder of the Dresden Expressionist artists' group Die Brücke (The Bridge) in 1905. His art was suppressed as "degenerate" by the Nazis in 1937.

Kiwanga, Kapwani (1978–)
French Canadian mixed-media artist of Tanzanian ancestry. Informed by a background in anthropology and social sciences, Kiwanga embraces a subjective reading of history and its corresponding archives, exploring ideas around spirituality, mythology, colonialism, and the economics of material production. These interests are articulated across a range of media,

including installation, photography, video, and performance.

Lam, Wifredo (1902–1982)
Cuban painter. Work was influenced by Picasso and Surrealism, and often based on African sculpture. Following his return to Cuba and his travels throughout the Caribbean, also strongly influenced by such Africa-derived religions as *Santería* and *Vodun*.

Lawrence, Jacob (1917–2000)
Prolific African American painter with a singular talent for depicting the high drama of black life and history. He began exhibiting in the 1930s, and is arguably the most popular black artist of the century.

Lawson, Deana (1979–)
African American photographer. Challenges conventional representations of black identities. Drawing on family albums, studio portraiture, staged *tableaux*, and documentary pictures, Lawson explores black culture as seen through the body's ability to channel personal narratives and spirituality. Lawson's works are made in collaboration with her subjects, who both embrace and confront the camera, destabilizing the idea of photography as a passive, voyeuristic medium.

Lee, Spike (1957–)
African American filmmaker and producer, born Shelton Jackson Lee. Notable since the mid-1980s for films depicting the dilemma of American race-relations, and the intra-group tensions of black culture—especially issues turning on class, color, and gender. Best known for *She's Gotta Have It* (1986), *School Daze* (1988), *Do the Right Thing* (1989), and *Malcolm X* (1992).

Leigh, Simone (1967–)
African American sculptor of Jamaican ancestry. Creates objects that celebrate blackness and reframe stereotypes associated with black women. Grounded in materiality, Leigh's sculptures utilize iconographies (such as cowrie shells and cornrowed hairstyling) that reference culture throughout the African diaspora and are imbued with symbolic meaning.

Levinthal, David (1949–)
White American photographer, especially recognized for his theatrical, psychologically complex still lifes of miniature toy soldiers, vintage American bric-a-brac, and racist memorabilia.

Lewis, Norman (1909–1979)
African American painter of Caribbean parentage who began in the 1930s as a Social Realist painter of black urban life. Following World War II, he embraced Abstract Expressionism. Yet, his non-representational paintings remained based in natural and urban milieux and were never wholly given over to emotion and technique.

Lichfield, Patrick (1939–2005)
White British fashion and portrait photographer. Best known for his portraits of the British royal family.

Ligon, Glenn (1960–)
African American painter. Seeks through his work to transform specific cultural experiences and current events into wider explorations of race and identity. He is especially concerned with the power of language to define, dictate, and marginalize.

Liking, Werewere (1950–)
Cameroon-born playwright, theater director, performance artist, and novelist. Prominent in France and French-speaking Africa for dramatic, highly symbolic plays often based in Bassa initiation and healing rituals—among them *La Queue du diable* (*The Devil's Tail*) 1979, and *La Rougeole arc-en-ciel* (*The Rainbow Measles*) 1987. In 1984, she founded the Ki-Yi Mbock Théâtre, a theatrical troupe and artists' collective.

Lois, George (1931–)
White American graphic designer. In the early 1960s he was one of the first designers to move successfully from art direction into the business side of advertising. Trailblazing in his use of celebrities and star athletes in commercial advertising.

Loving, Al (1935–2005)
African American, self described "material abstractionist." His collages—constructed from oils, fabrics, dyes, and paper—explore the ranges and possibilities of color.

McGruder, Aaron (1974–)
African American cartoonist. His controversial comic strip *The Boondocks*, which features a mostly African American cast of offbeat, discontented youth, has enjoyed phenomenal popularity since first nationally syndicated in 1999.

Manley, Edna (1900–1987)

English-born sculptor of wood and stone, living and working in Jamaica from the early 1920s. Her busts of Jamaican notables, and Cubist renderings of the island's populace were exhibited in London from the late 1930s. Her efforts in arts education led to the founding of the Jamaica School of Art.

Mapplethorpe, Robert (1946–1989)

White American photographer. His work dealt predominantly with issues of sexuality and race. His subjects were human figures, flowers, and portraits of personalities from the gay social scene of the 1980s.

Marshall, Kerry James (1955–)

African American figure painter, prominent since the early 1980s for representational paintings rich in metaphor and symbol, yet feigning simplicity. His work complicates the received wisdom concerning the ideas of beauty, and deconstructs unyielding American categories of racial and cultural identity.

MASS Design Group, Ltd. (est. 2008)

American and Rwandan architectural firm. Founded by students at the Harvard Graduate School of Design, MASS Design Group collaborates with local communities to advocate for architecture that promotes justice, healing, and human dignity. The firm, whose name is derived from the motto "A Model of Architecture Serving Society," is best known for the National Memorial for Peace and Justice in Montgomery, Alabama, which has been called "the single greatest work of American architecture of the 21st century."

Maurice, Richard D. (1893–1955)

Trailblazing Afro-Cuban filmmaker. Between 1920 and 1928, his Detroit-based Maurice Film Corporation produced a number of serious-minded, didactic black dramas—among them *Our Christianity a.k.a. Nobody's Children* (1920) and *Eleven p.m.* (1928).

Mehretu, Julie (1970–)

Ethiopian American painter. Conceived in diagrammatic and architectonic terms, Mehretu's paintings present fictional topographies realized through collaged imagery and a formal vocabulary of line, color, markings, and grids, all stratified and overlaid onto the canvas's surface. Her works engage both "the psychogeography of space" and non-objective art, and pose questions about the relationship between utopian impulses and abstraction.

Mills, Lev (1940–)

African American graphic artist and printmaker, whose work contemplates contemporary notions of racial identity and manhood, while exploiting and reflecting the ever-growing technology available to present-day artists.

Miner, Leigh Richmond (1864–1935)

White American educator and photographer. Taken in the 1910s and 1920s, his sympathetic but unsentimental portraits of blacks at St. Helena Island, South Carolina, and Hampton, Virginia, offer a corrective to the prevailing photographic record of rural blacks from the period.

Minnelli, Vincente (1903–1986)

White American stage and film director. Highly regarded for film and Broadway musicals, and winner of several Academy awards in the 1950s. Directed black casts in *Cabin in the Sky* and *I Dood It* (1943).

Mr. Imagination, né Gregory Warmack (1948–2012)

Self-taught African American sculptor. Since the early 1970s, known locally in Chicago as a street artist, sign maker, and neighborhood art teacher. In the 1980s his work with found materials—industrial sandstone, nails, bottle caps, old paint brushes, etc.—earned him national acclaim as an intuitive artist.

Moore, Philip (1921–2012)

Guyanese painter and sculptor. Especially concerned with the artistic maintenance of a larger Afro-Caribbean memory.

Morgan, Sister Gertrude (1900–1980)

African American singer, preacher, and self-taught painter. In the 1970s, her brilliantly colored, religiously oriented work gained her recognition in New Orleans and later nationwide as a highly talented folk artist.

Morrison, Keith (1942–)

Jamaica-born painter working in San Francisco. His expansive and deeply colored canvases deploy and rework symbols from the folklore and mythology of Africa and Afro-America.

Motley Jr., Archibald J. (1891–1981)

African American painter. Highly acclaimed

during the 1920s and 1930s for sympathetic black portraiture, and for his vibrant, frenetic portrayals of black social life in the US and abroad.

Muholi, Zanele (1972–)
South African visual activist and photographer. Driven "to rewrite a black queer and trans visual history of South Africa for the world to know of our resistance and existence...." Following studies with photographer David Goldblatt, Muholi has singlehandedly constructed a visual archive of South Africa's lesbians, ays, bisexuals, and transgender and intersex persons: portraits that provide an outlet for self-representation, and that respond to continuing discrimination and violence.

Mutu, Wangechi (1972–)
Kenyan American mixed-media artist. Engages in a visual myth-making in which the combining of fact with fiction opens up the possibilities for symbolic female depictions markedly different from those in either art history or popular culture. Mutu's works propose worlds within worlds—populated by powerful hybridized female figures—in which ecology and an alternate course for black history are ever-present themes.

Ofili, Chris (1968–)
Black British painter of Nigerian descent. In the late 1990s garnered both top critical honors—the Turner Prize—and condemnation from many cultural conservatives for his provocative art, which combined lively, brilliantly painted surfaces with unconventional, arguably scatological, collaged elements.

O'Grady, Lorraine (1940–)
African American of Jamaican descent. Conceptual and performance artist, and cultural critic. Renowned in the early 1980s for staging art criticism as guerrilla performance in several New York galleries—*Mlle Bourgeoisie Noire*. Since the 1990s has concentrated on portraiture and photomontage—taking as her subject the exigencies of race, class, and gender in contemporary Afro America.

Overstreet, Joe (1934–2019)
African American painter who used huge canvases, bright and bold colors, and three-dimensional geometric shapes. In the 1970s his canvases were usually stretched by wood and rope, suggesting sculpture as well as painting.

Palcy, Euzhan (1957–)
Martiniquan filmmaker. Her first feature film, *Rue Cases-Nègres* (*Sugar Cane Alley*) in 1983—a moving, beautifully shot period drama of 1930s Martinique—opened to great acclaim in France. Her American début was *A Dry White Season* (1989).

Perry, Sondra (1986–)
African American media artist. Known for video installations, performances, and internet works that foreground the tools of digital production as a way to critically reflect on new technologies of representation and to remobilize their potential.

Pettit, H.M. (Harry McEwen) (1867–1941)
White American architectural painter and illustrator who enjoyed a long career from the 1890s to the 1930s.

Pierce, Elijah (1892–1984)
African American sculptor, carver, and painter of Biblical and slave scenes. At age seventy-nine gained widespread recognition as a folk artist.

Pindell, Howardena (1943–)
African American abstract artist. Her collaged paintings and mixed-media works offer engrossing explorations of her personal development and life travels—especially her visits to Asia and Africa.

Piper, Adrian (1948–)
African American performance and conceptual artist. Recognized since the 1960s for confronting audiences with the stark personal consequences of race and gender discrimination, and for exploring the complexities of modern notions of identity.

Piper, Keith (1960–)
Black British media artist. Since the early 1980s has used video, photocollage, and other technologies to analyze the social and political issues around contemporary images of black masculinity.

Piper, Rose (1917–2005)
African American painter. In the late 1940s began a series of folk paintings fusing the growing impulse toward abstraction with a studied, painterly improvisation reminiscent of African American rhythms.

Phokela, Johannes (1966–)
Black South African painter, based in London.

By consciously referencing and transforming the moralizing compositions of sixteenth- and seventeenth-century Netherlandish art, this postmodernist rejuvenates the old-fashioned pictorial allegory for twenty-first-century viewers.

Pope.L. (1955–)
African American performance artist. Works with an array of media to shatter preconceived notions about race, class, and gender. Pope.L is famous for his "crawls": street performances during which he drags his body along the ground, expressing the vulnerability of homelessness. Pope.L's performances, art historian Kristine Stiles has stated, "belong to the mental, social and political theater of the absurd."

Powers, Harriet (1837–1911)
African American homemaker and quilter. Her vibrant, narrative quilts—some exhibited in local southern fairs in the late nineteenth century—are indicative of a larger, though long unrecognized, domestic artistic tradition.

Puryear, Martin (1941–)
African American sculptor of large studio pieces, museum installations, and environmental pieces. Works primarily in wood and often from African-inspired designs. Always exhibits remarkable imagination and superior craftsmanship.

Rand, Archie (1949–)
White American painter. Often frames his work explicitly in relation to the outpourings and inspirations of other artists and intellectuals. His series *The Letter Paintings* incorporated and referred to the work of various jazz, blues, and doowop groups.

Reiss, Winold (1886–1953)
German painter and muralist, and graphic and interior designer. Lived and worked in New York during the 1920s and 1930s. Noted for his sensitive pastel renderings of American ethnics, especially blacks and Native Americans.

Renoir, Jean (1894–1979)
French-born filmmaker. Left France after the German invasion in 1941 and became a US citizen. Among his early films was the controversial fantasy *Sur un air de Charleston* (1927). From the late 1930s, developed a reputation for Social Realist filmmaking—especially for *Toni* (1935) and *The Southerner* (1945).

Riggs, Robert (1896–1970)
White American artist and illustrator. In the early 1930s, began a series of pugilism prints that earned him the reputation as the first artist of boxing. Also remembered for subsequent series of circus and hospital prints.

Ringgold, Faith (1930–)
African American painter, soft sculptor, and performance artist. Recognized from the 1960s for work exploring American feminism and race relations. Subsequently has gained significant popular appeal for her watercolors and quilting, which were used as subjects for illustrated children's books.

Rivers, Larry (1923–2002)
White American painter. Started as a jazz musician, and turned seriously to painting only in his mid-twenties. Recognized since the early 1950s for his ironic riffs on classic paintings and grand themes from art history, as well as for his artistic translations of everyday items.

Robinson, John (1912–1994)
African American painter. From the mid-1930s—while working full-time as a cook—his portraiture, landscapes, and church murals were well-known and sought after in the Anacostia and Garfield regions of Washington, DC. Concentrated on his art after his retirement from catering, and from the mid-1970s was acclaimed by a national audience for the warmth and intimacy of his work.

Rockwell, Norman (1894–1978)
White American painter and illustrator. From the late 1910s through the 1960s his covers for the *Saturday Evening Post* and other periodicals portrayed middle-class Americans in an uncritical light.

Rose, Tracey (1974–)
South African conceptual artist of Khosian and German ancestry. Fusing performance with photographic self-portraiture, this artist spans contemporary visual media in her probing interrogations of identity and history.

Saar, Alison (1956–)
African American sculptor and artist. Her installations tend toward a didactic mysticism, and draw simultaneously on contemporary urban motifs as well as

African and African American mythologies. Daughter of the renowned artist *Betye Saar.

Saar, Betye (1926–)
African American artist whose assemblages and collages—often composed of found and natural materials—reflect her interest in folk culture and mythology. She frequently employs stereotyped black imagery in order to subvert its traditional meaning.

Saunders, Raymond (1934–)
African American abstract artist. His brightly colored, textured paintings attempt to express through symbols and letters the fragmentary nature of memory and experience, and the grain of American urban life.

Savage, Augusta (1892–1962)
African American sculptor. Her wide-ranging work with Depression-era WPA arts projects, and her signal contributions to the organization of the Harlem Artists Guild place her among the most important African American art educators of the century.

Savain, Petion (1906–1973)
Haitian painter and writer. Grounded his fiction and visual art in the folklore, physical environment, and peasant life of Haiti—best exemplified in the text and illustrations of his 1939 novel *La Case de Damballah* (*Damballah's Hut*). One of the generation of Haitian painters encouraged by William Scott's artistic mission to the island in the early 1930s.

Scott, John T. (1940–2007)
African American sculptor and printmaker. Prominent in the 1980s for work addressing historical themes. Lately celebrated for kinetic sculptures of painted metal.

Scott, Joyce J. (1948–)
African American jewelry maker, quilter, sculptor, and performance artist. An accomplished artist in several scales—from brooches to environmental site installations—her work pays close attention to black cultural agency in contexts of pronounced racism.

Sekoto, Gerard (1913–1993)
Pioneering, black South African painter, expatriate in Paris from 1947. Oils and watercolors executed both before and following his emigration capture the soul and

travail of South African townships—especially Sophiatown, District Six, and Eastwood.

Sembène, Ousmane (1923–2007)
Award-winning Senegalese novelist and filmmaker. From the mid-1960s gained international fame for his trenchant yet often satirical cinematic critiques of African neocolonialism—among them, *La Noire de...* (*Black Girl*, 1966), *Mandabi* (*The Money Order*, 1968), and *Xala* (*Impotence*, 1974).

Shonibare, Yinka (1962–)
Black British artist of Nigerian descent. Critically acclaimed for his sculptural installations of upholstered furniture and fiberglass mannequins dressed in period costumes, made from Western-manufactured, so-called "African" printed cloth, and several large-scale photographic series that feature the artist in historical and literary parodies.

Simmons, Gary (1964–)
African American painter and installation artist, who is especially concerned with recording and subverting modern representations of black masculinity.

Simpson, Coreen (1942–)
African American photographer and jewelry designer. In the mid-1980s embarked on a documentary project dedicated to capturing contemporary urban street culture—most notably hip hop and transvestism.

Simpson, Lorna (1960–)
African American photographer and installation artist. Conceptually her portraits and phototexts address contemporary constructions of race and gender; technically, they challenge traditional methods of framing a subject.

Smith, Albert Alexander (1896–1940)
African American painter, printmaker, and musician. An expatriate in Paris from the early 1920s, he often made fellow black performers the subject of his work.

Snowden, Sylvia (1942–)
African American painter. A figurative expressionist whose works are bold, intensely colored, contorted, and, at times, violent.

Spriggs, Edward (1934–)
African American graphic artist and filmmaker.

An early director of the Studio Museum in Harlem, and then Head of Atlanta's Hammonds House Museum.

Stone III, Charles S. (1966–)

African American video and film director, whose mix of satire, narrative subtleties, and visual panache has garnered much commercial and critical praise, opening the way to assorted feature-length film projects.

Sulter, Maud (1960–2008)

Black British photographic and installation artist. Especially concerned with confronting the challenges and catastrophes of race in the modern history of the Western world.

Sy, Oumou (1952–)

Senegalese designer. Founder of an experimental fashion and jewelry design workshop in Dakar, Senegal, and the creator and frequent director of that city's Carnival: a dazzling spectacle of inventive fashions, impromptu performances, and street happenings.

Tanner, Henry Ossawa (1859–1937)

The most acclaimed African American painter of the late nineteenth century. He began as a painter of land and seascapes, but toward the turn of the century began executing religious subjects and detailed genre scenes of African American life, of which the *The Banjo Lesson* (1893) is perhaps the best known.

Télémaque, Hervé (1937–)

Haitian-born painter and collagist working in Paris since 1961. Painterly agility, a bright palette, and a thoughtful though often muted recourse to symbolism characterize the otherwise diverse developments in his subject matter and style.

Thomas, Alma (1891–1978)

African American painter and educator. Became a full-time artist only on retirement from secondary school teaching in 1960. In 1924, was the first student to graduate from the Howard University art department. An abstract artist, she used systemics and color theory in the creation of her paintings.

Thomas, Hank Willis (1976–)

African American photographer and mixed-media artist. Addresses issues of identity, politics, and commercialization as pertaining to mass-media pictures of African Americans. Thomas digitally manipulates familiar images from photographic archives, advertisements, etc., interrogating the underlying messages these representations transmit, and critiquing the distortions that lie behind much photography-based black imagery.

Thomas, Mickalene (1971–)

African American painter and mixed-media artist. Draws attention to stereotypes of African American women and the accouterments of glamour, while also hailing constructions of femininity as a source of power. Blurring the distinctions between object and subject, parody and sincerity, and real and imaginary, Thomas employs black women, art history, and popular culture to create heretofore unplumbed representations of beauty, joy, and agency.

Thompson, Bob (1937–1966)

Shortlived, but prolific African American painter, a figurative expressionist. In the 1960s his brilliantly colored reinterpretations of European masters—Goya and Titian among them—brought him contemporary recognition and, later, significant posthumous fame.

Tseng, Kwong Chi (1950–1990)

Hong Kong-born photographer working in New York from 1978. Best known for his series of globe-trotting, sometimes surreal self-portraits, *East Meets West.*

Ulmann, Doris (1882–1934)

White American photographer who worked in the pictorialist tradition of photography as did her teacher and mentor Clarence White. Her photographs of black Southerners from the Lang Syne Plantation in South Carolina accompanied Julia Peterkin's text in the sentimental, but now valuable period piece *Roll, Jordan, Roll* (1933).

VanDerZee, James (1886–1983)

African American commercial photographer, recognized many years later for his artistry. His portraits of Jazz-Age Harlem speak eloquently to the substance of black identity and aspiration in the 1920s and 1930s.

Van Peebles, Melvin (1932–)

Iconoclastic African American film director, and screenwriter. Critically acclaimed for *The Story of a Three Day Pass* (1968), but propelled into the public imagination for the independent making, marketing, and distribution of *Sweet Sweetback's Baadasssss Song* (1971).

Van Vechten, Carl (1880–1964)
White American critic, photographer, and novelist. Significant in the 1920s and 1930s—especially in New York—for his patronage and portraits of black artists.

Vári, Minnette (1968–)
White South African conceptual artist. Employing photography, computer technology, and occasionally mass-marketing techniques, this artist excavates the art of portraiture and, using her own image and personal history, dismantles postmodernism's most inviolable subjects: race and gender.

Walker, Kara (1969–)
African American graphic artist, painter, and installation artist who, from the 1990s was applauded, publicly vilified, and internationally recognized for her mural-size, meticulously conceived, black paper silhouette cut-outs of previously unimagined master/slave narratives.

Warhol, Andy (1928–1987)
White American artist and filmmaker, and a main exponent of American Pop Art. In 1984–85 collaborated with *Jean-Michel Basquiat.

Waring, Laura Wheeler (1887–1948)
African American painter. Noted for her still lifes, and for warmly colored, affectionate portraits of black notables—*Alma Thomas and W.E.B. Du Bois among them. She taught at and later headed the art department at Cheyney State Teachers College in Pennsylvania.

Watts, Ouattara (1957–)
Côte d'Ivoire painter working in Paris from 1977, and in New York since 1989. His work—shot through with symbols and iconography of West African initiation—interrogates intersections of spirituality and technology. Physically his paintings often consist of mixed media incorporated in acrylic.

Weems, Carrie Mae (1953–)
African American photographer working in the documentary tradition. A self-described "image maker," she has been especially concerned with how images inform and reflect contemporary notions of race, class, and gender.

Wells, James Lesesne (1902–1993)
African American painter, and printmaker of mainly religious, mythical, and natural subjects.

Aspects of his work borrow from German Expressionism and Cubism. Founder of Howard University's graphic arts department.

White, Charles (1918–1979)
African American painter and draftsman. Heroically resisted the artistic movements that swept up many of his contemporaries—Minimalism, Abstract Expressionism, and Conceptualism. From the 1940s through the 1970s he produced masterfully drafted pieces dedicated almost exclusively to social and economic themes in black America.

Whitten, Jack (1939–2018)
African American painter. His philosophically loaded, optically complex work qualify him as one of the leading abstract artists in the US.

Wiley, Kehinde (1977–)
African American painter of Nigerian ancestry. Recognized for reinvigorating the art of portraiture, paradoxically via appropriations of the genre's bodily rhetoric. Wiley paints his black urban subjects, their simulated poses adopted from original masterworks, against decorative backgrounds, supporting a socio-political narrative relevant to black and brown lives and their precarious positions in the world.

Williams, Aubrey (1926–1990)
Guyanese painter living in Britain from the mid-1950s. Prominent in the London-based Caribbean Artists' Movement in the 1960s and 1970s. His work mines the Pre-Columbian impulse in Caribbean art and culture.

Williams, Spencer (1893–1969)
African American actor and director. Active as a Hollywood writer and performer from the late 1920s, he later made a series of films centered on black religious experience—*The Blood of Jesus* (1941) and *Go Down Death!* (1944) among them. With Oscar Micheaux, one of the pioneering black filmmakers, though perhaps best known as Andy in the 1950s sitcom *Amos 'n' Andy*.

Williamson, Sue (1941–)
White, English-born artist and writer living in South Africa since the age of eight. In the Apartheid era, her prints and installations—celebrated as subtle yet powerful examples of political or protest art—surveyed gender and racial injustice in South Africa. Lately an

important critic and curator of contemporary South African art.

Wilson, Fred (1954–)

African American installation artist. His provocative yet deeply contemplative exhibitions probe and attempt to counter the tendency of American art, letters, and history to obscure the contributions and voices of American blacks.

Withers, Ernest C. (1922–2007)

African American photojournalist. Noted for work during the American civil rights movement—especially his photographs of the open-casket funeral for the brutalized Emmett Till, and his pictures of Martin Luther King Jr. during the the civil rights leader's last days.

Woodruff, Hale (1900–1980)

African American painter and educator. From the late 1920s his style and subject matter ranged from Cubism to Abstract Expressionism, and from picturesque French cityscapes to abstract riffs on African sculpture. Best known for his historical murals at Talladega College in Alabama (1939), Clark Atlanta University in Georgia (1950–51), and the Golden State Mutual Insurance Company in California (1949).

Yiadom-Boakye, Lynette (1977–)

Ghanaian painter based in the UK. Composes and paints fictional black people, culled from scrapbooks, drawings, and her imagination. Yiadom-Boakye's subjects are depicted with loose brushwork and floating against ambiguous backgrounds that contribute to a sense of timelessness. Working rapidly and intuitively, she often completes a composition in a day and considers the physical properties of paint to be at the core of her practice.

Select Bibliography and Sources

There are several key works that provide basic art-historical information on black diasporal cultures in twentieth-century art, and these are listed in the General section below. Many other books, monographs, exhibition catalogues, directories, articles, and essays that have been published on this topic and that have provided source material are included in the bibliographical notes that follow for each chapter; these are grouped under subject headings and are listed in the order in which the points and quotations appear in the text. Where n.p. appears in the place of a page reference, the publication has no pagination.

General

Araeen, Rasheed, *The Other Story: Afro-Asian Artists in Post-war Britain*, South Bank Centre, London, 1989.

Archer Straw, Petrine and Kim Robinson, *Jamaican Art*, Kingston Publishers, Kingston, 1990.

Chambers, Eddie, ed., *The Routledge Companion to African American Art History*, Routledge, New York, 2019.

"Critical Decade: Black British Photography in the 80s," *Ten.8* 2, Spring 1992.

Dover, Cedric, *American Negro Art*, The New York Graphic Society, Greenwich, CT, 1960.

Doy, Gen, *Black Visual Culture: Modernity and Postmodernity*, I. B. Tauris, London, 1999.

Driskell, David C., *Hidden Heritage: Afro-American Art, 1800–1950*, Bellevue Art Museum, Bellevue, Washington, DC, 1985.

Fine, Elsa Honig, *The Afro-American Artist: A Search for Identity*, Harcourt Brace Jovanovich, New York, 1973.

Igoe, Lynn Moody and James Igoe, *Two Hundred and Fifty Years of Afro-American Art: An Annotated Bibliography*, R. R. Bowker, New York, 1981.

Kennedy, Jean, *New Currents, Ancient Rivers: Contemporary African Artists in a Generation of Change*, Smithsonian Institution Press, Washington, DC, 1992.

Lewis, Samella, *African American Art and Artists*, University of California Press, Berkeley, 1990.

Lippard, Lucy R., *Mixed Blessings: New Art in a Multicultural America*, Pantheon Books, New York, 1990.

Owusu, Kwesi, ed., *Storms of the Heart: An Anthology of Black Arts & Culture*, Camden Press, London, 1988.

Perry Reginia, *Free Within Ourselves: African American Artists in the Collection of the National Museum of American Art*, Pomegranate Artbooks, San Francisco, 1992.

Porter, James A., *Modern Negro Art* (first published 1943), Howard University Press, Washington, DC, 1992 edn.

Rodman, Selden, *Where Art is Joy, Haitian Art: The First Forty Years*, Ruggles de Latour, New York, 1988.

Thompson, Robert Farris, *Flash of the Spirit: African and Afro-American Art and Philosophy*, Random House, New York, 1983.

Walmsley, Anne, *The Caribbean Artists Movement, 1966–1972: A Literary and Cultural History*, New Beacon, London, 1992.

Young, Kevin, *The Grey Album: On the Blackness of Blackness*, Graywolf Press, Minneapolis, MN, 2012.

The following journals, magazines, and periodicals have also been especially informative: *African American Review, African Arts, American Art, Artist and Influence, BWIA Caribbean Beat, Callaloo, International Review of African American Art, Jamaica Journal, Nka: Journal of Contemporary African Art, Revue Noire, Screen, Ten.8, Third Text, Transition.*

Also useful, but not specifically concerned with black culture:

Blocker, Jane, *Becoming Past: History in Contemporary Art*, University of Minnesota Press, Minneapolis, 2016.

Clifford, James, *The Predicament of Culture: Twentieth-Century Ethnography, Literature, and Art*, Harvard University Press, Cambridge, MA, 1988.

Deleuze, Gilles, *Cinema 1: The Movement-Image*, University of Minnesota Press, Minneapolis, 1986.

— *Cinema 2: The Time-Image*, University of Minnesota Press, Minneapolis, 1989.

Foster, Hal, ed., *Recodings: Art, Spectacle, Cultural Politics*, Bay Press, Seattle, 1985.

Foucault, Michel, trans. and ed. Colin Gordon, *Power/Knowledge: Selected Interviews and Other Writings, 1972–1977*, Pantheon Books, New York; Harvester Press, Brighton, 1980.

Freedberg, David, *The Power of Images: Studies in the History and Theory of Response*, University of Chicago Press, Chicago, 1989.

Geertz, Clifford, *The Interpretation of Cultures*, Basic Books, New York, 1973.

Kristeva, Julia, *The Kristeva Reader*, Columbia University Press, New York, 1986.

Petro, Patrice, ed., *Fugitive Images: From Photography to Video*, Indiana University Press, Bloomington, 1995.

Simpson, Bennett, *Blues for Smoke*, Museum of Contemporary Art, Los Angeles, 2012.

Spivak, Gayatri Chakravorty, *In Other Worlds: Essays in Cultural Politics*, Methuen, London and New York, 1987.

Stafford, Barbara Maria, *Body Criticism: Imaging the Unseen in Enlightenment Art and Medicine*, MIT Press, Cambridge, MA, 1991.

Tagg, John, *The Burden of Representation: Essays on Photographies and Histories*, University of Minnesota Press, Minneapolis, 1988.

Wallis, Brian, ed., *Art after Modernism: Rethinking Representation*, New Museum of Contemporary Art, New York, 1984.

Wood, Paul and Francis Frascina, Jonathan Harris, and Charles Harrison, *Modernism in Dispute: Art Since the Forties*, Yale University Press, New Haven, 1993.

Introduction: The Dark Center

Defining "Blackness": Fanon, Frantz, trans. Charles Lam Markmann, *Black Skin, White Masks* (*Peau noire, masques blancs*, 1952), Grove, New York, 1967, p. 135. Vlach, John Michael, *The Afro-American Tradition in Decorative Arts*, Cleveland Museum of Art, Cleveland, 1978, pp. 20–22. Tibbles, Anthony, ed., *Transatlantic Slavery: Against Human Dignity*, HMSO, London, 1994, pp. 110, 152. Thompson, Robert Farris, "The Flash of the Spirit: Haiti's Africanizing Vodun Art," in Ute Stebich, ed., *Haitian Art*, The Brooklyn Museum, Brooklyn, 1978, pp. 26–37. Curtin, Philip D., *The Atlantic Slave Trade: A Census*, University of Wisconsin Press, Madison, 1969.

Patterson, Orlando, *Slavery and Social Death: A Comparative Study*, Harvard University Press, Cambridge, MA, 1982. Jahn, Janheinz, *Muntu: The New African Culture*, Grove, New York, 1961. Jordan, Winthrop D., "The Bodies of Men: The Negro's Physical Nature," in *White Over Black: American Attitudes Toward the Negro, 1550–1812*, Pelican Books, Baltimore, 1969, pp. 216–65. Gates, Henry Louis Jr., "The Blackness of Blackness: A Critique of the Sign and the Signifying Monkey," in *Figures in Black: Words, Signs, and the "Racial" Self*, Oxford University Press, New York and Oxford, 1987, pp. 235–76. Sáiz, María Concepción García, *The Castes: A Genre of Mexican Painting*, Olivetti, Milan, 1989, pp. 180–81. "La Pintura de Castas," *Artes de México* 8, 1990.

Locating and describing black cultures: Hall, Stuart, "What is this 'Black' in Black Popular Culture," in Gina Dent, ed., *Black Popular Culture*, Bay Press, Seattle, 1992, pp. 21–33. Bastide, Roger, *African Civilizations in the New World*, Harper Torchbooks, New York, 1972. Jaynes, Gerald David and Robin M. Williams Jr., eds., *A Common Destiny: Blacks and American Society*, National Academy Press, Washington, DC, 1989. Powell, Richard J., *African and Afro-American Art: Call and Response*, Field Museum of Natural History, Chicago, 1984. Blier, Suzanne, *African Vodun: Art, Psychology, and Power*, University of Chicago, Chicago, 1995. Blackwell, James E., *The Black Community: Diversity and Unity*, 2nd edn, Harper & Row, London and New York, 1985.

Theories of black subjectivity: Murray, Freeman H.M., *Emancipation and the Freed in American Sculpture*, privately published, Washington, DC, 1916; particularly pp. 135–36. Powell, Richard J., "Face to Face: Elizabeth Catlett's Graphic Work," in *Elizabeth Catlett: Works on Paper, 1944–1992*, Hampton University Museum, Hampton, 1993, pp. 49–53. Hassan, Salah, "The Modernist Experience in African Art: Visual Expressions of the Self and Cross-Cultural Aesthetics," *Nka: Journal of Contemporary African Art* 2, Spring/ Summer 1995, pp. 30–33, 72. West, Cornel, *Race Matters*, Beacon Press, Boston, 1993. Locke, Alain, *The Negro in Art: A Pictorial Record of the Negro Artist and of the Negro Theme in Art*, Associates in Negro Folk Education, Washington, DC, 1940. Parry, Ellwood C., *The Image of the Indian and the Black Man in American Art, 1590–1900*, George Braziller, New York, 1974. Honour, Hugh, *The Image of the Black in Western Art, Volume IV, From the American Revolution to World War I*, Harvard University Press, Cambridge, MA, 1989. Wardlaw, Alvia, *Black Art, Ancestral Legacy: The African Impulse in African-American Art*, Dallas Museum of Art, Dallas, 1989. McElroy, Guy C., *Facing History: The Black Image in American Art, 1710–1940*, Bedford Arts, San Francisco, 1990. Pieterse, Jan Nederveen, *White on Black: Images of Africa and Blacks in Western Popular Culture*, Yale University Press, New Haven, 1992. Harris, Michael D., *Colored Pictures: Race and Visual Representation*, University of North Carolina Press, Chapel Hill, NC, 2003. Fusco, Coco and Wallis, Brian, *Only Skin Deep: Changing Visions of the American Self*, Harry N. Abrams, New York, 2003. Mercer, Kobena, ed., *Cosmopolitan Modernisms*, MIT Press, Cambridge, MA, 2005. Mercer, Kobena, *Discrepant Abstraction*, MIT Press, Cambridge, MA, 2006. Mercer, Kobena, ed., *Pop Art and Vernacular Cultures*, MIT Press, Cambridge, MA, 2007. English, Darby, *How to See a Work of Art in Total Darkness*, MIT Press, Cambridge, MA, 2007. Cooks, Bridget, *Exhibiting Blackness: African Americans and the American Art Museum*, University of Massachusetts Press, Amherst, 2011. Fleetwood, Nicole, *Troubling Vision: Performance, Visuality and Blackness*, University of Chicago Press, Chicago, 2011. Copeland, Huey Copeland, *Bound to Appear: Art, Slavery, and the Site of Blackness in Multicultural America*, University of Chicago Press, Chicago, 2013.

Key writings by Jeff Donaldson, Paul Gilroy, Robert Farris Thompson: Donaldson, Jeff, "10 in Search of a Nation," *Black World* 19, October 1970, pp. 80–89; and "TransAfrican Art," *The Black Collegian* 11, October/ November 1980, pp. 90–101. Gilroy, Paul, *The Black Atlantic: Modernity and Double Consciousness*, Harvard University Press, Cambridge, MA, 1993; *Against Race: Imagining Political Culture beyond the Color Line*, Harvard University Press, Cambridge, MA, 2000. Thompson, Robert Farris, "African Influence on the Art of the United States" (1969), in William Ferris, ed., *Afro-American Folk Art and Crafts*, G.K. Hall, Boston, 1983, pp. 27–63; *Flash of the Spirit: African and Afro-American Art and Philosophy*, Random House, New York, 1983; *Face of the Gods: Art and Altars of Africa and the African Americas*, Museum for African Art, New York, 1993; and with Joseph Cornet, *The Four Moments of the Sun: Kongo Art in Two Worlds*, National Gallery of Art, Washington, DC, 1981; *Aesthetic of the Cool: Afro-Atlantic Art and Music*, Periscope Publishing, Ltd, New York, 2011.

Feminist theory: De Lauretis, Teresa, *Alice Doesn't*, Indiana University Press, Bloomington, 1984. Trinh, T. Minh-ha, *Woman, Native, Other: Writing Postcoloniality and Feminism*, Indiana University Press, Bloomington, 1989. Alcoff, Linda, "Cultural Feminism Versus Post-Structuralism: The Identity Crisis in Feminist Theory," *Signs: Journal of Women in Culture and Society* 13, 1988, pp. 405–36. King, Deborah K., "Multiple Jeopardy, Multiple Consciousness: The Context of Black Feminist Ideology" (1988), in Beverly Guy-Sheftall, ed., *Words of Fire: An Anthology of African-American Feminist Thought*, The New Press, New York, 1995, pp. 293–317. Crenshaw, Kimberle, "Demarginalizing the Intersection of Race and Sex: A Black Feminist Critique of Antidiscrimination Doctrine, Feminist Theory and Antiracist Politics," *University of Chicago Legal Forum*, 1989, pp. 139–67. hooks, bell, *Black Looks: Race and Representation*, South End Press, Boston, MA, 1992. Broude, Norma and Garrard, Mary D., eds., *The Expanding Discourse: Feminism and Art History*, Icon Editions, New York, 1992. Nochlin, Linda, *Representing Women*, Thames & Hudson, London, 1999. Nochlin, Linda, *The Body in Pieces: The Fragment as a Metaphor of Modernity*, Thames & Hudson, London, 2001. Spillers, Hortense J., "Mama's Baby, Papa's Maybe: An American Grammar Book," in "Culture and Countermemory: The 'American' Connection," special issue, *Diacritics* 17, Summer 1987, pp. 64–81. Bobo, Jacqueline, ed., *Black Feminist Cultural Criticism*, Blackwell, Malden, MA, 2001. Pollock, Griselda, *Vision and Difference: Feminism, Femininity, and the Histories of Art*, Routledge, London, 2003. Quashie, Kevin Everod, *Black Women, Identity, and Cultural Theory: (Un)becoming the Subject*, Rutgers University Press, New Brunswick, 2004. Chadwick, Whitney, *Women, Art, and Society*, Thames & Hudson, London, 2012. Gumbs, Alexis Pauline, *Spill: Scenes of Black Feminist Fugitivity*, Duke University Press, Durham, NC, 2016.

Art histories and postmodernism: Smalls, James, "A Ghost of a Chance: Invisibility and Elision in African American Art Historical Practice," *Art Documentation* 13, Spring 1994, pp. 3–8. Nicodemus, Everlyn, "The Center of Otherness," in Jean Fisher, ed., *Global Visions: Towards a New Internationalism in the Visual Arts*, Kala Press, London, 1994, pp. 91–104. Bailey, David A., "Mirage: Enigmas of Race, Difference, and Desire," in *Mirage: Enigmas of Race, Difference and Desire*, Institute of Contemporary Arts, London, 1995, pp. 57–96. Thompson, Krista, *Shine: The Visual Economy of Light in African Diasporic Aesthetic Practice*, Duke University Press, Durham, NC, 2015.

Post-Black: defined and described: Isaak, Jo Anna, ed., *Looking Forward, Looking Black*, Hobart and William Smith Colleges Press, Geneva, NY, 1999. Golden, Thelma, ed., *Freestyle*, Studio Museum in Harlem, New York, 2001. Golden, Thelma, ed., *Frequency*, Studio Museum in Harlem, New York, 2005. Murray, Derek Conrad, "Post Post-Black: Some Politically Incorrect Thoughts on the Reception and Contemplation of African American Art," *Art Journal* 66, 2007, pp. 112–14. *African American Review (Post-Soul Aesthetic* issue) 41, Winter 2007.

Multiple categories of outsiderness: Arnett, Paul and Arnett, William S., *Souls Grown Deep, Vol. 1: African American Vernacular Art of the South*, Tinwood Books, Atlanta, GA, 2000. Fine, Gary Alan, *Everyday Genius: Self-Taught Art and the Culture of Authenticity*, University of Chicago Press, Chicago, 2004. Russell, Charles, *Groundwaters: A Century of Art by Self-Taught and Outsider Artists*, Prestel, New York, 2011. Muñoz, José Esteban, *Disidentifications: Queers of Color and the Performance of Politics*, University of Minnesota Press, Minneapolis, 1999. Murray, Derek Conrad, *Queering Post-Black Art: Artists Transforming African-American Identity after Civil Rights*, I. B. Tauris, London, 2016. Burton, Johanna and Bell, Natalie, *Trigger: Gender as a Tool and a Weapon*, The New Museum, New York, 2017.

Rediscovering the Harlem Renaissance and the Black Arts Movement: Goeser, Caroline, *Picturing the New Negro: Harlem Renaissance Print Culture and Modern Black Identity*, University Press of Kansas, Lawrence, 2007. Kirschke, Amy Helene, ed., *Women Artists of the Harlem Renaissance*, University Press of Mississippi, Jackson, 2014. Collins, Lisa Gail and Crawford, Margo Natalie, eds., *New Thoughts on the Black Arts Movement*, Rutgers University Press, New Brunswick, NJ, 2006. Calo, Mary Ann, *Distinction and Denial: Race, Nation, and the Critical Construction of the African American Artist, 1920–40*, University of Michigan Press, Ann Arbor, 2007. Jones, Kellie, "Now Dig This!" *Art and Black Los Angeles, 1960–1980*, Hammer Museum, University of California, Los Angeles, 2013. Godfrey, Mark and Whitley, Zoé, eds., *Soul of a Nation: Art in the Age of Black Power*, Tate, London and D.A.P/Distributed Art Publishers Inc., New York, 2017.

Historical revisions: Jones, Kellie, *Energy/Experimentation: Black Artists and Abstraction, 1964–1980*, Studio Museum in Harlem, New York, 2006. Sirmans, Franklin, *NeoHoodoo: Art for a Forgotten Faith*, Menil Collection, Houston,

2008. Thompson, Krista, "A Sidelong Glance: The Practice of African Diaspora Art History in the United States," *Art Journal* 70, 2011, pp. 6–31. Francis, Jacqueline, *Making Race: Modernism and "Racial Art" in America*, University of Washington Press, Seattle, 2012. Harper, Phillip Brian, "Black Personhood in the Maw of Abstraction," *Abstractionist Aesthetics: Artistic Form and Social Critique in African American Culture*, New York University Press, New York, 2015, pp. 17–67.

International Blackness: Enwezor, Okwui, *The Short Century: Independence and Liberation Movements in Africa, 1945–1994*, Prestel, Munich, 2001. Barson, Tanya and Gorschluter, Peter, eds., *Afro-Modern: Journeys through the Black Atlantic*, Tate Liverpool, 2010. Bindman, David and Gates, Henry Louis Jr., eds., *The Image of the Black in Western Art, V, Part 2, The Twentieth Century: The Rise of Black Artists*, Harvard University Press, Cambridge, 2014. Soutif, Daniel, ed., *The Color Line: Les Artistes africains-américains et la ségrégation, 1865–2016*, Flammarion, Paris, 2016. Pedrosa, Adriano, ed., *Histórias Afro-Atlânticas*, Museu de arte de São Paulo, 2018.

Chapter 1
Art, Culture, and "The Souls of Black Folk"

Black images at the turn of the century: Geiss, Imanuel, *The Pan-African Movement*, Methuen, London, 1974. Honour, Hugh, *The Image of the Black in Western Art, 4: From the Revolution to World War I, Part 1*, Harvard University Press, Cambridge, MA, 1989, pp. 259–304. Kemble, Edward Windsor, *Kemble's Coons: A Collection of Southern Sketches*, R. H. Russell, New York, 1896. Fletcher, Tom, *100 Years of the Negro in Show Business!*, Burdge, New York, 1954. Mosby, Dewey F., *Henry Ossawa Tanner*, Rizzoli, New York, 1991, pp. 10–53, 116–20. Long, Richard A., *Black Americana*, Crescent Books, New York, 1993, pp. 11–21. Perry, Regenia A., *Harriet Powers's Bible Quilts*, Rizzoli, New York, 1994. Johnson, James Weldon, *The Autobiography of an Ex-Colored Man* (first published 1912), Avon Books, New York, 1965 edn, pp. 393–511. Johnson, James Weldon, *Along This Way*, Viking Press, New York, 1933, pp. 151–59.

Stuart Davis and Ernst Ludwig Kirchner: Boyajian, Ani, ed., *Stuart Davis: A Catalogue Raisonne, Vol. 1*, Yale University Art Gallery, New Haven, 2007. Höper, Corinna, ed., *Ernst Ludwig Kirchner: Die Unbekannte Sammlung*, Sandstein, Dresden, 2018.

In response to cultural assaults on "the race": Gates, Henry Louis Jr., "The Trope of a New Negro and the Reconstruction of the Image of the Black," *Representations* 24, Fall 1988, pp. 129–155. Du Bois, W. E. B., *The Souls of Black Folk* (first published 1903), Avon Books, New York, 1965, pp. 209–389. Washington, Booker T., *Up From Slavery* (first published 1901) Avon Books, New York, 1965, pp. 145–50. Dunbar, Paul Laurence, *Candle-Lightin' Time*, Dodd Mead, New York, 1901, pp. 117–27. Adams, John Henry Jr., "The Modern Cyrenian's Cross, or the Black Man's Burden," *Voice of the Negro* 4, July 1907, p. 285. Du Bois, W. E. B., "Roosevelt," *The Horizon: A Journal of the Color Line* 1, January 1907, pp. 2–10. Dixon, Thomas, *The Leopard's Spots: A Romance of the White Man's Burden, 1865–1900*, Doubleday, Page, New York, 1902.

Isaac Scott Hathaway, Meta Vaux Warrick Fuller and Edwin A. Harleston: "The Isaac Hathaway Art Company," *The Crisis* 15, November 1917, p. 46. Ater, Renée, *Remaking Race and History: The Sculpture of Meta Warrick Fuller*, University of California Press, Berkeley, 2011. Brawley, Benjamin G., *The Negro in Literature and Art in the United States*, Duffield, New York, 1918, pp. 113–24. Murray, Freeman Henry Morris, *Emancipation and the Freed in American sculpture: A Study in Interpretation*, Murray Brothers, Washington, DC, 1916, pp. 55–66, 183. Casely Hayford, J.E., *Ethiopia Unbound: Studies in Race Emancipation* (first published 1911), Frank Cass, London, 1969. McDaniel, M. Akua,"The Life of Edwin Augustus Harleston, Portrait Painter" (unpublished Ph. D. dissertation, Emory University), 1994. Franklin, John Hope and Alfred A. Moss Jr., *From Slavery to Freedom: A History of African Americans*, McGraw-Hill, New York, 1994, pp. 323–60.

Preludes to the "New Negro": Du Bois, W. E. B., "Letters from Dr. Du Bois," *The Crisis* 17, February 1919, pp. 169. Johnson, James Weldon, "Preface to Original Edition," *The Book of American Negro Poetry* (first published 1922), Harcourt, Brace & World, New York, 1958.

Chapter 2
Enter and Exit the "New Negro"

Race and Modernity: Smith, Terry, *Making the Modern: Industry, Art, and Design in America*, University of Chicago Press, Chicago, 1993. Gates, Henry Louis Jr., "The Trope of a New Negro and the Reconstruction of the Image of the Black," *Representations* 24, Fall 1988, pp. 129–55. Lewis,

David Levering, *When Harlem Was In Vogue*, Alfred A. Knopf, New York, 1981. Douglas, Ann, *Terrible Honesty: Mongrel Manhattan in the 1920s*, Farrar, Straus & Giroux, New York, 1995. "Harlem: Mecca of the New Negro," *Survey Graphic* 6, March 1925. Locke, Alain, ed., *The New Negro: An Interpretation* (first published 1925), Atheneum, New York, 1980.

Winold Reiss and Aaron Douglas: Stewart, Jeffrey C., *To Color America: Portraits by Winold Reiss*, Smithsonian Institution Press, Washington, DC, 1989. Earle, Susan, ed., *Aaron Douglas: African American Modernist*, Yale University Press, New Haven, 2007. Douglas, Aaron, "The Harlem Renaissance," unpublished manuscript, 18 March 1973, Special Collections, Fisk University Library, Nashville. Douglas, Aaron, interview by L. M. Collins, 16 July 1971, Special Collections, Fisk University Library, Nashville. Douglas, Aaron, letter to Langston Hughes, 21 December 1925, as quoted in Richard J. Powell, "Art History and Black Memory: Toward a Blues Aesthetic," in Genevieve Fabre and Robert O'Meally, eds., *History and Memory in African American Culture*, Oxford University Press, New York, 1994, pp. 228–43.

Representing the "New Negro": Hughes, Langston, "The Negro Artist and the Racial Mountain," *Nation* 122, 23 June 1926, pp. 692–94. Rampersad, Arnold, *The Life of Langston Hughes, Vol. 1: 1902–1941, I, Too, Sing America*, Oxford University Press, New York, 1986. Gaines, Jane, "Fire and Desire: Race, Melodrama, and Oscar Micheaux," in Manthia Diawara, *Black American Cinema*, Routledge, London and New York, 1993, pp. 49–70. Toomer, Jean, *Cane* (first published 1923), Harper & Row, 1969. *The Darkness and The Light: Photographs by Doris Ulmann*, Aperture, Millerton, New York, 1974. Foucault, Michel, "Powers and Strategies," trans. and ed. Colin Gordon, *Power/Knowledge: Selected Interviews and Other Writings, 1972–1977*, Pantheon, New York, 1980, pp. 134–45. Reynolds, Gary A. and Beryl J. Wright, *Against the Odds: African-American Artists and the Harmon Foundation*, Newark Museum, Newark, 1989. Powell, Richard J. *Homecoming: The Art and Life of William H. Johnson*, Rizzoli, New York, 1991.

The evolution of the "Harlem Renaissance" concept: Brawley, Benjamin G., "The Negro Literary Renaissance," *The Southern Workman* 56, April 1927, pp. 177–84. Hughes, Langston, *The Big Sea* (first published 1940) in David Levering Lewis, ed., *The Portable Harlem Renaissance Reader*, Penguin, New York, 1994, pp. 77–91. Franklin, John Hope, "A Harlem Renaissance," in *From Slavery to Freedom: A History of American Negroes*, Alfred A. Knopf, New York, 1947, pp. 489–511. Huggins, Nathan, *Harlem Renaissance*, Oxford University Press, New York, 1971. Campbell, Mary Schmidt, *Harlem Renaissance: Art of Black America*, Abrams, New York, 1987. Anderson, Jervis. *This Was Harlem: A Cultural Portrait, 1900–1950*, Farrar, Straus & Giroux, New York, 1982. Johnson, James Weldon, *Black Manhattan*, Alfred A. Knopf, New York, 1930, pp. 264–80. Porter, James A., *Modern Negro Art* (first published 1943), Howard University Press, Washington, DC, 1992, pp. 86–101. Williams, Adriana, *Covarrubias*, University of Texas, Austin, 1994, pp. 17–58. Robinson, Jontyle Theresa and Wendy Greenhouse, *The Art of Archibald J. Motley Jr.*, Chicago Historical Society, Chicago, 1991. De Jongh, James L., "The Image of Black Harlem in Literature," in Christopher Mulvey and John Simons, eds., *New York: City as Text*, Macmillan, London, 1990, pp. 131–46. Wright, John S., "A Scintillating Send-Off For Falling Stars: The Black Renaissance Reconsidered," in *A Stronger Soul Within A Finer Frame: Portraying African-Americans in the Black Renaissance*, University of Minnesota, Minneapolis, 1990, pp. 12–45.

Jazz, blues and the performance paradigm: Van Vechten, Carl, "Memories of Bessie Smith," *Jazz Record* 58, September 1947, pp. 6–7. Morand, Paul, *Black Magic*, Viking Press, New York, 1929, pp. v–vi. Powell, Richard J., *The Blues Aesthetic: Black Culture and Modernism*, Washington Project for the Arts, Washington, DC, 1989.

Black culture in Jazz-Age Paris: Leininger-Miller, Teresa, "The Transatlantic Tradition: African American Artists in Paris, 1830–1940," in Asake Bomani and Belvie Rooks, eds., *Paris Connections: African American Artists in Paris*, Q. E. D. Press, San Francisco, 1992, pp. 9–23. Blake, Jody, *Le Tumulte noir: Modernist Art and Popular Entertainment in Jazz-Age Paris, 1900–1930*, Pennsylvania State University Press, University Park, 1999. Viry-Babel, Roger, *Jean Renoir: Le jeu et la règle* (first published 1986), Editions Ramsay, Paris, 1994, pp. 38–39. Archer-Straw, Petrine, *Negrophilia: Avant-Garde Paris and Black Culture in the 1920s*, Thames & Hudson, London, 2000.

Primitivism, Africa, and the "race renewal": Vendryes, Margaret Rose, *Barthé: A Life in*

Sculpture, University Press of Mississippi, Jackson, 2008. Torgovnick, Marianna, *Gone Primitive: Savage Intellects, Modern Lives*, University of Chicago Press, Chicago, 1990. Mudimbe, V. Y., *The Invention of Africa: Gnosis, Philosophy, and the Order of Knowledge*, Indiana University Press, Bloomington, 1988, pp. 1–23. McKay, Claude, *A Long Way from Home*, Lee Furman, New York, 1937, pp. 348–54. Locke, Alain, "The Negro: 'New' or Newer: A Retrospective Review of the Literature of the Negro for 1938," in Jeffrey C. Stewart, ed., *The Critical Temper of Alain Locke*, Garland Publishing, New York, 1983, pp. 271–83.

Chapter 3
The Cult of the People
Art and culture in the 1930s: Montgomery, Evangeline J., "Sargent Claude Johnson," in *San Francisco Art Commission Honors Award Show*, San Francisco Art Commission Gallery, San Francisco, 1977. Powell, Richard J., ed., *Archibald Motley: Jazz Age Modernist*, Nasher Museum of Art at Duke University, Durham, 2014. Hills, Patricia, *Social Concern and Urban Realism: American Painting of the 1930s*, Boston University Art Gallery, Boston, 1983. Park, Marlene and Gerald E. Markowitz, *New Deal for Art*, Gallery Association of New York State, Hamilton, New York, 1977. Doss, Erika, *Benton, Pollock, and the Politics of Modernism: From Regionalism to Abstract Expressionism*, University of Chicago Press, Chicago, 1991. Gordon, Allan, *Echoes of Our Past: The Narrative Artistry of Palmer C. Hayden*, The Museum of African American Art, Los Angeles, 1988. Wright, Richard, *Lawd Today* (first published 1963), Northeastern University Press, Boston, 1986. Duberman, Martin, *Paul Robeson*, Alfred A. Knopf, New York, 1988, pp. 207–208. Spencer, Jon Michael, *Blues and Evil*, The University of Tennessee Press, Knoxville, 1993, pp. 1–34. Oliver, Paul, *Songsters and Saints*, Cambridge University Press, Cambridge, 1984, pp. 109–39. Anderson, Jervis, "Harlem Explodes," in *This Was Harlem: A Cultural Portrait, 1900–1950*, Farrar, Straus & Giroux, New York, 1982, pp. 295–98. Greene, Lorenzo J. and Carter G. Woodson, *The Negro Wage Earner*, The Association for the Study of Negro Life and History, Washington, DC, 1930. Pells, Richard, *Radical Visions and American Dreams: Culture and Social Thought in the Depression Years*, Harper & Row, New York, 1973, pp. 43–95. Hurlburt, Laurance P., "New Workers School, 1933," in *The Mexican Muralists in the United States*, University of New Mexico Press, Albuquerque, 1989, pp. 175–93.

Stange, Maren, *Symbols of Ideal Life: Social Documentary Photography in America, 1890–1950*, Cambridge University Press, Cambridge, 1989. King-Hammond, Leslie, "Black Printmakers and the W. P. A.," in *Alone in a Crowd: Prints of the 1930s–40s by African-American Artists*, American Federation of Arts, New York, 1993, pp. 10–20. M.M.S., "Comments on Art Exhibitions," *Parnassus* 7, March 1935, p. 24. Hayes, Jeffreen M., *Augusta Savage: Renaissance Woman*, D. Giles, Ltd, London, 2018.

Edward Burra and Walker Evans: Martin, Simon, *Edward Burra*, Lund Humphries, London, 2011. Chéroux, Clément, ed., *Walker Evans*, DelMonico Books, Prestel, Munich, 2017.

The Negritude and Indigenist movements: Harris, Wilson, *The Womb of Space: The Cross-Cultural Imagination*, Greenwood Press, Westport, CT, 1983. Kutzinski, Vera, "The Carnivalization of Poetry: Nicolas Guillen's Chronicles," in *Against the American Grain: Myth and History in William Carlos Williams, Jay Wright, and Nicolás Guillén*, The John Hopkins University Press, Baltimore, 1987, pp. 131–235. Vaillant, Janet G., *Black, French, and African: A Life of Léopold Sédar Senghor*, Harvard University Press, Cambridge, MA, 1990, pp. 87–116. Douglas, Aaron, "Forge Foundry," *La Revue du monde noir* I, 1931, p. 4. Benjamin, Tritobia H., *The Life and Art of Loïs Mailou Jones*, Pomegranate Artbooks, San Francisco, 1994, pp. 26–44. Lerebours, Michel-Philippe, *Haïti et ses Peintres de 1804 à 1980: souffrances & espoirs d'un Ppeuple*, L'Imprimeur II, Port-au-Prince, 1989. Césaire, Aimé, *Cahiers d'un retour au pays natal* (first published 1939), Brentano's, New York, 1947, n.p. Shelton, Marie-Denise, *Image de la Société dans le roman haïtien*, L'Harmattan, Paris, 1993, pp. 7–31, 55–76. Savain, Petion, *La Case de Damballah* (first published 1939), Kraus Reprint, Nendeln, 1970.

Black diasporal religions and art: Mead, Chris, *Champion: Joe Louis, Black Hero in White America*, Scribner, New York, 1985. Herskovits, Melville J., "Les Noirs du Nouveau Monde: sujet de recherches africanistes," *Journal de la Societé du Africanistes* 8, 1938, pp. 65–82. Archer Straw, Petrine and Kim Robinson, *Jamaican Art*, Kingston Publishers, Kingston, 1990, pp. 5–10. Beckwith, Martha Warren, "The Pukkemerians," in *Black Roadways: A Study of Jamaican Folk Life: The Black Folk Hero*, The University of North Carolina Press, Chapel Hill, 1929, pp. 176–82. Hemenway, Robert E., *Zora Neale Hurston: A*

Literary Biography, University of Illinois Press, Urbana, 1977. Metcalf, Eugene, "Black Art, Folk Art, and Social Control," *Winterthur Porfolio 18*, Winter 1983, pp. 271–89. Preece, Harold, "The Negro Folk Cult," *The Crisis* 43, 1936, pp. 364, 374. Fuller, Edmund L., *Visions in Stone: The Sculpture of William Edmondson*, University of Pittsburgh Press, Pittsburgh, 1973. Radin, Paul, "Status, Fantasy, and the Christian Dogma," in *God Struck Me Dead: Religious Conversion Experiences and Autobiographies of Ex-Slaves*, ed. Clifton H. Johnson, Pilgrim Press, Philadelphia, 1969, pp. vii-xiii. Hall, Michael D., *Legacy in Wood: Elijah Pierce at the Columbus Museum of Art*, Columbus Museum of Art, Columbus, OH, 2013. Bearden, Romare, "The Negro Artist and Modern Art," *Opportunity* 12, December 1934, pp. 371–72.

Chapter 4
Pride, Assimilation, and Dreams

Negro Cavalcade" of the 1940s: Ottley, Roi, *New World A-Coming*, Houghton Mifflin, Boston, 1943. Robinson, John N., "John N. Robinson: An Autobiographical Sketch," in *John N. Robinson: A Retrospective*, Smithsonian Institution Press, Washington, DC, 1976, pp. 13–18. "Karl Broodhagen," in *Pioneer Artists of the Pre-Independence Era*, Art Collection Foundation, Bridgetown, 1993. Lamming, George, *In the Castle of My Skin*, McGraw-Hill, New York, 1953. Thomas, Jesse O., *Negro Participation in the Texas Centennial Exposition*, The Christopher Publishing House, Boston, MA, 1938. Locke, Alain, *Contemporary Negro Art*, Baltimore Museum of Art, Baltimore, 1939. Locke, Alain, "Up Till Now," in *The Negro Artist Comes of Age*, Albany Institute of History and Art, Albany, 1945, pp. iii-vii. Locke, Alain, *The Negro in Art*, Associates in Negro Folk Education, Washington, DC, 1940. Porter, James A., *Modern Negro Art* (first published 1943), Howard University Press, Washington, DC, 1992.

Jacob Lawrence and William H. Johnson: Nesbett, Peter T. and DuBois, Michelle, eds., *Over the Line: The Art and Life of Jacob Lawrence*, University of Washington Press, Seattle, 2001. Powell, Richard J., *Homecoming: The Art and Life of William H. Johnson*, Rizzoli, New York, 1991.

Eldzier Cortor and the "folk cult" revisited: Naremore, James, "Uptown Folk: Cabin in the Sky (1943)," in *The Films of Vincente Minnelli*, Cambridge University Press, Cambridge, 1993, pp. 51–70. Cortor, Eldzier, letter to Homer St. Gaudens, 15 September 1947, Archives of American Art, Smithsonian Institution, Washington, DC. Jennings, Corrine L., "Eldzier Cortor: The Long Consistent Road," in *Three Masters: Eldzier Cortor, Hughie Lee-Smith, Archibald John Motley Jr.*, Kenkeleba Gallery, New York, 1988, pp. 12–22. Vlach, John Michael, "Contemporary Plain Painters: New Forms, New Criteria," in *Plain Painters: Making Sense of American Folk Art*, Smithsonian Institution, Washington, DC, 1988, pp. 161–75.

John Dunkley and Hector Hyppolite: Nawi, Diana, ed., *John Dunkley: Neither Day or Night*, Prestel, Munich, 2017. Rodman, Selden, *Where Art Is Joy*, Ruggles de Latour, New York, 1988. Breton, André, "Hector Hyppolite," in *Surrealism and Painting* (1965), reprint, Icon Editions, New York, 1972, pp. 308–12. *Mystical Imagination: The Art of Haitian Master Hector Hyppolite*, The Haitian Art Society, Washington, DC, 2012. Glissant, Edouard, "On Haitian Painting," in *Caribbean Discourse*, University of Virginia Press, Charlottesville, 1992, pp. 155–57.

James Hampton and Minnie Evans: Powell, Richard J., "Art, History, and Vision," *Art Bulletin* 77, September 1995, pp. 379–82. Kahan, Mitchell Douglas, *Heavenly Visions: The Art of Minnie Evans*, University of North Carolina Press, Chapel Hill, 1986.

Black culture and abstract art: Gibson, Ann, "Two Worlds: African-American Abstraction in New York at Mid-Century," in *The Search for Freedom: African American Abstract Painting, 1945–1975*, Kenkeleba Gallery, New York, 1991, pp. 11–53. Frascina, Francis, "Attitudes: Origins and Cultural Difference," in *Modernism in Dispute: Art Since the Forties*, Yale University Press, New Haven, 1993, pp. 124–57. "Leading Young Artists," *Ebony* 13, April 1958, pp. 33–38. Fine, Ruth, ed., *Procession: The Art of Norman Lewis*, University of California Press, Berkeley, 2015. Wilson, Judith, "Go Back and Retrieve It: Hale Woodruff, Afro-American Modernist," in *Selected Essays: Art & Artists from the Harlem Renaissance to the 1980s*, National Black Arts Festival, Atlanta, 1988, pp. 41–49. Woodruff, Hale, letter to Charles Alston, 18 February 1947, Archives of American Art, Smithsonian Institution, Washington, DC. Rosenberg, Harold, as quoted in Charles Childs, "The Artist Caught between Two Worlds," *Tuesday Magazine*, April 1967, pp. 8–10, 23. Harris, Shawnya L., *Richard Hunt: Synthesis*, Georgia Museum of Art, University of Georgia, Athens,

2018. Walmsley, Anne, ed., *Guyana Dreaming: the Art of Aubrey Williams*, Dangaroo Press, Coventry and Sydney, 1990. Powell, Richard J., "Drawing the Color Line: The Art of Ollie Harrington," in *Going There: Black Visual Satire*, Yale University Press, New Haven, 2020, pp. 52–100.

Sartre, universality, and the "Orphic" myth: Fabre, Michel, *From Harlem to Paris: Black American Writers in France, 1840–1980*, University of Illinois Press, Urbana, 1991. Wilson, Sarah, "Paris Post War: In Search of the Absolute," in Frances Morris, *Paris Post War: Art and Existentialism, 1945–55*. Tate Gallery, London, 1993, pp. 25–52. Diop, Alioune, "Niam n'goura ou les raisons d'être de *Présence Africaine*," *Présence Africaine* 1, October–November 1947, p. 7. Sartre, Jean-Paul, "Black Orpheus" (1948), English translation, *The Massachusetts Review* 6, Autumn/Winter 1964–65, pp. 13–52. Fanon, Frantz, trans. Charles Lam Markmann, *Black Skin, White Masks*, Grove, New York, 1967, pp. 109–40. David, Catherine, *Wifredo Lam*, Centre Pompidou, Paris, 2015. Ellison, Ralph, *Invisible Man*, Random House, New York, 1952. Moraes, Vinicius de, *Orfeu da Conceição*, Editôra Dois Amigos, Rio de Janeiro, 1967. Trémois, Claude-Marie, "Comment Camus a tourné *Orfeu Negro*," *Nouveaux Films Français* 474 (1960). Miller-Keller, Andrea, *Bob Thompson: Matrix 90*, Wadsworth Atheneum, Hartford, 1986. Canterbury, Patricia Sue, *Beauford Delaney: From New York to Paris*, Minneapolis Institute of Arts, Minneapolis, 2005. Porter, Thomas J., "Skunder Boghossian: Spaces," in *Skunder*, Trisolini Gallery of Ohio University, Athens, 1980, n.p.

Black figuration and protest: Spiro, Lesley, *Gerard Sekoto: Unsevered Ties*, Johannesburg Art Gallery, Johannesburg, 1989. *Elizabeth Catlett: The Negro Woman*, Barnett-Aden Gallery, Washington, DC, 1947. Herzog, Melanie Ann, *Elizabeth Catlett: An American Artist in Mexico*, University of Washington Press, Seattle, 2005. Hansberry, Lorraine, "Foreword," in *Charles White*, ACA Gallery, New York, 1961, n.p. Oehler, Sarah Kelly, ed., *Charles White: A Retrospective*, Art Institute of Chicago, 2018. Bush, Martin H., *The Photographs of Gordon Parks*, Edwin A. Ulrich Museum of Art, Wichita, 1983. Hughes, Langston, and Roy DeCarava, *The Sweet Flypaper of Life*, Simon and Schuster, New York, 1955. Frank, Robert, *The Americans*, Grove, New York, 1959. *Let Us March On! Selected Civil Rights Photographs of Ernest C. Withers, 1955–1968*,

Massachusetts College of Art, Boston, 1992. *102 Favorite Paintings by Norman Rockwell*, Crown, New York, 1978.

Chapter 5
"Black is a Color"
Romare Bearden and the metamorphosis of identity: Jones, LeRoi, "blackhope," in *Home*, William Morrow, New York, 1966, pp. 234–37. Childs, Charles, "Bearden: Identification and Identity," *Art News* 63, October 1964, pp 24–25, 54, 61–62. Fine, Ruth, ed., *The Art of Romare Bearden*, National Gallery of Art, Washington, DC, 2003.

Barbara Chase-Riboud and Raymond Saunders: Selz, Peter, *Barbara Chase-Riboud: Sculptor*, Harry N. Abrams, New York, 1999. Fanon, Frantz, trans. Charles Lam Markmann, *Black Skin, White Masks*, Grove, New York, 1967, pp. 109–40. Saunders, Raymond, *Black Is A Color*, privately printed, San Francisco, *c.* 1968, n.p. Powell, Richard J. "The Art of Raymond Saunders: Colored," *New Observations* 97, September/October 1993, pp. 10–15.

Alma Thomas and Sam Gilliam: Kingsley, April, *Afro-American Abstraction*, The Art Museum Association, San Francisco, 1982. Berry, Ian, *Alma Thomas*, Prestel, Munich, 2016. Binstock, Jonathan P., *Sam Gilliam: A Retrospective*, University of California Press, Berkeley, 2005. Morrison, Keith, *Art in Washington and its Afro-American Presence: 1940–1970*, Washington Project for the Arts, Washington, DC, 1985. Powell, Richard J., *Circle Dance: The Art of John T. Scott*, University Press of Mississippi, Jackson, 2005.

Hervé Télémaque and Emilio Cruz: Briend, Christian, *Hervé Télémaque*, Somogy éditions d'art, Paris, 2015. Fleminger, Susan, *Emilio Cruz: Spilled Nightmares, Revelations and Reflections*, Studio Museum in Harlem, New York, 1987.

Joe Overstreet and Al Loving: Fine, Elsa Honig, *The Afro-American Artist: A Search for Identity*, Holt, Rinehart and Winston, New York, 1973, pp. 234–35, 261–62. Reed, Ishmael, *Mumbo Jumbo*, Doubleday, New York, 1972. Siegel, Katy, *Al Loving: Torn Canvas*, Gary Snyder Gallery, New York, 2015

Edward Clark and Jack Whitten: Rajaratnam, Sukanya, *Ed Clark: A Survey*, Mnuchin Gallery, Los Angeles, 2018. Wright, Beryl J., *Jack Whitten*, The Newark Museum, Newark, 1990, pp. 7–13. Kittelmann, Udo, *Jack Whitten*, Prestel, Munich, 2019.

Uzo Egonu and Frank Bowling: Oguibe, Olu, *Seen/ Unseen*, Bluecoat Gallery, Liverpool, 1994. Araeen, Rasheed, *The Other Story: Afro-Asian artists in post-war Britain*, South Bank Centre, London, 1989, pp. 37–41, 119–21. Bowling, Frank, "Is Black Art About Color?" in Rhoda L. Goldstein, ed., *Black Life and Culture in the United States*, Thomas Crowell, New York, 1971, pp. 302–21. Crippa, Elena, *Frank Bowling*, Tate Publishing, London, 2019.

African Americans and the media: McLuhan, H. Marshall, *Understanding Media: The Extensions of Man*, Routledge and Kegan Paul, London; McGraw-Hill, New York, 1964. Campbell, Mary Schmidt, *Tradition and Conflict: Images of a Turbulent Decade, 1963–1973*, Studio Museum in Harlem, New York, 1985. Donaldson, Jeff, *The Civil Rights Yearbook*, Henry Regnery, Chicago, 1964. Shecter, Leonard, "The Passion of Muhammad Ali," *Esquire* 69, April 1968, pp. 128–31, 140, 148–60. Bogle, Donald, *Toms, Coons, Mulattoes, Mammies, and Bucks: An Interpretive History of Blacks in American Film*, Viking Press, New York, 1973, pp. 232–35.

Black cultural signifiers: "Beauty Bulletin: The Natural," *Vogue* 153, January 1969, pp. 134–37. Lewis, Samella, *African American Art and Artists*, University of California Press, Berkeley, 1994. Willis-Thomas, Deborah, *Introspect: the Photographs of Anthony Barboza*, Studio Museum in Harlem, New York, 1982. *afri-cobra iii*, University Art Gallery, University of Massachusetts at Amherst, Amherst, 1973. Donaldson, Jeff, "10 in Search of a Nation," *Black World* 19, October 1970, pp. 80–89.

The black nude: Childs, Charles, "Larry Ocean Swims the Nile, Mississippi and other Rivers," in *Some American History*, Institute for the Arts, Rice University, Houston, 1971, pp. 9–20. Wilson, Judith, "Getting Down to Get Over: Romare Bearden's Use of Pornography and the Problem of the Black Female Body in Afro-U.S. Art," in Gina Dent, ed., *Black Popular Culture*, Bay Press, Seattle, 1992, pp. 112–22. *Murry DePillars: Paintings*, Studio Museum in Harlem, New York, 1976. Farrington, Lisa E., *Faith Ringgold*, Pomegranate Communications, Petaluma, CA, 2004. Chandler, Dana, *If The Shoe Fits, Hear It! Paintings and Drawings, 1967–1976*, Northeastern University, Boston, 1976. Schoonmaker, Trevor, ed., *Barkley L. Hendricks: Birth of the Cool*, Nasher Museum of Art at Duke University, Durham, 2008. Willis, Deborah, ed., *Picturing Us: African American*

Identity in Photography, The New Press, New York, 1994. Mercer, Kobena, "Reading Racial Fetishism: The Photographs of Robert Mapplethorpe," in *Welcome to the Jungle: New Positions in Black Cultural Studies*, Routledge, London and New York, 1994, pp. 171–219. Ribas, João and Ramos, Maria, *Robert Mapplethorpe: Pictures*, Fundação de Serralves, Porto, 2018. Walker, Alice, *Meridian*, Deutsch, London; Harcourt Brace Jovanovich, New York, 1976, p. 130.

Alternatives to the "Black Arts" movement agenda: Driskell, David C., *Two Centuries of Black American Art*, Alfred A. Knopf, New York, 1976. Diawara, Manthia, ed., *Black American Cinema*, Routledge, London, 1993. Carpenter, Jane H. and Saar, Betye, *Betye Saar*, Pomegranate Communications, Petaluma, CA, 2003. Gordon, Allan, "Nommo Muse: Black Improvisation in California," *New Art Examiner* 7, June 1980, pp. 6–7. Bryant, Linda Goode and Marcy S. Philips, *Contexures*, Just Above Midtown Gallery, New York, 1978, pp. 38–45. Jones, Kellie, *David Hammons: Five Decades*, Mnuchin Gallery, Los Angeles, 2016.

Reimaging "Africa" after colonialism: Beier, Ulli, *Art in Nigeria*, Cambridge University Press, Cambridge, 1960. Thompson, Alison, *Son et Lumière: The Paintings of Francis Griffith*, Barbados Museum and Historical Society, Bridgetown, 1995. Bender, Wolfgang, *Rastafari Kunst aus Jamaica*, Übersee-Museum, Bremen, 1984. VanDyke, Rebecca, *Designing a New Tradition: Loïs Mailou Jones and the Aesthetics of Blackness*, Penn State University Press, State College, PA, 2020. Poinsett, Alex, "Festac '77," *Ebony* 32, May 1977, pp. 33–49.

Music, art, and the black ethos: Powell, Richard J., *The Blues Aesthetic: Black Culture and Modernism*, Washington Project for the Arts, Washington, DC, 1989. Archie Rand, *The Groups: Paintings by Archie Rand*, Museum of Art, Carnegie Institute, Pittsburgh, 1983. *Ernie Barnes/Artist*, The Company of Art, Los Angeles, 1979.

"Folk," "fine," and reconciliations of black culture: Livingston, Jane and John Beardsley, *Black Folk Art in America: 1930–1980*, University of Mississippi Press, Jackson, 1982. Poupeye-Rammelaere, Veerle, "The Rainbow Valley: The Life and Work of Brother Everald Brown," *Jamaica Journal* 21, May–July 1988, pp. 2–14. Childs, Adrienne L., *Margo Humphrey*, Pomegranate

Communications, Petaluma, CA, 2009. Tate, Greg, "Cult-Nats Meet Freaky-Deke," *Flyboy in the Buttermilk: Essays on Contemporary America*, Fireside Book, New York, 1992, pp. 198–210.

Chapter 6
Culture as Currency

Lyle Ashton Harris, Alison Saar, and Martin Puryear: Coblentz, Cassandra, ed., *Lyle Ashton Harris: Blow Up*, Gregory R. Miller & Company, New York, 2008. Krane, Susan, *Art at the Edge: Alison Saar/Fertile Ground*, High Museum of Art, Atlanta, 1993. Doll, Nancy and Tallman, Susan, *Mirror, Mirror: The Prints of Alison Saar*, Jordan Schnitzer Family Foundation, Portland, OR, 2019. Kamin Rapaport, Brooke, ed., *Martin Puryear: Liberty Libertà*, Gregory R. Miller & Company, New York, 2019.

Culture as an artistic currency: Tate, Greg, "Start Black-Owned Conceptual Bomber," *Vibe* 3, February 1995, p. 32. *The Decade Show: Frameworks of Identity in the 1980s*, Museum of Contemporary Hispanic Art/The New Museum of Contemporary Art/The Studio Museum in Harlem, New York, 1990. "Critical Decade: Black British Photography in the 80s," *Ten.8* 2, Spring 1992. West, Cornel, "Nihilism in Black America," in Gina Dent, ed., *Black Popular Culture*, Bay Press, Seattle, 1992, pp. 36–47. Hall, Stuart, "What is this 'Black' in Black Popular Culture?" in Gina Dent, ed., *op. cit.*, pp. 20–33. *Interrogating Identity*, Grey Art Gallery and Study Center, New York University, New York, 1991.

Black signs and symbols: Reed, Dock, Henry Reed, and Vera Hall, "Handwriting on the Wall" (1937), in Alan Lomax, ed., *Afro-American Spirituals, Work Songs, and Ballads*, Library of Congress AFS L3. Buchhart, Dieter, ed., *Jean-Michel Basquiat*, Fondation Louis Vuitton, Paris, 2018. Hughes, Robert, "Jean-Michel Basquiat: Requiem for a Featherweight," in *Nothing If Not Critical: Selected Essays on Art and Artists*, Alfred A. Knopf, New York, 1990, pp. 308–12. *Tam Joseph: Learning to Walk*, Bedford Hill Gallery, London, 1989. Enwezor, Okwui, "Ouattara: Beyond Shamanism," *Nka: Journal of Contemporary African Art* 2, Spring/Summer 1995, pp. 24–29. Powell, Richard J., unpublished notes on meeting with Ras Ishi Butcher, St. John, Barbados, 13 March 1995.

Mr. Imagination and Philip Moore: Patterson, Tom, "Manifesting the World of Mr. Imagination," in *Reclamation and Transformation: Three Self-Taught Chicago Artists*, Terra Foundation for the Arts, Chicago, 1994, pp. 34–63. Moore, Philip, unpublished notes on his work, 8 April 1992, Mervyn Awon Archives, St. Michael, Barbados.

Martha Jackson Jarvis and Melvin Edwards: Swift, Mary, "The Power of One: Martha Jackson Jarvis," *Washington Review* 20, February/March 1995, pp. 3–5. Potts, Alex, ed., *Melvin Edwards: Five Decades*, Nasher Sculpture Center, Dallas, 2015.

Placement/displacement: Grynsztejn, Madeleine, *About Place: Recent Art of the Americas*, Art Institute of Chicago, Chicago, 1995. Simon, Joan, *Lorna Simpson*, Prestel, Munich, 2013. Morrison, Toni, *The Bluest Eye* (first published 1970), Pocket Books, New York, 1972, pp. 17–18. Storr, Robert, *Dislocations*, Museum of Modern Art, New York, 1991. Wilson, Fred, "The Silent Message of the Museum," in Jean Fisher, ed., *Global Visions: Towards a New Internationalism in the Visual Arts*, Kala Press, London, 1994, pp. 152–60. Jacob, Mary Jane, *Places with a Past: New Site-Specific Art at Charleston's Spoleto Festival*, Rizzoli, New York, 1991, pp. 138–45. Sims, Lowery Stokes, "Home is Where the Heart is: Beverly Buchanan's Shack Sculpture in Context," in *Beverly Buchanan: Shack Works, a 16-Year Survey*, Montclair Art Museum, Montclair, 1994, pp. 33–39. Molesworth, Helen, ed., *Kerry James Marshall: Mastry*, Skira Rizzoli Publications, New York, 2016. Solomon, Andrew, "The Artists of South Africa: Separate, and Equal," *New York Times Magazine*, 27 March 1994, p. 78. Williamson, Sue, letter to Richard J. Powell, 28 November 1995. Grynsztejn, Madeleine, *op. cit.*, pp. 31–33.

Fred Wilson, Sonia Boyce, Conwill/De Pace/Majozo and Alfredo Jaar: Fleming, Jeff, "Ground-Truthing," in *Insight/In Site/In Sight/Incite: Memory/Artist and the Community: Fred Wilson*, Southeastern Center for Contemporary Art, Winston-Salem, 1994, pp. 15–19. Wilson, Fred and Globus, Doro, eds., *Fred Wilson: A Critical Reader*, Ridinghouse, London, 2011. Tawadros, Gilane, "Peeping Toms," in *Peep: Sonia Boyce*, Institute of International Visual Arts, London, 1995, n.p. Majozo, Estella Conwill, "To Search for the Good and make it Matter," in Suzanne Lacy, ed., *Mapping the Terrain: New Genre Public Art*, Bay Press, Seattle, 1995, pp. 88–93. Gilroy, Paul, *The Black Atlantic: Modernity and Double Consciousness*, Harvard University Press, Cambridge, MA, 1993. Siitari, Pirkko, *Tonight no poetry will serve: Alfredo Jaar/*

Kun runous ei riitä: Alfredo Jaar, Nykytaiteen museo Kiasma, Helsinki, 2014.

Identities in flux: Fleming, Jeff, "Ground-Truthing," in *Insight/In Site/In Sight/Incite: Memory/Artist and the Community: Fred Wilson*, Southeastern Center for Contemporary Art, Winston-Salem, 1994, pp. 15–19. Wilson, Fred and Globus, Doro, eds., *Fred Wilson: A Critical Reader*, Ridinghouse, London, 2011. Tawadros, Gilane, "Peeping Toms," in *Peep: Sonia Boyce*, Institute of International Visual Arts, London, 1995, n.p. Majozo, Estella Conwill, "To Search for the Good and make it Matter," in Suzanne Lacy, ed., *Mapping the Terrain: New Genre Public Art*, Bay Press, Seattle, 1995, pp. 88–93. Gilroy, Paul, *The Black Atlantic: Modernity and Double Consciousness*, Harvard University Press, Cambridge, MA, 1993. Siitari, Pirkko, *Tonight no poetry will serve: Alfredo Jaar/Kun runous ei riitä: Alfredo Jaar*, Nykytaiteen museo Kiasma, Helsinki, 2014. Appiah, Kwame Anthony, *In My Father's House: Africa in the Philosophy of Culture*, Oxford University Press, New York, 1992, p. 176.

Philip Mallory Jones and Albert Chong: Levin, Julie, "Visions of Diaspora: Five Video Works by Philip Mallory Jones," in *1992 Dallas Video Festival*, Dallas Museum of Fine Arts, Dallas, 1992, p. 63. *Ancestral Dialogues: The Photographs of Albert Chong*, The Friends of Photography, San Francisco, 1994.

Lorraine O'Grady and Emma Amos: Reid, Calvin, "A West Indian Yankee in Queen Nefertiti's Court," *New Observations* 97, September/ October 1993, pp. 5–9. hooks, bell, "Aesthetic Intervention," in *Emma Amos: Changing the Subject, Paintings and Prints, 1992–1994*, Art in General, New York, 1994, pp. 5–12.

Coreen Simpson, Dawoud Bey, and Maud Sulter: Ashford, Nickolas and Valerie Simpson, *Ashford & Simpson: Gimme Something Real* (1973), Warner Bros. Records BS 2739. Birt, Rodger, "Coreen Simpson: An Interpretation," *Black American Literature Forum* 21, Fall 1987, pp. 289–304. *Dawoud Bey: Seeing Deeply*, University of Texas Press, Austin, 2018. Sulter, Maud, *Zabat*, Urban Fox Press, West Yorkshire, 1989. Hambourg, Maria Morris, François Heilbrun, Philippe Néagu, *Nadar*, Abrams, New York, 1995, pp. 238–40.

Social narratives and "color" concepts: Merewether, Charles, "Banality and Tragedy.

A History of the Present in Haiti," in *Edouard Duval-Carrié*, Museo de Arte Contemporáneo de Monterrey, Monterrey, 1993, pp. 19–23. Gill, Susan, "Sue Coe's Inferno," *Art News* 86, October 1987, pp. 110–15. Thomas, Jo, "Black Youths Riot in London District," *New York Times*, 29 September 1985, pp. 1, 20.

Adrian Piper and Howardena Pindell: Cherix, Christophe, ed., *Adrian Piper: A Synthesis of Intuitions, 1965–2016*, Museum of Modern Art, New York, 2018. Stepto, Robert B., *From Behind the Veil: A Study of Afro-American Narrative*, Urbana, University of Illinois Press, 1979. *Howardena Pindell: Paintings and Drawings*, Roland Gibson Gallery, Potsdam, New York, 1992. Beckwith, Naomi and Cassel Oliver, Valerie, eds., *Howardena Pindell: What Remains to be Seen*, DelMonico Books/Prestel, Munich, 2018.

Glenn Ligon/Byron Kim and Robert Colescott: Harrison, Helen, "Skin Pigmentation as a Determinant of Attitudes," *New York Times*, 1 December 1991, section 12, p. 22. Rothkopf, Scott, ed., *Glenn Ligon: America*, Yale University Press, New Haven, 2011. Bailey, David A., "Mirage: Enigmas of Race, Difference, and Desire," in *Mirage: Enigmas of Race, Difference, and Desire*, Institute of Contemporary Arts, London, 1995, p. 78. Platow, Raphaela and Sims, Lowery Stokes, eds., *Art and Race Matters: The Career of Robert Colescott*, Rizzoli Electa, New York, 2019.

Keith Morrison and Stanley Greaves: Ater, Renée, *Keith Morrison*, Pomegranate Communications, Petaluma, CA, 2005. Roopnaraine, Rupert, *The Primacy of the Eye: The Art of Stanley Greaves*, Peepal Tree Press Ltd, Leeds, 2005. Greaves, Stanley, letter to Richard J. Powell, 13 June 1995.

Bodily acts of black art: Henderson, Stephen, *Understanding the New Black Poetry: Black Speech & Black Music as Poetic References*, William Morrow, New York, 1972. *Other Sources: An American Essay*, San Francisco Art Institute, San Francisco, 1976. King-Hammond, Leslie and Lowery Stokes Sims, *Art As A Verb: The Evolving Continuum/ Installations, Performances, and Videos by 13 African-American Artists*, Maryland Institute, College of Art, Baltimore, 1988. *The Decade Show: Frameworks of Identity in the 1980s*, Museum of Contemporary Hispanic Art/ The New Museum of Contemporary Art/The Studio Museum in Harlem, New York, 1990. Sims, Lowery Stokes, "Aspects of Performance in the Work of Black American Women Artists," in Arlene Raven, ed., *Feminist Art Criticism: An Anthology*, UMI Research Press, Ann Arbor, 1988, pp. 207–25. Thompson, Robert Farris, *Face of the Gods: Art and Altars of Africa and the African Americas*, Museum for African Art, New York, 1993. Fusco, Coco, "Performance and the Power of the Popular," in Catherine Ugwu, ed., *Let's Get it On: The Politics of Black Performance*, Bay Press, Seattle, 1995, pp. 158–75.

Keith Haring/Tseng Kwong Chi/Bill T. Jones: Pih, Darren, ed., *Keith Haring*, Tate Publishing, London, 2019. Mercer, Kobena, "Reading Racial Fetishism: The Photographs of Robert Mapplethorpe," in *Welcome to the Jungle: New Positions in Black Cultural Studies*, Routledge, London and New York, 1994, pp. 171–219.

Ben Jones and Sherman Fleming: Patrick, John, "The Big Picture: Multiculturalism evoked in Jersey City exhibit," *The Jersey Journal*, 6 January 1995, p. E7. Spriggs, Edward S., ed., *Deliverance: The Art of Ben Jones, 1970–2008*, Jersey City Museum, Jersey City, NJ, 2009. Stiles, Kristine, "Rodforce: Thoughts on the Art of Sherman Fleming," *High Performance* 10, 1987, pp. 34–39. "Other Bloods/ Dagboek Aldert Mantje," *De Maat Schappy Arti et Amicitiæ* 3, March 1995, pp. 5–7. Riefenstahl, Leni, *The Last of the Nuba*, Harper & Row, New York, 1974; Collins, London, 1976.

Black women artists performing "the body": *Sokari Douglas Camp: Play and Display*, Museum of Mankind, London, 1995. Magnier, Bernard, "A la rencontre de... Werewere Liking," *Notre Librairie* 79, 1985, pp. 17–21. James, Curtia, "Joyce J. Scott: Generic Interference/ Genetic Engineering," *Art Papers*, September/ October 1993, p. 66. Schneider, Gary Garrido, *Joyce J. Scott: Harriet Tubman and Other Truths*, Grounds for Sculpture, Hamilton, NY, 2018. Delmez, Kathryn W., ed., *Carrie Mae Weems: Three Decades of Photography and Video*, Yale University Press, New Haven, 2013.

Chapter 7
Through a Glass, Diasporally

Toward a definition of "black film": Cripps, Thomas, "Oscar Micheaux: The Story Continues," in Manthia Diawara, ed., *Black American Cinema*, Routledge, London and New York, 1993, pp. 71–79. Bill Cosby, "Introduction," in Middleton A. Harris, Morris Levitt, Roger Furman, and Ernest Smith, eds., *The Black Book*, Random House, New York, 1974, p. i. Snead, James, *White Screens/Black Images: Hollywood from the Dark Side*, Routledge, London and New York, 1994.

Vincente Minelli and Spencer Williams: Cripps, Thomas, "Oscar Micheaux: The Story Continues," in Manthia, Diawara, ed., *Black American Cinema*, Routledge, London and New York, 1993, pp. 71–79. Bill Cosby, "Introduction," in Middleton A. Harris, Morris Levitt, Roger Furman, and Ernest Smith, eds., *The Black Book*, Random House, New York, 1974, p. i. Snead, James, *White Screens/Black Images: Hollywood from the Dark Side*, Routledge, London and New York, 1994.

Realities and pleasures via the cinematic artifice: Stephenson, Ralph and J. R. Debrix, *The Cinema as Art*, Penguin, London, 1965, pp. 13–36. Callenbach, Ernest, "Film Reviews: Orfeu Negro," *Film Quarterly* 13, Spring 1960, pp. 57–58. Sainville, Leonard, "Le Cinéma: Orfeu Negro," *Présence Africaine* 26, June–July 1959, pp. 130–31. Dent, Gina, "Black Pleasure, Black Joy: An Introduction," in Gina Dent, ed., *Black Popular Culture*, Bay Press, Seattle, 1992, pp. 1–19. Diawara, Manthia, "Black American Cinema: The New Realism," in Manthia Diawara, ed., *Black American Cinema*, Routledge, London and New York, 1993, pp. 3–25. Hemphill, Essex, "Brother to Brother: Interview with Isaac Julien," *Black Film Review* 5, Summer 1989, pp. 14–17. Mercer, Kobena, "Dark and Lovely: Black Gay Image-Making," *Welcome to the Jungle: New Positions in Black Cultural Studies*, Routledge, London and New York, 1994, pp. 220–32. Gates, Henry Louis Jr., "Looking for Modernism," in Manthia Diawara, ed., *Black American Cinema*, pp. 200–207. Diawara, Manthia and Phyllis R. Klotman, "Ganja and Hess: Vampires, Sex, and Addictions," and Diawara, Manthia, "The Nature of Mother in Dreaming Rivers," in *Black American Literature Forum* 25, Summer 1991, pp. 283–98 and 299–314. Smith, Valerie, "Facing the Spectre of Racism," *Emerge* 6 (October 1994), pp. 60–61.

Spike Lee and Felix de Rooy: Lee, Spike, and Lisa Jones, *Uplift the Race: The Construction of School Daze*, Fireside Book, New York, 1988. Fusco, Coco, "Stateless Hybrids: An Introduction," *Hybrid State Films*, Exit Art, New York, 1991, n.p. Malbert, Roger, "Felix de Rooy," *In Fusion: New European Art*, The South Bank Centre/Ikon Gallery, Birmingham, 1993, p 42.

Ousmane Sembène and Euzhan Palcy: Ukadike, Nwachukwu Frank, *Black African Cinema*, University of California Press, 1994, pp. 182–84. Pfaff, Françoise, *The Cinema of Ousmane Sembène, A Pioneer of African Film*, Greenwood Press, Westport, CT, 1984. De Stefano, George, "Sugar Cane Alley," *Cineaste* 13, 1984, pp. 42–45.

Julie Dash and Haile Gerima: Dash, Julie, *Daughters of the Dust: The Making of an African American Woman's Film*, The New Press, New York, 1992. Brown, Georgia, "The haunting," *Village Voice* 39, 12 April 1994, p. 56.

Broadcast television and music videos: MacDonald, J. Fred, *Blacks and White TV: African Americans in Television since 1948*, Nelson-Hall Publishers, Chicago, 1992. Rose, Tricia, "Voices from the Margins: Rap Music and Contemporary Black Cultural Production," *Black Noise: Rap Music and Black Culture in Contemporary America*, University Press of New England, 1994, pp. 1–20. Laing, Dave, "Music Video: Industrial Product, Cultural Form," *Screen* 26, March–April 1985, pp. 78–83. Durgnat, Raymond, "Amazing Grace," *American Film* 11, January–February 1986, pp. 31–35.

Keith Piper and black British video initiatives: Mercer, Kobena, "Recording Narratives of Race and Nation," *Black Film/British Cinema: ICA Documents* 7, 1988, pp. 4–14. Piper, Keith, "Introduction," *The Exploded City*, Center 181 Gallery, London, 1994, n.p.

Jonathan Demme, Steve McQueen, and Charles Stone III: Morrison, Toni, *Beloved*, Alfred A. Knopf, New York, and Chatto & Windus, London, 1987. Winfrey, Oprah, *Journey to Beloved*, Hyperion, New York, 1998. Dobrzynski, Judith H., "A Convert Spreads the Word for Haitian Art," *New York Times*, June 10, 1997. Laurenz Foundation, ed., *Steve McQueen: Works*, Kehrer, Heidelberg, 2012. O'Kane, Paul, "Reviews: Steve McQueen: ICA, London, England," *Zing Magazine* 10, Summer 1999, see www.zingmagazine.com. Powell, Richard J., unpublished notes on meeting with Charles Stone III, Durham, North Carolina, 5 April 1995. Elliot, Stuart, "Responsible Party: Charles Stone III; A Buzzword Rises from an Inside Joke," *New York Times*, April 16, 2000.

The "Cut and Mix" Aesthetic: Oguibe, Olu, "African Cinema Today: Interview with Mark Reid," *Nka* 9, Fall/Winter 1998, pp. 58–61. Miller,

Paul D., "Time and The Cinematic Image: Notes for the Oberhausen Film Festival 2001," see www.djspooky.com. Moten, Fred, *In the Break: The Aesthetics of the Black Radical Tradition*, University of Minnesota Press, Minneapolis, 2003. Thompson, Krista, "The Sound of Light: Reflections on Art History in the Visual Culture of Hip-Hop," *Art Bulletin* 91, 2009, pp. 481–505. Gad, Amira and Joseph Constable, *Arthur Jafa: A Series of Utterly Improbable, Yet Extraordinary Renditions*, Walter Koenig Books, Berlin, 2018. Cimini, Amy, "Walking to the gallery: Sondra Perry's 'It's in the game' in San Diego in five fragments," *Sound Studies* 4, 2018, pp. 178–200. Sales, Liz, "Rendering the Real: Interview with Gilles Elie-Dit-Cosaque," *ARC Magazine*, August 18, 2014. https://www.arcthemagazine.com/arc/2014/08/rendering-the-real-liz-sales-interviews-matinician-descent-artist-gilles-elie-dit-cosaque. Accessed May 5, 2020.

Chapter 8
Fin-de-Siècle Blues
The Allure and Loathing of Blackness: Deliss, Clementine, ed., *Seven Stories about Modern Art in Africa*, Flammarion, Paris, 1995. *Freestyle*, Studio Museum in Harlem, New York, 2001. Doy, Gen, *Black Visual Culture: Modernity and Postmodernity*, I. B. Tauris Publishers, London, 2000. *Septima Bienal de la Habana*, Centro de Arte Contemporaneo Wifredo Lam, Havana, 2000. Bedford, Emma, "Dak'Art 2000: In Search of the Magic Moment," *Nka* 13/14, Spring/Summer 2001, pp. 14–17. Enwezor, Okwui, *Trade Routes: History and Geography*, 2nd Johannesburg Biennale, Johannesburg, 1997. Gilroy, Paul, *Against Race: Imagining Political Culture Beyond the Color Line*, Belknap Press of Harvard University, Cambridge, 2000.

Kara Walker, David Levinthal, and other visual provocateurs: Vergne, Philippe, ed., *Kara Walker: My Complement, My Enemy, My Oppressor, My Love*, Walker Art Center, Minneapolis, 2007. Lott, Tommy, "Kara Walker Speaks: A Public Conversation on Racism, Art, and Politics," *Black Renaissance/Renaissance Noire* 3, Fall 2000: pp. 66–91. *David Levinthal: Works from 1975–1996*, D.A.P., New York, 1997. *David Levinthal: Blackface*, Arena Editions, Santa Fe, New Mexico, 1999. *Re/Righting History: Counternarratives by Contemporary African-American Artists*, Katonah Museum of Art, Katonah, New York, 1999. Allen, James, *Without Sanctuary: Lynching Photography in America*, Twin Palms Publishers, Santa Fe, New Mexico, 2000.

Renée Cox, Aaron McGruder, and Chris Ofili: Isaak, Jo Anna, *Looking Forward, Looking Black*, Hobart and William Smith Colleges Press, Geneva, New York, 1999. Nyong'o, Tavia, "Racial Kitsch and Black Performance," *The Yale Journal of Criticism* 15, 2002, p. 383. McGruder, Aaron, *Fresh for '01 You Suckas!*, Andrews McMeel Publishing, Kansas City, 2001. Gioni, Massimiliano, ed., *Chris Ofili: Night and Day*, Skira Rizzoli, New York, 2014. Hirschberg, Lynn, "How Black Comedy Got the Last Laugh," *The New York Times Magazine*, September 3, 2000.

African Artists in the Global Imagination: Enwezor, Okwui, *The Short Century: Independence and Liberation Movements in Africa, 1945–1994*, Prestel, Munich, 2001. Enwezor, Okwui, "Between Worlds: Postmodernism and African Artists in the Western Metropolis," in Olu Oguibe and Okwui Enwezor, eds., *Reading the Contemporary: African Art from Theory to the Marketplace*, in IVA, London, 1999. M.I.T. Press, Cambridge, MA, 1999, pp. 244–75. *In/sight: African Photographers, 1940 to the Present*, Guggenheim Museum, New York, 1996. Oguibe, Olu, "Beyond Visual Pleasures: A Brief Reflection on the Work of Contemporary African Women Artists," in Salah M. Hassan, ed., *Gendered Visions: The Art of Contemporary Africana Women Artists*, Trenton, Africa World Press, Inc., 1997, pp. 63–72. Williamson, Sue and Ashraf Jamal, *Art in South Africa: The Future Present*, David Philip, Cape Town, 1996. Hassan, Salah M., and Olu Oguibe, *Authentic/Ex-Centric: Conceptualism in Contemporary African Art*, Forum for African Arts, Ithaca, 2001. Haines, Bruce, "Johannes Phokela: Changing the Title," in Salah M. Hassan and Iftikhar Dadi, eds., *Unpacking Europe: Towards a Critical Reading*, Museum Boijmans Van Beuningen and NAI Publishers, Rotterdam, 2001, pp. 380–83. Williamson, Sue, "Artbio: Tracey Rose," *Artthrob* 43, March 2001, see www.artthrob.co.za. Mosquera, Gerardo, "Good-Bye Identity, Welcome Difference: From Latin American Art to Art From Latin America," *Third Text* 56, Autumn 2001, pp. 25–32. Kasfir, Sidney Littlefield, *Contemporary African Art*, Thames & Hudson, London, 1999. Enwezor, Okwui, "Reframing the Black Subject: Ideology and Fantasy in Contemporary South African Representation," in Oguibe and Enwezor, eds., *Reading the Contemporary*, 1999, pp. 377–99. *Mode/Fashion* (Special Issue), *Revue Noire* 27, December 1997/January & February 1998. Mustafa, Hudita Nura, "Sartorial Ecumenes: African Styles in a Social and Economic Context," in *The Art of African Fashion*, Prince Claus Fund, The Hague, 1998, pp. 13–45.

In response to the "post-black" phenomenon: Berger, Maurice, *Adrian Piper: A Retrospective*, D.A.P., New York, 1999. Berger, Maurice, "The Critique of Pure Racism: An Interview with Adrian Piper," *Afterimage* 18, October 1990, pp. 5–9. Huntington, Patricia, "Fragmentation, Race, and Gender: Building Solidarity in the Postmodern Era," in Lewis Gordon, ed., *Existence in Black: An Anthology of Black Existential Philosophy*, Routledge, New York, 1997, pp. 185–202. *Chakaia Booker: New Sculptures*, Marlborough Galleries, New York, 2001. *Siempre Vuelvo: Colografís de Belkis Ayón*, VII Bienal de la Habana/Galería Habana, Havana, 2000. Cassel Oliver, Valerie, *Double Consciousness: Black Conceptual Art Since 1970*, Contemporary Art Museum, Houston, 2005. Smith, Cherise, *Enacting Others: Politics of Identity in Eleanor Antin, Nikki S. Lee, Adrian Piper, and Anna Deavere Smith*, Duke University Press, Durham, NC, 2011. Walker, Hamza, *Black Is, Black Ain't*, The Renaissance Society, Chicago, 2013. Bessire, Mark H.C., ed., *William Pope.L: The Friendliest Black Artist in America*, MIT Press, Cambridge, MA, 2002. Obadike, Keith, "Blackness for Sale," originally posted August 18, 2001. https://obadike.squarespace.com/#/blackness/. Accessed May 5, 2020.

Chapter 9
The Price of Blackness

Artistic Acclamations and Afropessimism: Smith, Roberta, "A Sea Change in the Art World, Made by Black Creators," *New York Times*, November 24, 2019. Hartman, Saidiya, *Lose Your Mother: A Journey along the Atlantic Slave Route*, Farrar, Strauss & Giroux, New York, 2007. Wilderson, Frank III, *Afropessimism*, Liveright, New York, 2020. Hill, Anita, Smee, Sebastian and Butler, Connie, *Mark Bradford*, Phaidon Press, Inc., New York, 2018. Cubbs, Joanne, ed., *Hard Truths: The Art of Thornton Dial*, Delmonico/Prestel, New York, 2011. Vogel, Susan Mullin, *El Anatsui: Art and Life*, Prestel, Munich, 2012. Shiff, Richard, "Our Life in Signs," in *Julie Mehretu/Mural*, Goldman Sachs, New York, 2013, pp. 11–71.

Black Cameras: Dolan, Julia, ed., *Hank Willis Thomas: All Things Being Equal*, Aperture, New York, 2018. Widholm, Julie Rodrigues, *Rashid Johnson: Message to Our Folks*, Museum of Contemporary Art, Chicago, 2012. Smith, Zadie, *Deana Lawson*, Aperture, New York, 2018.

Willis, Deborah, *Reflections in Black: A History of Black Photographers from 1840 to the Present*, W.W. Norton, New York, 2000.

List of illustrations

Black Portraitures: Powell, Richard J., *Cutting a Figure: Fashioning Black Portraiture*, University of Chicago Press, Chicago, 2008. Beckwith, Naomi, *Lynette Yiadom-Boakye*, Prestel, New York, 2014. Tsai, Eugenie, ed., *Kehinde Wiley: A New Republic*, DelMonico/Prestel, New York, 2015.

La Noire de…: Farrington, Lisa E., *Creating Their Own Image: The History of African American Women Artists*, Oxford University Press, New York, 2005. McMillan, Uri, *Embodied Avatars: Genealogies of Black Feminist Art and Performance*, New York University Press, New York, 2015. Andersson, Andrea and Crooks, Julie, eds., *Mickalene Thomas: Femmes Noires*, Art Gallery of Ontario, Toronto, 2018. Mussai, Renée, *Zanele Muholi: Somnyama Ngonyama, Hail the Dark Lioness*, Aperture, New York, 2018. Musser, Amber Jamilla, "Toward Mythic Feminist Theorizing: Simone Leigh and the Power of the Vessel," *differences* 30, 2019, pp. 63–91. Smith, Roberta, "Sugar? Sure, but Salted with Meaning," *New York Times*, May 11, 2014.

David Adjaye and MASS Design Group: Adjaye, David and Peter Allison, *David Adjaye – Works 1995–2007: Houses, Pavilions, Installations, Buildings*, Thames & Hudson, 2020. Allison, Peter, ed., *David Adjaye: Constructed Narratives*, Thames & Hudson, 2017. Ryan, Zoë, ed., *David Adjaye: Form, Heft, Material*, Art Institute of Chicago, Chicago, 2015. Murphy, Michael, ed., *Justice is Beauty: MASS Design Group*, The Monacelli Press, New York, 2019. Hood, Walter and Grace Mitchell Tada, eds., *Black Landscapes Matter*, University of Virginia Press, Charlottesville, 2020.

Afrofuturism and its artistic reverberations: Nelson, Alondra, "AfroFuturism: Past-Future Visions," *Colorlines: Race, Culture, Action* 3, Spring 2000, pp. 34–37. Eshun, Kodwo, "Further Considerations of Afrofuturism," *CR: The New Centennial Review* 3, Summer 2003, pp. 287–302. Ose, Elvira Dyangani, *Nick Cave: Epitome*, Prestel, New York, 2014. Price, Marshall N., ed., *Nina Chanel Abney, Royal Flush*, Nasher Museum of Art at Duke University, Durham, NC, 2017. Umolu, Yesomi, *Kapwani Kiwanga: Structural Adjustments*, Reva and David Logan Center for the Arts, Chicago, 2018. Schoonmaker, Trevor, ed., *Wangechi Mutu: A Fantastic Journey*, Nasher Museum of Art at Duke University, Durham, NC, 2013.

Measurements are given in centimetres followed by inches, height preceding width

1 Sylvia Snowden, *Mamie Harrington*, 1985 (detail). Acrylic on masonite 48½ × 67 (123.2 × 170.2). National Gallery of Art, Washington, D.C. Corcoran Collection, The Evans-Tibbs Collection, Gift of Thurlow Evans Tibbs, Jr. 2015.19.210. © Sylvia Snowden
2 *Slave drum*, late seventeenth century. Wood, 41 × W 28 (16¼ × 11⅛). Photo Trustees of the British Museum, London
3 Anonymous, *Las Castas*, late eighteenth century. Oil on canvas, 266.7 × 269.2 (105 × 106). Museo Nacional del Virreinato, Tepotzotlan. The Picture Art Collection/Alamy
4 Arthur Drummond, *The Empress*, 1901. Oil on canvas, 343 × 203 (135 × 79⅞). Private Collection. Christie's Images, London/Scala, Florence
5 Sosa Adede, *King Glele in the Guise of a Lion*, late nineteenth century. Wood, pigment, H 170 (66⅞). Musée du quai Branly, Paris. Photo RMN-Grand Palais/Patrick Gries
6 Elizabeth Catlett, *Negro es Bello II*, 1969. Lithograph, 85.1 × 64.1 (33⅝ × 25¼). Photo Detroit Institute of Arts, USA/Museum Purchase, Octavia W. Bates Fund/Bridgeman Images. © Elizabeth Catlett
7 Jeff Donaldson, *Victory in Zimbabwe*, 1977–80. Mixed media on acid-free corrugated board, 106.7 × 114.3 (41 × 45). Photo Smithsonian American Art Museum/Art Resource/Scala, Florence. Courtesy the artist
8 Cover of sheet music for "All Coons Look Alike to Me" by Ernest Hogan, 1896. 34 × 26.4 (13⅜ × 10⅜). New York Public Library, Music Division
9 Henry Ossawa Tanner, *The Banjo Lesson*, 1893.

Oil on canvas, 124.5 × 90.2 (49 × 35½). Hampton University Museum, Virginia
10 Harriet Powers, *Bible Quilt, c.* 1895–98. Pieced, appliquéd and printed on cotton embroidered with plain and metallic yarns, 175 × 267 (69 × 105). Museum of Fine Arts, Boston
11 H. M. Pettit, *Close Competition at the Cake Walk*, 1899. From Leslie's Weekly, 1899. Photo courtesy the author
12 Stuart Davis, *Negro Dance Hall*, 1913. Crayon and ink on paper, 53.7 × 42.2 (21¼ × 16⅝). Paul Kasmin Gallery, New York. © Estate of Stuart Davis/VAGA at ARS, NY and DACS, London 2021
13 Ernst Ludwig Kirchner, T*apdancing Negro*, 1914. Lithograph. Lothar Buchheim Collection, Munich
14 Leigh Richmond Miner, frontispiece for Paul Laurence Dunbar's *Candle-Lightin' Time*, 1901. Smithsonian Library, Washington, D.C.
15 John Henry Adams Jr., *The Modern Cyrenian's Cross*, or *The Black Man's Burden*, 1907. Drawing from *Voice of the Negro*. Perkins Library, Duke University, Durham, North Carolina
16 D. W. Griffith, *The Birth of a Nation*, 1915. Photo BFI Stills, Posters & Designs
17 Isaac Scott Hathaway, *Frederick Douglass*, 1919. Plaster, H 81 (32). Roscoe Conklin Simmons Papers, Harvard University Archives, Cambridge. Photo Harvard College Photographic Services
18 Meta Warrick Fuller, *The Awakening of Ethiopia, c.* 1920. Bronze, 170.2 × 40.6 × 50.8 (67 × 16 × 20). Art and Artifacts Division, Schomburg Center for Research in Black Culture, New York Public Library
19 Advertisement for Banania, 1917. Colour lithograph, 164 × 123 (65 × 48⅜). Kharbine-Tapabor/Shutterstock
20 Edwin A. Harleston, *The Soldier*, 1919. Oil on canvas. Whereabouts unknown. Photo courtesy the National Archives, Washington, D.C.
21 Winold Reiss, *Langston Hughes, c.* 1925. Pastel on illustration board, 76.3 × 54.9 (30¹⁄₁₆ × 21⅝). National Portrait Gallery, Smithsonian Institution, gift of W. Tjark Reiss, in memory of his father, Winold Reiss. © Estate of Winold Reiss
22 Aaron Douglas, *Dance Magic*, 1929–30. Mural in the College Room Inn, Sherman Hotel, Chicago. Destroyed. Photo courtesy the author. © Heirs of Aaron Douglas/VAGA at ARS, NY and DACS, London 2021
23 Aaron Douglas, *Harriet Tubman*, 1931. Mural at Bennett College, Greensboro, North Carolina. Oil on canvas, 137 × 183 (54 × 72). © Bennett College, Greensboro, NC. All Rights Reserved

24 Carl Van Vechten, *Aaron Douglas*, 1933. Gelatin print, 25.2 × 20.2 (10 × 8). Beinecke Rare Book & Manuscript Library, Yale University. © Van Vechten Trust
25 Doris Ulmann, *Baptism,* 1929–30. Photograph, 21.6 × 16.4 (8½ × 6½). Ulmann Collection, CN 3423, Special Collections, University of Oregon Library
26 William H. Johnson, *Self-Portrait*, 1929. Oil on canvas, 59 × 46.3 (23¼ × 18¼). Photo Smithsonian American Art Museum/Art Resource/Scala, Florence
27 Laura Wheeler Waring, *Anna Washington Derry, c.* 1927. Oil on canvas, 50.8 × 40.6 (20 × 16). Photo Smithsonian American Art Museum/Art Resource/Scala, Florence
28 James VanDerZee, *Untitled (West 127th Street, Harlem)*, 1932. Gelatin silver print, 19.5 × 24.7 (7⅝ × 9¾). © James VanDerZee
29 Albert Alexander Smith, *A Tap Dancer, c.* 1928. Etching, 25 × 17 (9⅞ × 6⅜). Library of Congress, Washington, D.C.
30 Advertisement for Memphis Julia Davis's "Black Hand Blues", from The Chicago Defender, 1925. Perkins Library, Duke University, Durham, North Carolina
31 Archibald J. Motley Jr., *Jockey Club*, 1929. Oil on canvas, 65.4 × 81.3 (25¾ × 32). Art and Artifacts Division, Schomburg Center for Research in Black Culture, New York Public Library. © Archibald J. Motley Jr.
32 Jean Renoir, *Sur un air de Charleston*, 1926. Photo BFI Stills, Posters & Designs
33 Paul Colin, from *Le Tumulte noir, c.* 1927. Pochoir print, 46 × 31 (18 × 12). The Stapleton Collection/Bridgeman Images. © ADAGP, Paris and DACS, London 2021
34 Richmond Barthé, *African Dancer*, 1933. Plaster, 110.5 × 43.3 × 37.3 (43½ × 17¹⁄₁₆ × 14¹¹⁄₁₆). Photo Whitney Museum of American Art, New York/Scala, Florence
35 Alfred Janniot, sculptural relief for the façade of the Palais de la Porte Dorée, Paris, 1931. Limestone, H 13 m (43 ft). Photo RMN-Grand Palais/Jacques Chirac
36 Charles C. Dawson, advertisement for Madagasco Hair Straightener, from *The Chicago Defender*, 1925. Perkins Library, Duke University, Durham, North Carolina
37 Miguel Covarrubias, "*To Hold as t'Were the Mirror Up to Nature*," from *Vanity Fair*, 1929. Perkins Library, Duke University, Durham, North Carolina
38 Sargent Johnson, *Negro Woman, c.* 1935. Terracotta, 23.5 × 12.7 × 15.2 (9¼ × 5 × 6).

Assembly, c. 1950–64. Gold and silver aluminium foil, colour Kraft paper and plastic sheets over wood, paperboard and glass. 180 pieces in overall configuration, 3.2 m × 8.23 m × 4.42 m (10 ft 6 × 7 ft × 14 ft 6). Photo Smithsonian American Art Museum/Art Resource/Scala, Florence

64 Minnie Evans, *A Dream*, 1959. Oil and ink on canvas board, 30.3 × 40.6 (11⅞ × 16). North Carolina Museum of History, Raleigh, N.C.

65 Rose Piper, *Slow Down Freight Train*, 1946. Oil on canvas, 74 × 58.7 (29½ × 23⅛). The Ackland Art Museum, The University of North Carolina at Chapel Hill, Ackland Fund

66 Norman Lewis, *Every Atom Glows: Electrons in Luminous Vibration*, 1951. Oil on canvas, 137.2 × 86.4 (54 × 34). Photo Museum of Fine Arts, Boston. The John Axelrod Collection—Frank B. Bemis Fund, Charles H. Bayley Fund, and The Heritage Fund for a Diverse Collection. Courtesy of Michael Rosenfeld Gallery LLC, New York. © Estate of Norman Lewis

67 Hale Woodruff, *Art of the Negro* murals, Panel 5: *Influences*, 1950–51. Oil on canvas, 3.66 m × 3.66 m (12 ft × 12 ft). Courtesy of Clark Atlanta University, Collection of African-American Art, Atlanta, Georgia. © Estate of Hale Woodruff/VAGA at ARS, NY and DACS, London 2021

68 Richard Hunt, *Arachne*, 1956. Welded steel, 76 × 62.2 × 71.7 (30 × 24½ × 28¼) including base. Digital image The Museum of Modern Art, New York/Scala, Florence

69 Aubrey Williams, *Guyana*, 1965. Courtesy Eve Williams. © Aubrey Williams

70 Ollie Harrington. "No, it don't make no sense to me neither Bootsie. But white folks jus' won't buy nothin' if it makes sense!", 1959. Pencil and ink on paper, 21.6 × 36.8 (18½ × 14½). Collection of Dr. Walter Evans, Detroit

71 Wifredo Lam, *The Eternal Presence*, 1944. Oil on canvas, 215.9 × 196.9 (85 × 77½). Rhode Island School of Design, Providence. © ADAGP, Paris and DACS, London 2021

72 Marcel Camus, *Orfeu Negro (Black Orpheus)*, 1959. Photo BFI Stills, Posters & Designs

73 Bob Thompson, *Garden of Music*, 1960. Oil on canvas, 202.9 × 364.5 (78⅞ × 143½). Wadsworth Atheneum Museum of Art, Hartford, CT. The Ella Gallup Sumner and Mary Catlin Sumner Collection Fund, 1987.4. Photo Allen Phillips/Wadsworth Atheneum. © Michael Rosenfeld Gallery LLC, New York. Courtesy of Michael Rosenfeld Gallery, London

74 Beauford Delaney, *Self-Portrait*, 1962. Oil on canvas, 58.4 × 48.3 (23 × 19). Photo Detroit Institute of Arts, USA/Founders Society Purchase, City of Detroit by exchange/Bridgeman Images. © Beauford Delaney

75 Skunder Boghossian, *Ju-Ju's Wedding*, 1964. Tempera and metallic paint on cut-and-torn cardboard, 53.6 × 50.7 (21⅛ × 20). Digital image The Museum of Modern Art, New York/Scala, Florence

76 Gerard Sekoto, *Woman Ironing*, c. 1940–41. Oil on hardboard, 71.1 × 61 (28 × 24). Hampton University Museum, Virginia. © Gerard Sekoto Foundation/DALRO, South Africa/DACS, London 2021

77 Elizabeth Catlett, *…and a special fear for my loved ones*, 1947. Linocut, 38.5 × 28.7 (15¼ × 11⅜). The Art Institute of Chicago, restricted gift of the Leadership Advisory Committee/Bridgeman Images. © Catlett Mora Family Trust/VAGA at ARS, NY and DACS, London 2021

78 Charles White, *Oh, Mary, Don't You Weep*, 1956. Graphite and pen and ink on board, 99.7 × 102.9 (39¼ × 41½). Crystal Bridges Museum of American Art, Bentonville, Arkansas. © The Charles White Archives, Inc.

79 Ernest C. Withers, cover of *Complete Photo Story of Till Murder Case*, 1955. Offset print, 20.3 × 25.4 (8 × 10). Memphis Brooks Museum of Art. Courtesy the artist

80 Norman Rockwell, *The Problem We All Live With*, 1964. Oil on canvas, 91.5 × 147.5 (36 × 58). Norman Rockwell Museum, Vermont. Artwork Approved by the Norman Rockwell Family Agency

81 Romare Bearden, *Summertime*, 1967. Collage, 142.2 × 111.8 (56 × 44). Saint Louis Art Museum, Missouri, Museum Minority Artists Purchase Fund/Bridgeman Images. © Romare Bearden Foundation/VAGA at ARS, NY and DACS, London 2021

82 Barbara Chase-Riboud, *Confessions for Myself*, 1972. Bronze, painted black, and black wool, 304.8 × 101.6 × 30.5 (120 × 40 × 12). University of California, Berkeley Art Museum

83 Raymond Saunders, *Jack Johnson*, 1972. Gouache, chalk, tickets, masking tape on paper, 48.3 × 58.4 (19 × 23). Yale University Art Gallery, New Haven. © Raymond Saunders

84 Alma Thomas, *Red Azaleas Singing and Dancing Rock and Roll Music*, 1976. Acrylic on canvas, 183.5 × 398.3 (72¼ × 156¾). Photo Smithsonian American Art Museum/Art Resource/Scala, Florence

85 Sam Gilliam, *Lion's Rock Arc*, 1981. Acrylic on canvas, 208.3 × 484.1 (82 × 191). The Studio Museum Harlem, New York. © Sam Gilliam

115 Lois Mailou Jones, *Magic of Nigeria*, 1971. Watercolour, 86.4 × 56 (34 × 22). Private Collection
116 Archie Rand, *The Groups*, 1970. Acrylic and wax crayon on canvas, 68.6 × 398.8 (27 × 157). Collection of the artist. © Archie Rand
117 Ernie Barnes, *The Sugar Shack*, 1972–76. Acrylic on canvas, 91.4 × 121.9 (36 × 48) Collection Mr. and Mrs. Eddie Murphy. Courtesy of The Company of Art, Los Angeles
118 Sister Gertrude Morgan, *Come in my Room, Come on in the Prayer Room*, c. 1970. Tempera, acrylic, ballpoint pen and pencil on paperboard, 30.7 × 58.4 (12⅛ × 23). Photo Smithsonian American Art Museum/Art Resource/Scala, Florence
119 Margo Humphrey, *The Last Bar-B-Que*, 1988–89. Lithograph with goldleaf, 55.9 × 121.9 (22 × 48). Collection of the artist
120 Everald Brown, *Dove Harp*, 1996. Private Collection
121 Lyle Ashton Harris, *For Cleopatra*, 1994. Unique Polaroid, 50.8 × 61 (20 × 24). Courtesy Jack Tilton Gallery, New York/Lyle Ashton Harris
122 Alison Saar, *Terra Rosa*, 1993. Latex, wax, dirt and polymer on wood, 138.4 × 39.4 × 63.5 (54½ × 15½ × 25). © Alison Saar. Courtesy of the artist
123 Martin Puryear, *His Eminence*, 1993–95. Red cedar and pine, 248.9 × 113.7 × 246.4 (98 × 44¾ × 97). Photo Museum Voorlinden, Wassenaar. Courtesy Matthew Marks Gallery. © Martin Puryear
124 Gary Simmons, *Black Chalkboard (Double Grin)*, 1993, from the *Erasure* series. Oak, masonite, slate paint and chalk with fixative, 121.9 × 152. 4 (48 × 60). Princeton University Art Museum. Courtesy of the artist and Metro Pictures, New York
125 Jean-Michel Basquiat, *Flexible*, 1984. Acrylic and oilstick on wood, 259 × 190.5 (102 × 75) Private Collection. © The Estate of Jean-Michel Basquiat/ ADAGP, Paris and DACS, London 2021
126 Tam Joseph, *Learning to Walk*, 1988. Sand, acrylic medium and pigment, 201 × 386 (79⅛ × 152). Arts Council Collection, London. © Tam Joseph
127 Outtara Watts, *Hip-Hop Jazz Makoussa*, 1994. Mixed media on wood, 281.9 × 365.8 (111 × 144). Courtesy the artist
128 Ras Ishi Butcher, *400 Years New World Order*, 1995. Oil and sand on canvas, 32 × 28 (12⅝ × 11). Collection of Meryvn Awon. Courtesy the artist
129 Mr. Imagination, *Portrait Head Paintbrush Tree*, 1991. Mixed media, 165.4 × 57.8 × 47.6 (65⅛ × 22¾ × 18 ¾). Photo Smithsonian American Art Museum/Art Resource/Scala, Florence

130 Philip Moore, *King Sparrow in Sacred Wonder Heart*, 1992. Oil on canvas, 48 × 36 (18⅞ × 14⅛). Collection of Meryvn Awon. Courtesy the artist
131 Melvin Edwards, Tambo, 1993. Welded Steel, 71.5 × 64.2 × 55.9 (28⅛ × 25¼ × 22). Smithsonian American Art Museum, Washington, D.C. © Melvin Edwards
132 Martha Jackson Jarvis, *Last Rites: Sarcophagi II (Earth)*, 1992–93. Clay, glass, pigmented cement, wood, iron, 10.2 × 14 × 6.4 (4 × 5½ × 2½). Photo Harlee Little. © Martha Jackson Jarvis
133 Lorna Simpson, *Five Rooms* (detail of Room One). Installation at Spoleto Festival USA, Charleston, South Carolina, 1991. Glass water bottles, wooden stools, engraved plastic plaques, 4-colour polaroid prints; dimensions variable. © Lorna Simpson
134 Beverly Buchanan, *Red Shack*, c. 1990. Tin and wood, 68.6 × 38.1 × 27.9 (27 × 15 × 11). Courtesy of Andrew Edlin Gallery, New York
135 Sue Williamson, *Mementoes of District Six*, 1993. Various objects preserved in lucite, steel, rubble, dirt, lights, sound, 83.2 × 109.2 (32¾ × 43). Birmingham Museum of Art, Alabama. © Sue Williamson
136 Kerry James Marshall, *Better Homes Better Gardens*, 1994–95. Acrylic on canvas, 254 × 365.8 (100 × 144). Denver Art Museum. © Kerry James Marshall
137 Fred Wilson, *Insight: In Site: In Sight: Incite: Memory*. Installation in St Philip's Church, Old Salem, Winston-Salem, North Carolina, 1994. One room filled with gourds; dimensions variable. Photo Jackson Smith. Photo courtesy of the Southeastern Center for Contemporary Art and Fred Wilson, New York
138 Sonia Boyce, *Peep*. Installation view, intervention in Cultures Gallery, Brighton Museum and Art Gallery, Sussex, 1995. 50 glass cases covered with tracing paper. Commissioned by the Institute of International Visual Arts, London. Photo David Catchpole. © Sonia Boyce
139 Houston Conwill, Joseph de Pace, Estella Conwill Majozo, *The New Ring Shout*, 1995. Ted Weiss Federal Building, New York. Photo Carol M. Highsmith/Buyenlarge/Getty Images
140 Alfredo Jaar, *Real Pictures*, 1995. Colour photographs in archival boxes, silkscreen, overall dimensions variable. Courtesy Galerie Lelong & Co. and the artist, New York. © Alfredo Jaar
141 Achamyeleh Debela, *Artist Under a Mask*, 1990–91. Cibachrome print, 50.8 × 76.2 (20 × 30). Collection of the artist
142 Philip Mallory Jones, *First World Order*, 1994. Video. Courtesy of Electronic Arts Intermix, New York

143 Albert Chong, *Winged Desire*, 1994. Gelatin silver print with incised copper mat, 61 × 50.8 (24 × 20). Courtesy the artist
144 Lorraine O'Grady, *The Strange Taxi: From Africa to Jamaica to Boston in 200 Years*, 1991. Black-and-white photomontage, dimensions variable. © Lorraine O'Grady
145 Emma Amos, *Confederates*, 1994. Collagraph and photo transfer, 45.7 × 50.8 (18 × 20). Courtesy RYAN LEE Gallery, New York. © Emma Amos
146 Coreen Simpson, *Jamien*, 1984, from the *B-Boy* series. Gelatin silver print, 101.6 × 152.4 (40 × 60). © Coreen Simpson
147 Dawoud Bey, *Sara, Martin David and Tolani*, 1992. Colour polaroid (triptych), 76.2 × 167.6 (30 × 66). Addison Gallery of American Art, Museum purchase/Bridgeman Images. © Dawoud Bey
148 Maud Sulter, *Calliope*, from the *Zabat* series, 1989. Cibachrome print 60 × 48 (152.4 × 121.9). Image Arts Council Collection, Southbank Centre. © Estate of Maud Sulter. All rights reserved, DACS/Artimage 2021
149 Edouard Duval-Carrié, *Un Touriste chez lui*, 1981. Oil on canvas, 147.3 × 195.6 (58 × 77). Collection Ann Duval. Courtesy Gutierrez Fine Arts, Miami Beach. © Edouard Duval-Carrié
150 Sue Coe, *Woman Shot in the Back*, 1985. Graphite and gouache on off-white Bristol board, 55.8 × 76.2 (22 × 30). Courtesy Galerie St Etienne, New York. © 1985 Sue Coe
151 Byron Kim and Glenn Ligon, *Rumble, Young Man, Rumble (Version No. 2)*, 1993. Paintstick canvas punch bag, 106.7 × 35.6 × 35.6 (42 × 14 × 14). Photo Dennis Cowley. Walker Art Center, Minneapolis. Courtesy Max Protech Gallery, New York
152 Adrian Piper, *My Calling (Card) No. 2*, 1986. Guerrilla performance with printed calling card, 5 × 8.9 (2 × 3½). Courtesy John Weber Gallery, New York
153 Howardena Pindell, *Separate but Equal Genocide: AIDS*, 1991–92. Mixed media on canvas, 191.8 × 231.1 (75½ × 91). Courtesy the artist and Garth Greenan Gallery, New York
154 Robert Colescott, *Lightening Lipstick*, 1994. Acrylic on canvas, 228.6 × 289.6 (90 × 114). Photo Eskenazi Museum of Art/Kevin Montague. © ARS, NY and DACS, London 2021
155 Keith Morrison, *Chariot*, 1987. Oil on canvas, 162.6 × 221 (64 × 87). Collection of the artist. © Keith Morrison
156 Stanley Greaves, *The Presentation No. 2*, 1992, from *There is a Meeting Here Tonight* series. Acrylic, 120 × 104.5 (47¼ × 41⅛). Collection of the artist. © Stanley Greaves

157 Tseng Kwong Chi and Keith Haring, *Bill T. Jones*, 1983. Photograph. © 1983 Tseng Kwong Chi. Courtesy of the estate of Keith Haring
158 Ben Jones, *Shango* wall installation (detail), 1994. Multi-media, length 9.15 m (30 ft). Collection of the artist. © Ben Jones
159 Sherman Fleming, *UN/SUB: De Jacht op Zwarte Piet*, 1995. Performance held at Art et Amichitiae, Amsterdam. Courtesy of the artist
160 Sokari Douglas Camp, *Gelede From Top to Toe*, 1995. Steel and wood, 183 × 41 × 94 (72 × 16⅛ × 37) Collection of the artist. Photo Peter White. © Sokari Douglas Camp
161 Werewere Liking, *Un Touareg s'est marié à une pygmée*, 1992. Performance held at Création au Festival des Francophonies, Limoges, France. Photo © Catherine Millet
162 Joyce J. Scott, *Generic Interference, Genetic Engineering*, 1992. Performance held at the Baltimore Museum of Art, Maryland. © Joyce J. Scott
163 Carrie Mae Weems, *Ode to Affirmative Action*, 1989. Silver print, record and label, 61 × 76.2 (24 × 30). Courtesy of the artist and Jack Shainman Gallery, New York. © Carrie Mae Weems
164 Spencer Williams, *The Blood of Jesus*, 1941. Photo Southwest Film/Video Archives
165 Richard D. Maurice, *Eleven p.m.*, 1928. Photo Library of Congress, Washington, D.C.
166 Edward Spriggs and Fred Padula, *Ephesus*, 1966. Courtesy of the artist
167 Isaac Julien, *Looking for Langston*, 1989. Photo Sunil Gupta/BFI Stills, Posters and Designs. © Sankofa Film and Video 1989
168 Martina Attille, *Dreaming Rivers*, 1988. Photo Christine Parry. © Sankofa Film and Video 1988
169 Camile Billops and James Hatch, *The KKK Boutique Ain't Just Rednecks*, 1994. Photo Mary Ellen Andrews. © 1994 Mom and Pop Productions
170 Spike Lee, *School Daze*, 1988. Columbia/Kobal/Shutterstock
171 Felix de Rooy, *Ava & Gabriel: A Love Story*, 1990. Photo BFI Stills, Posters & Designs
172 Ousmane Sembene, *Ceddo*, 1976. Photo BFI Stills, Posters & Designs
173 Euzhan Palcy, *Rue Cases-Nègres (Sugar Cane Alley)*, 1983. Photo BFI Stills, Posters & Designs
174 Julie Dash, *Daughters of the Dust*, 1991. American Playhouse/Wmg/Geechee/Kobal/Shutterstock
175 Haile Gerima, *Sankofa*, 1993. Photo Mypheduh Production/WDR
176 Jean-Paul Goude, album cover for *Island Life*, Grace Jones, 1985. Courtesy of Island Records Ltd.

177 Keith Piper, *Reckless Eyeballing*, Installation, Ferens Art Gallery, Hull, UK, June-July 1995. Interactive installation with video projection from laser disk triggered by spectators stepping on to three lecterns. Installation controlled by Apple Macintosh computer running SampleCell and Max. Courtesy the artist

178 Jonathan Demme, *Beloved*, 1998. Courtesy Harpo Productions. Photo Ken Regan/Camera 5. © Touchstone Pictures Company, All Rights Reserved

179 Charles S. Stone III, *You Got Me*, 1998. Videos still. Courtesy of Erykah Badu, Charles S. Stone III, MCA Records and Universal/Motown Group

180 DJ Spooky (a.k.a Paul D. Miller), *Rebirth of a Nation*, 2002. © 2002 Paul D. Miller/Subliminal Kid Publishing

181 Gilles Elie-Dit-Cosaque ,*Twinkl/Zétwal,* 2008. © Gilles Elie-Dit-Cosaque

182 Arthur Jafa, *Dreams are Colder than Death*, 2013. © Arthur Jafa

183 Sondra Perry, *IT'S IN THE GAME '17 or Mirror Gag for Vitrine and Projection*, 2017. Installation. Courtesy of the artist, Bridget Donahue, New York and Electronic Arts Intermix (EAI), New York

184 Kara Walker, *African/American*, 1998. Linoleum cut, 116.8 × 153.7 (46 × 60.5). Museum of Modern Art, New York. Courtesy of Sikkema Jenkins & Co., New York. Artwork © Kara Walker

185 David Levinthal, *Blackface*, 1995. Colour polaroid, 61 × 50.8 (24 × 20). © ARS, NY and DACS, London 2021

186 Renée Cox, *The Liberation of Lady J. and U. B.*, 1998. Cibachrome print, 121.9 × 152.4 (48 × 60). © Renée Cox

187 Aaron McGruder, strip from *The Boondocks*, 2000. BOONDOCKS © Aaron McGruder. Distributed by UNIVERSAL PRESS SYNDICATE. Reprinted with permission. All rights reserved

188 Chris Ofili, *Afrodizzia (second version),* 1996. Acrylic, oil, polyester resin, paper collage, glitter, map pins and elephant dung on linen, 243.8 × 182.8 (96 × 72). Courtesy the artist and Victoria Miro. © Chris Ofili

189 Yinka Shonibare, *Cloud* 9, 1999–2000. Dutch wax printed cotton textile, fiberglass figure, helmet, flagpole and flag. Astronaut, 212 × 63 × 56 (83½ × 24¾ × 22) Flag height, 183 (72). Exhibition presented at Camden Arts Centre, London, 2000. Photo Andy Keate. Courtesy Stephen Friedman Gallery, London. © Yinka Shonibare CBE. All Rights Reserved, DACS 2021

190 Yinka Shonibare, *Dorian Gray, Scene 7*, 2001. Black-and-white resin print, 134 × 165 (52⅞ × 65). Image courtesy Stephen Friedman Gallery,

London. © Yinka Shonibare CBE. All Rights Reserved, DACS/Artimage 2021

191 Johannes Phokela, *Pantomime Art Trilogy*, 1999. Oil on canvas, 183 × 168 (72 × 66⅛). Courtesy of the artist

192 Minnette Vári, *Self-Portrait 2*, 1995. Photographic print, 75 × 102 (29½ × 40⅛). Courtesy of the artist and Serge Ziegler Galerie, Zurich

193 Tracey Rose, *Span II*, 1997. Performance/video installation. Photo Michael Hall

194 Oumou Sy, *Cyberdress*, 1997. Photo Mamadou Touré Béhan, Dakar Senegal © Prince Claus Fund

195 Chakaia Booker, *Wrench (Wench) II*, 2001. Steel, rubber, wood, 228.6 × 116.8 × 53.4 (90 × 46 × 21). Courtesy Marlborough Gallery, New York. © Chakaia Booker

196 Belkis Ayón, *La Cena (The Dinner),* 1991. Collagraph, 6 panels, each 133.6 × 1505. (52⅝ × 59¼). Collection of the Norton Family Foundation, Santa Monica, CA. © Belkis Ayón

197 Pope.L, *Eating the Wall Street Journal*, at The Sculpture Centre, New York, 2000. Digital c-print on gold fibre silk paper, 15.2 × 22.9 (6 × 9). All files courtesy of the artist and Mitchell-Innes & Nash, New York. © Pope.L

198 Mark Bradford, *Mithra*, 2008. Mixed media, dimensions variable. Photo Sean Shim-Boyle. Courtesy the artist and Hauser & Wirth. © Mark Bradford

199 Thornton Dial, *Lost Americans*, 2008. Wood chest, chair parts, mannequin parts, corrugated tin, metal, letterman's jacket, clothing, quilted fabric, rope, nails, metal banding, found wood, tree stump, faux leather, and enamel on wood, 182.9 × 243.8 × 34.5 (72 × 96 × 13.5). Montgomery Museum of Fine Arts, Alabama. Pitkin Studio/Art Resource, New York. © ARS, NY and DACS, London 2021

200 El Anatsui, *In the World But Don't Know the World*, 2009. Aluminium and copper wire, 56 × 100 (22⅛ × 39⅜). Photo Maximilian Geuter. Courtesy of the artist and Jack Shainman Gallery, New York. © El Anatsui

201 Julie Mehretu, *Mural*, 2009. Ink and acrylic on canvas, 22 × 80 feet. Collection Goldman, Sachs & Co. Photo Tom Powel Imaging. Courtesy of the artist and Marian Goodman Gallery, New York. © Julie Mehretu

202 Rashid Johnson, *Self-Portrait Laying on Jack Johnson's Grave*, 2006. Lambda print, 103 × 125 (40½ × 49½). Courtesy the artist and Hauser & Wirth. © Rashid Johnson

203 Hank Willis Thomas, *Branded Head*, from the series *B®anded*, 2003. Lambda photograph, 96.5 × 71.1 (38 × 28¾). Courtesy of the artist and

Jack Shainman Gallery, New York. © Hank Willis Thomas

204 Deana Lawson, *The Garden, Gemena, DR Congo*, 2015. Inkjet print photograph, 140.2 × 176.7 (55³⁄₁₆ × 69⁹⁄₁₆). Courtesy of Sikkema Jenkins & Co., New York, Rhona Hoffman Gallery, Chicago and David Kordansky Gallery, Los Angeles. © Deana Lawson

205 John Akomfrah, *Precarity*, 2017. Three channel HD colour video installation, 7.1 sound. Dimensions variable, 46 minutes 3 seconds. Courtesy Smoking Dogs Films and Lisson Gallery. © Smoking Dogs Films

206 Lynette Yiadom-Boakye, *8am Cadiz*, 2017. Oil on linen, 200 × 250 (78¾ × 98⅜). Baltimore Museum of Art. Photo Marcus Leith. Courtesy the Artist, Corvi-Mora, London, and Jack Shainman Gallery, New York

207 Kehinde Wiley, *President Barack Obama*, 2018. Oil on canvas, 213.7 × 147 (84⅛ × 57⅞). Courtesy of the National Portrait Gallery, Smithsonian Institution. The National Portrait Gallery is grateful to the following lead donors for their support of the Obama Portraits: Kate Capshaw and Steven Spielberg; Judith Kern and Kent Whealy; Tommie L. Pegues and Donald A. Capoccia. © Kehinde Wiley

208 Iona Rozeal Brown, *Whoshi (ANA.ROGU-The Sender), (After Yoshitoshi's 'The Ghost Of Taira No Tomomori Appears At Diamotsu Bay')*, 2008. Acrylic and printed paper collage on panel, 157.5 × 127.7 (62 × 50¼). © Iona Rozeal Brown

209 Mickalene Thomas, *Les dejeurner sur l'herbe: Les Trois Femmes Noires*, 2010. Rhinestone, acrylic and enamel on panel, 304.8 × 731.5 (120 × 288). Seattle Art Museum. © ARS, NY and DACS, London 2021

210 Zanele Muholi, *ZaVa, Amsterdam*, 2014. Gelatin silver print, 96.5 × 124 (38 × 48.8) Courtesy of Stevenson, Cape Town/Johannesburg and Yancey Richardson, New York. © Zanele Muholi

211 Simone Leigh, *Brick House*, 2019. Bronze, 4.9 m (16 ft). Photo Timothy Schenck. Courtesy of the High Line. © Simone Leigh

212 Kara Walker, *A Subtlety, or the Marvelous Sugar Baby, an Homage to the unpaid and overworked Artisans who have refined our Sweet tastes from the cane fields to the Kitchens of the New World on the Occasion of the demolition of the Domino Sugar Refining Plant*, 2014. Polystyrene foam, sugar, 10.8 m × 7.9 m × 23 m (35.5 ft × 26 ft × 75.5 ft). Photo Jason Wyche. Courtesy of Sikkema Jenkins & Co., New York. Artwork © Kara Walker

213 Freelon/Adjaye/Bond/SmithGroup, National Museum of African American History and Culture, Smithsonian Institution, Washington, DC, 2016. Photo Jahi Chikwendiu/The Washington Post via Getty Images

214 MASS Design Group, Ltd/Equal Justice Initiative, National Memorial for Peace and Justice, Montgomery, Alabama, 2018. Photo Raymond Boyd/Getty Images

215 Kapwani Kiwanga, performing AFROGALACTICA: A Brief History of the Future at FRAC Champagne-Ardenne, Reims, France, 2015. Photo Martin Argyroglo. © ADAGP, Paris and DACS, London 2021

216 Nick Cave, *Soundsuits*, 2013. Mixed media including fabric, crochet blanket, doilies, sequins and mannequin, 251.5 × 66 × 45.7 (99 × 26 × 18). Photo James Prinz Photography. Courtesy of the artist and Jack Shainman Gallery, New York. © Nick Cave

217 Nina Chanel Abney, *Untitled*, 2017. Enamel on panel, 228.6 × 746.8 (90 × 294) Courtesy of the artist and Jack Shainman Gallery, New York. © Nina Chanel Abney

218 Wangechi Mutu, *The Seated II*, from *The newOnes, will free Us*, 2019. Installation view. Metropolitan Museum of Art, New York. Photo Bruce Schwarz. Courtesy of the artist and Gladstone Gallery, New York and Brussels

Index

Lawson, Deana 286–9; *204*
Le déjeuner sur l'herbe: Les Trois Femmes Noires (Thomas) 292; *209*
Le Tumulte Noir (Colin) 66; *33*
Learning to Walk (Joseph) 184; *126*
Lee, Spike 235–6, 250, 252; *170*
Lee, Stagger 180
Leigh, Simone 296–7; *211*
Leonardo da Vinci 277
Les Fétiches (Jones) 85; *46*
lesbianism 23
Levinson, Andre 66
Levinthal, David 259; *185*
Lewis, Norman 80, 112–14; *66*
Lewis, Samella 25, 169
Liberation of Lady J. and U.B., The (Cox) 259–60, 263; *186*
Lichfield, Patrick 156, 161; *100*
Life magazine 79, 130
Lift Every Voice and Sing (The Harp) (Savage) 80; *43*
Lightening Lipstick (Colescott) 212–13; *154*
Ligon, Glenn 23, 212, 213; *151*
Liking, Werewere 219–21, 269; *161*
Lion's Rock Arc (Gilliam) 139–42; *83*
Locke, Alain 16, 25, 48–50, 55, 61, 70, 72, 99–100, 169
Lois, George 155; *98*
London 149, 209, 242, 255, 269
Long, Richard A. 30
Look magazine 131
Looking for Langston (Julien) 231–3; *167*
Lost Americans (Dial) 278–9; *199*
Louis, Joe 88
Louis, Morris 139
Lovers (Crichlow) 79–80; *42*
Loving, Al 144, 146; *91*
lynchings 41, 47, 128, 300–2

M
Machado, Gerardo 82
Madagasco hair straightener (Dawson) 70; *36*
Madden, Owney 48
Magic of Nigeria (Jones) 172; *115*
Majozo, Estella Conwill 197; *139*
Makeba, Miriam 172
Malbert, Roger 236

Malcolm X 151, 152
Mamie Harrington (Snowden) 144; *1*; *88*
Manda (Biggers) 102; *58*
Mandela, Nelson 183
Manet, Édouard 160, 292
Manley, Edna 87–92; *48*
Mantegna, Andrea 155
Mapplethorpe, Robert 164, 216, 233; *110*
Markle, Meghan 295
Marsh, Reginald 76, 80
Marsha Hunt (Lichfield) 156, 161; *100*
Marshall, Kerry James 192–5, 240, 275, 282; *136*
Martin, Trayvon 289
Martinique 236–8, 250–1
Marvel Studios 303
Marxism 119
masculinity 164
Mask No. II (Jackson) 97–8; *54*
mass culture 72
Mass Design Group, Ltd 300–2; *214*
mass media 49, 151
Maupassant, Guy de 29
Maurice, Richard D. 227–8; *165*
McDonald, Laquan 289
McGruder, Aaron 261; *187*
McKay, Claude 66, 72, 80
McLuhan, H. Marshall 151
McQueen, Steve 247, 275
Mehretu, Julie 282; *201*
Mello, Breno 229
Mementoes of District Six (Williamson) 192–5; *135*
Memphis 62
Menil Foundation 160
Mercer, Kobena 25, 216, 233
Messenger, The (monthly) 78
Mexico 128; Spanish-speaking elite 8–11
Micheaux, Oscar 55, 224
middle classes 139, 182, 183
Midsummer Night in Harlem (Hayden) 76, 77; *40*
migration 17, 58–9, 95–6, 277, 279–82
Miller, Henry 125
Miller, Paul D. 249–50, 254; *180*
Mills, Irving 48
Mills, Lev 156–8; *101*
Miner, Leigh Richmond 39; *14*

Minnelli, Vincente 101–2, 224–6; *57*
Mithra (Bradford) 278; *198*
mixed race peoples 8–11, 34
Modern Cyrenian's Cross, The (Adams) 39–40; *15*
modern industrial design 51
Modern, the 48
modernism 48, 51, 52, 101, 107, 171, 272
modernity 48, 49, 50, 72
"moderns/primitives" artistic bond 107
Modigliani, Amedeo 114
Mokgosi, Meleko 290–1
Montañez Ortiz, Raphael 248
Moore, Henry 114
Moore, Philip 189; *130*
Morand, Paul 64–5, 66
Morgan, Sister Gertrude 175; *118*
Morris, Robert 135
Morrison, Keith 213; *155*
Morrison, Toni 192, 244, 245
Mosquera, Gerardo 268, 270
Motley, Archibald J., Jr. 60–1, 65, 75–6, 100; *31*; *39*
Mr. Imagination 189, 282; *129*
Mudimbe, V.Y. 70
Muholi, Zanele 294–5; *210*
Mural (Mehretu) 282; *201*
Murphy, Eddie 263
Murray, Freeman Henry Morris 15–16, 25
Museum of Modern Art (MoMA), New York 92, 126, 275
Mutu, Wangechi 309; *218*
My Calling (Card) No. 2 (Piper) 209–11; *152*

N
narrative control 211
Nashville 92
National Association for the Advancement of Colored People (NAACP) 41, 59, 80, 126, 151
National Endowment for the Arts–African American artists 167–9
National Memorial for Peace and Justice (Mass Design Group, Ltd/Equal Justice Initiative) 300–2; *214*

'The single most influential series of art books ever published' *Apollo*

'Outstanding ... exceptionally authoritative and well-illustrated' *Sunday Times*

'World of Art delivers real knowledge with crisp, useful clarity' *Guardian*

Comprehensive in coverage and accessible to all, the World of Art series explores both the newest and the perennial in all the arts, covering themes, artists and movements that straddle the centuries and the gamut of visual culture around the globe.

You may also like:

The Art of Contemporary China
Jiang Jiehong

Artists' Film
David Curtis

Caribbean Art
Veerle Poupeye

Central and Eastern European Art Since 1950
Maja and Reuben Fowkes

Contemporary African Art
Sidney Littlefield Kasfir

Contemporary Painting
Suzanne Hudson

Graffiti and Street Art
Anna Waclawek

Japanese Art
Joan Stanley-Baker

Movements in Art Since 1945
Edward Lucie-Smith

Women, Art, and Society
Whitney Chadwick

World of Art